Hands-On Security

Ensure continuous security, deployment, and delivery with
DevSecOps

Tony Hsu

BIRMINGHAM - MUMBAI

Hands-On Security in DevOps

Commissioning Editor: Vijin Boricha
Acquisition Editor: Heramb Bhavsar
Content Development Editor: Ronn Kurien
Technical Editor: Aditya Khadye
Copy Editor: Safis Editing
Project Coordinator: Kinjal Bari
Proofreader: Safis Editing
Indexer: Pratik Shirodkar
Graphics: Tom Scaria
Production Coordinator: Shantanu Zagade

First published: July 2018

Production reference: 1270718

Published by Packt Publishing Ltd.
Livery Place
35 Livery Street
Birmingham
B3 2PB, UK.

ISBN 978-1-78899-550-4

www.packtpub.com

mapt.io

Mapt is an online digital library that gives you full access to over 5,000 books and videos, as well as industry leading tools to help you plan your personal development and advance your career. For more information, please visit our website.

Why subscribe?

- Spend less time learning and more time coding with practical eBooks and Videos from over 4,000 industry professionals

- Improve your learning with Skill Plans built especially for you

- Get a free eBook or video every month

- Mapt is fully searchable

- Copy and paste, print, and bookmark content

PacktPub.com

Did you know that Packt offers eBook versions of every book published, with PDF and ePub files available? You can upgrade to the eBook version at www.PacktPub.com and as a print book customer, you are entitled to a discount on the eBook copy. Get in touch with us at service@packtpub.com for more details.

At www.PacktPub.com, you can also read a collection of free technical articles, sign up for a range of free newsletters, and receive exclusive discounts and offers on Packt books and eBooks.

Contributors

About the author

Tony Hsu is a senior security architect with over 20 years of experience in security services technology. He has rich experience with Secure Software Development LifeCycle (SSDLC), is deeply involved with security activities such as security requirements planning, threat modeling, secure architecture and design review, secure code review, automated security testing, and cloud services security monitoring. He is also in-house SDL trainer.

He is also a co contributor on OWASP projects such as OWASP testing guide, proactive control guide, and deserialization security cheatsheet.

I would like to thank my wife, Ya-Yu, my 3-year-boy, Wei-Jie, my parents, Wan-Te and Su-Ying for their love and full support especially during the period in the hospital when the book was in the writing phase. Thanks to all my friends for their encouragement. I would like to thank Ronn Kurien, Heramb Bhavsar, Aditya Khadye, and the editorial team for all of their feedback throughout this journey of book writing.

About the reviewer

Roshan Nagekar is an independent technology consultant with 10 years of experience in the field of DevOps and Site Reliability Engineering. He holds a master's degree in computer applications from Modern College, Pune. He has worked with companies such as Mphasis, IBM, Vuclip, and Western Union.

I would like to thank my wife, Poonam, my Mom and Dad, Pratibha and Gurunath Nagekar, and all my family and friends for all their support in producing this book.

Packt is searching for authors like you

If you're interested in becoming an author for Packt, please visit authors.packtpub.com and apply today. We have worked with thousands of developers and tech professionals, just like you, to help them share their insight with the global tech community. You can make a general application, apply for a specific hot topic that we are recruiting an author for, or submit your own idea.

Table of Contents

Preface

DevOps has provided speed and quality benefits with continuous development and deployment methods, but it does not guarantee the security of an entire organization. Hands-On Security in DevOps shows you how to adopt DevOps techniques to continuously improve your organization's security at every level, rather than just focusing on protecting your infrastructure.

This guide combines DevOps and security to help you to protect cloud services, and teaches you how to use techniques to integrate security directly in your product. You will learn how to implement security at every layer, such as for the web application, cloud infrastructure, communication, and the delivery pipeline layers. With the help of practical examples, you'll explore the core security aspects, such as blocking attacks, fraud detection, cloud forensics, and incident response. In the concluding chapters, you will cover topics on extending DevOps security, such as risk assessment, threat modeling, and continuous security.

By the end of this book, you will be well-versed in implementing security in all layers of your organization and be confident in monitoring and blocking attacks throughout your cloud services.

Who this book is for

This book is for system administrators, security consultants, and DevOps engineers who want to secure their entire organization. Basic understanding of Cloud computing, automation frameworks, and programming is necessary.

What this book covers

Chapter 1, *DevSecOps Drivers and Challenges*, we will cover external factors that drive the need for security such as security compliance, regulations, and the market.

Chapter 2, *Security Goals and Metrics*, we will discuss security practices from different perspectives based on the OWASP SAMM framework. We will also cover security activities in different roles such as security management, development, QA, and operation teams.

Chapter 3, *Security Assurance Program and Organization*, will cover how different organization structures may relate to the execution of a security assurance program. The role, responsibility and relationship of the security team in the organization structure also impact the success execution of a security assurance program. We will discuss these factors by case study.

Chapter 4, *Security Requirements and Compliance*, will cover security requirements covering four aspects: the security requirements for each release quality gate, the security requirements for general web applications, the security requirements for big data, and the security requirements for compliance with General Data Protection Regulation (GDPR).

Chapter 5, *Case Study - Security Assurance Program*, we will cover two case studies looking at the security assurance program and security practices in the DevOps process. Microsoft SDL and SAMM were introduced to apply to the security assurance program. In addition to the process, the non-technical parts, security training, and culture are also critical to the success of the security program. We will also give an example of how security tools and web security framework can help during the whole DevOps process

Chapter 6, *Security Architecture and Design Principles*, will cover security architecture and design principles. For security architects and developers, building software on a mature security framework will greatly reduce not only security risks with industry best practices but also implementation efforts. Therefore, this chapter introduces the key security elements of a cloud service architecture and some mature security frameworks, which can be applied based on the scenario

Chapter 7, *Threat Modeling Practices and Secure Design*, we will cover the importance of the whole team's involvement with threat modeling practices and the STRIDE examples (spoofing, tampering, repudiation, information disclosure, denial of service, and elevation of privilege).

Chapter 8, *Secure Coding Best Practices*, we will cover secure coding industry best practices, such as CERT, CWE, Android secure coding, OWASP Code Review, and the Apple secure coding guide. Based on those secure coding rules, we will establish secure coding baselines as part of the security policy and release criteria.

Chapter 9, *Case Study - Security and Privacy by Design*, we will examine a case study to discuss the implementation of security by design and privacy by design. The case study will show us the common challenges a DevOps team may have to face when applying security practices, and how the security team may help to provide best practices, tools, a security framework, and a training kit.

Chapter 10, *Security-Testing Plan and Practices*, will give an overview of a security-testing plan, security-testing domains, and the minimum set of security-testing scope. We will discuss a security testing plan, testing approaches, risk analysis, security domains, and industry practices, to build your security-testing knowledge base. In addition, we will introduce some industry best practices, testing approaches, and security tools, for security testing.

Chapter 11, *Whitebox Testing Tips*, will focus on whitebox testing tips. Whitebox code review can be most effective to identify certain specific security issues, such as XXE, deserialization, and SQL injection. However, a whitebox review can be time-consuming if there are no proper tools or strategies. To have an effective whitebox test, we need to focus on specific coding patterns and high-risk modules. This chapter will give tips, tools, and key coding patterns to identify high-risk security issues.

Chapter 12, *Security Testing Toolkits*, we will cover common (but not a comprehensive) set of security testing tools. The major elements of a network that involve security testing include web and mobile connections, configuration, communication, third-party components, and sensitive information. We will look at the testing tips and tools for each element. Furthermore, we will also learn how these tools can be executed both automatically and as tools that are built into continuous integration.

Chapter 13, *Security Automation with the CI Pipeline*, will focus on security practices in the development phases, as well as how to integrate tools such as Jenkins into continuous integration. In the development phases, we explored the techniques of using IDE plugins to secure code scanning, and suggested some static code analysis tools. For the build and package delivery, secure compiler configurations and dependency vulnerability checks will also be introduced. Finally, web security automation testing approaches and tips will also be discussed in this chapter.

Chapter 14, *Incident Response*, will cover incident responses for a security operation team. We will mainly discuss the key activities in the key phases of the incident response process: preparation, containment, detection, and post-incident analysis. The field of incident response includes how to handle public CVE vulnerability, how to respond to white hat or security attacks, how we evaluate each security issue, the feedback loop to the development team, and the tools or practices we may apply in incident response.

Chapter 15, *Security Monitoring*, will cover some security monitoring techniques. The objective of this chapter is to prepare our security monitoring mechanism to protect and prevent our cloud services from being attacked. To be prepared for this, our security monitoring procedures should include logging, monitoring the framework, threat intelligence, and security scanning for malicious programs.

Chapter 16, *Security Assessment for New Releases*, we will cover security assessment for new releases in this chapter. Cloud services may have frequent releases and updates. It's a challenge for the development, operations, and security teams to release their work within a short time frame and to finish the minimum required security testing before releases. In this chapter, we will look at the security review policies and the suggested checklist and testing tools for every release. For testing integration, the BDD security framework and other integrated security testing framework will also be introduced in this chapter.

Chapter 17, *Threat Inspection and Intelligence*, will cover threat inspection and intelligence. This chapter focuses on how to identify and prevent known and unknown security threats, such as backdoors and injection attacks, using various kinds of log correlation. We will introduce the logs that are needed, how those logs are connected, and the potential symptoms of attacks. Some open source threat detection will be introduced. Finally, we will introduce how to build your own in-house threat intelligence system.

Chapter 18, *Business Fraud and Service Abuses*, will cover business fraud and service abuses. Cloud services introduce new types of security risks, such as transaction fraud, account abuses, and promotion code abuses. This online fraud and abuse may result in financial losses or gains, depending on which side of the fence you sit. It will also provide guidelines and rules on how to detect these kinds of behaviors. We will discuss typical technical frameworks and technical approaches needed to build a service abuse prevention or online fraud detection system.

Chapter 19, *GDPR Compliance Case Study*, will cover GDPR compliance as a case study to apply to software development. It discusses the GDPR software security requirements it should include in coming releases. We will also explore some practical case studies, such as personal data discovery, data anonymization, cookie consent, data-masking implementation, and web privacy status.

Chapter 20, *DevSecOps - Challenges, Tips, and FAQs*, will cover some hands-on tips, challenges, and FAQs based on a functional roles perspective.

To get the most out of this book

Refer to the OWASP security projects, NIST, CSA, GDPR for updated security best practices. Try to install and apply the open source tools mentioned in the books.

Apply one security tool or practice at a time into the DevOps process.

Download the color images

We also provide a PDF file that has color images of the screenshots/diagrams used in this book. You can download it here: https://www.packtpub.com/sites/default/files/downloads/HandsOnSecurityinDevOps_ColorImages.

Conventions used

There are a number of text conventions used throughout this book.

`CodeInText`: Indicates code words in text, database table names, folder names, filenames, file extensions, pathnames, dummy URLs, user input, and Twitter handles. Here is an example: "Being able to establish the application resource (`TimeSheet.xls`) in a security relationship is a unique authorization model in OACC."

Bold: Indicates a new term, an important word, or words that you see onscreen.

 Warnings or important notes appear like this.

 Tips and tricks appear like this.

Get in touch

Feedback from our readers is always welcome.

General feedback: Email `feedback@packtpub.com` and mention the book title in the subject of your message. If you have questions about any aspect of this book, please email us at `questions@packtpub.com`.

Errata: Although we have taken every care to ensure the accuracy of our content, mistakes do happen. If you have found a mistake in this book, we would be grateful if you would report this to us. Please visit `www.packtpub.com/submit-errata`, selecting your book, clicking on the Errata Submission Form link, and entering the details.

Piracy: If you come across any illegal copies of our works in any form on the Internet, we would be grateful if you would provide us with the location address or website name. Please contact us at copyright@packtpub.com with a link to the material.

If you are interested in becoming an author: If there is a topic that you have expertise in and you are interested in either writing or contributing to a book, please visit authors.packtpub.com.

Reviews

Please leave a review. Once you have read and used this book, why not leave a review on the site that you purchased it from? Potential readers can then see and use your unbiased opinion to make purchase decisions, we at Packt can understand what you think about our products, and our authors can see your feedback on their book. Thank you!

For more information about Packt, please visit packtpub.com.

1
DevSecOps Drivers and Challenges

Due to the rapid release of cloud services, law enforcement, security incidents, and tenants' data protection, the security is indispensable to cloud/internet services. Moving security activities from right to left during the development lifecycle and having built-in security practices in the continuous integration pipeline are the goals of DevSecOps.

The business environment, culture, law compliance, and external market drive relate to how the DevSecOps security assurance program rolls out in an organization. The DevSecOps or security assurance program management involved with the whole organization across all business units and the key success to DevSecOps will require all stakeholders to agree with the goal and approaches.

We will cover the following topics in this chapter:

- Security compliance (ISO 2700x, FIPS, CSA-CCM)
- Legal/law compliance—**General Data Protection Regulation (GDPR)**
- New technology (third-party, cloud, containers, and virtualization)
- Cloud service hacks/abuse
- Rapid release

As shown in the following diagram, this is how external drivers and challenges impact on a team when delivering secure cloud services:

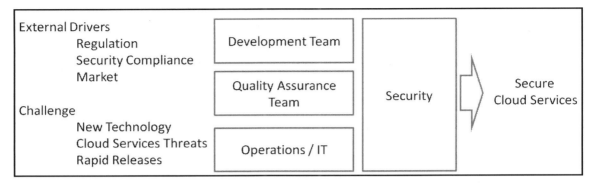

Security compliance

For cloud services, it's very important to have security compliance-ready. Security compliance not only shows how the security controls of the cloud service meet security standards but also demonstrates security trustworthiness for customers and partners. Security compliance provides an overview of a security assurance program, but it won't specifically tell us which security technical approach it should apply. For frequent cloud service releases, constantly monitoring and auditing to meet security compliance can be a big challenge.

Although most cloud service providers are security compliance ready (ISO, PCI, FedRAMP, SOC, and so on), it's still the cloud service customer's responsibility to secure data and manage their own application compliance assessment. Both cloud service customers and providers need to maintain system or application audit logs, configuration lists, and change histories for compliance assessment. The compliance assessment should be considered a continuous activity—not a one-time audit check.

In this chapter, we will introduce key cloud services security compliance as a reference to building a security assurance program, and how these security compliance standards relate to DevSecOps.

ISO 27001

ISO 27001 is an **information security management system (ISMS)**. It provides an overview of organization-level security assurance programs. ISO 27001 won't specify a technical security approach, but it provides a complete set of a security management programs. As the diagram shows, the segments in the upper parts may be more directly related to DevOps security practices, such as compliance, business continuity, operation security, access control, software development, cryptography, incident management, and communication. This will serve as a guideline to further developing our own DevOps security program:

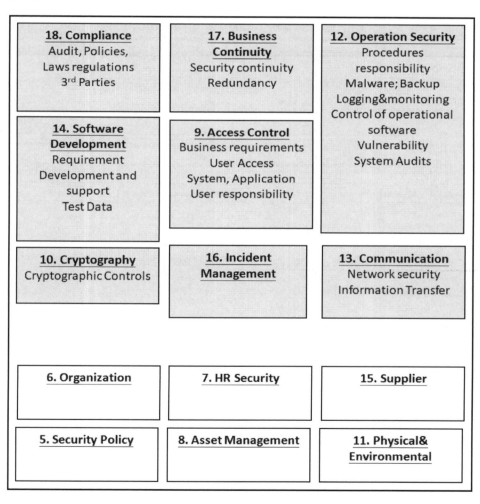

We won't introduce ISO 27001 details, but the following table summarizes how ISO 27001 relates to each role and the DevOps team:

Role	Company/organization security policy	Operation or DevOps team	Development team
ISO 27001 chapters	5 Information security policies 6 Organization of information security 7 Human resource security 8 Assess management 15 Supplier relationships 11 Physical and environmental security	9 Access Control 10 Cryptography 12 Operation security 13 Communication security 17 Information security aspects of business continuity management 16 Information security incident management 18 Compliance; with internal requirements, such as policies, and external requirements, such as laws 19 Cloud services control	14 System development 10 Cryptography 9 Access control

ISO 27017 and ISO 27018

ISO 27018 is mainly for the protection of **personally identifiable information (PII)** in the cloud. It's an extended security compliance based on ISO 27001 and ISO 27002. On top of ISO 27001/27002, ISO 27018 additionally defines PII protection security requirements

ISO 27017 provides both service providers and cloud service consumers with the ability to implement security controls for cloud services. ISO 27017 is an extension to ISO 27002 to address cloud-specific security issues.

Cloud Security Alliance (CSA)

As there are many cloud security compliance methods out there, we may get frustrated trying to follow each of them. The **CSA (Cloud Security Alliance) Cloud Controls Matrix (CCM)** consolidated most security compliance methods into one matrix called CCM. Take application and interface application security as an example—CCM includes all security compliance controls such as ISO, FedRAMP, and NIST 800-53 related to this area, and defines the control ID. The key benefit of referring to CCM is that we can simply focus on CCM and know all other security compliance regulations will be met as well.

In addition, CSA provides a **Consensus Assessments Initiative Questionnaire (CAIQ)**. It's a yes/no questionnaire for cloud consumers or cloud provides to do security self-assessment and to understand the requirements of security controls. **Google Vendor Security Assessment Questionnaires (VSAQ)** also provide a security assessment questionnaire in terms of Web Application Security, Security and Privacy Program, Infrastructure Security and Physical and Datacenter Security.

Furthermore, if you are looking for the top cloud threats and security control mitigations, **Cloud Security Alliance (CSA)** cloud top threats provide guidelines. At the time of writing, it defines the top 12 cloud threats, mappings to threat analysis, CCM/Control ID, and the domains of CSA Security Guidance reference. The following table shows related CSA security guides and how to apply security practices in your organization:

CSA security guides	What it is?	When to apply?
CSA Security Guidance reference	Cloud security white paper	If your organization needs a cloud service security guideline or white paper, this can be a good reference.
Cloud top threats	Top 12 cloud threats and mappings to threat analysis, CCM/Control ID, and domains of CSA Security Guidance reference	It can be the basis for cloud threat modeling.
CAIQ	Yes/no questionnaire	A list of yes/no questions for self-assessment to understand existing security control requirements.
CSA CCM	One consolidated worldwide security standard mapping	It's a great consolidated reference and includes most security compliance standards (ISO 27001, PCI, NIST, and so on). It's the only matrix you need to review security standards compliance.

Federal Information Processing Standards (FIPS)

The FIPS mainly defines minimum security requirements for the use of cryptographic modules. Every organization that is not going to get a FIPS certificate should also refer to it. It's highly recommended that you refer to *Security Requirements for Cryptographic Modules* to understand what cryptographic modules may be considered safe, legacy, or weak.

For developers who would like to learn how to implement cryptographic modules correctly, the following resources are recommended.

- OWASP Cryptographic Storage Cheat Sheet.
- OWASP Guide to Cryptography
- OWASP Key Management Cheat Sheet

Here is a summary of the minimum security requirements for each cryptography algorithm and its usage:

Usage scenario	Unsafe cryptography algorithm (key length)	Legacy Systems Only	Recommended cryptography algorithm
Symmetric encryption	Blowfish, DES, Skipjack, RC4	3 DES only when (key 1 != key 2 != key 3)	AES > 128 bits
Asymmetric encryption	RSA (< 1024 bits)	RSA (1024 bits)	RSA (> 1024 bits)
Hash	MD5	SHA1 (1024 bits)	SHA256
Digital signature	RSA (< 1024 bits) DSA (< 1024 bits) ECDSA (<= 160 bits)	DSA (1024 bits) RSA (1024 bits)	RSA (>=2048 bits) DSA (>=2048 bits) ECDSA (>=256 bits)
Hellman key exchange (DH)	DH (< 1024 bits)	DH (1024-2047 bits)	DH (>=2048 bits) ECDH(>-256 bits)

Center for Internet Security (CIS) and OpenSCAP – securing your infrastructure

The CIS defines security benchmarks and the **National Checklist Program** (**NCP**), defined by the NIST SP 800-70, provides guidance on the security configurations of the operating system, database, virtualization, framework, and applications.

The IT and operation team are primarily responsible for ensuring the security of the infrastructure. However, the development team may also share some responsibilities for securing the infrastructure. For example, the development team may decide to deliver the application package in the form of a container or to apply Infrastructure as Code frameworks, such as **Puppet or Chef**. These technologies allow development teams to define a secure configuration, even in the development stage, and the operation team just needs to apply the secure configuration definition during application deployment.

In addition, it's also the development team's job to provide a list of configuration changes for every release's deployment. This will allow the operation team to review if the configuration changes are secure and appropriate. Due to the complexity and the amount of configuration that needs to be reviewed, the adoption of scanning tools to check if all the configurations are secure and comply with industry best practices is necessary. Cloud service providers may provide such scanning services or tools. Here, we recommend open source tools such as CIS-CAT Lite provided by CIS and OpenSCAP.

The journey to secure the infrastructure and platform can be completed in three stages. The first stage is to define a secure configuration baseline by referring to industry practices such as CIS or NIST NCP. Then, we may apply tools such as Chef or Puppet to ensure every deployment includes a secure configuration as well. The final stage is to do constant monitoring of frequent configuration changes and security compliance assessment.

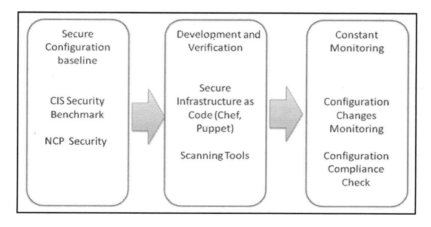

Typical infrastructure components are listed in the following table. CIS provides secure configuration suggestions to each system component and also tools to do the scanning against the security best practice baseline.

CIS provides the CIS Benchmark, which defines the secure configuration of operating systems, server software, cloud services, networking devices, and so on. It helps operation teams to understand how to secure and configure an infrastructure and platform.

Infrastructure layers	System
Web services	Apache, Nginx, IIS
Database	MS SQL, MySQL, Oracle, MongoDB
Virtualization/container	VMware, Docker, Kubernetes
Networking	Cisco devices
Operating systems	Windows, Linux, Ubuntu, CentOS, SUSE

In addition to CIS Benchmark documents, CIS also provides tools to infrastructure or operation teams for secure configuration scanning. The CIS Security website provides related security configuration scanning tools to download.

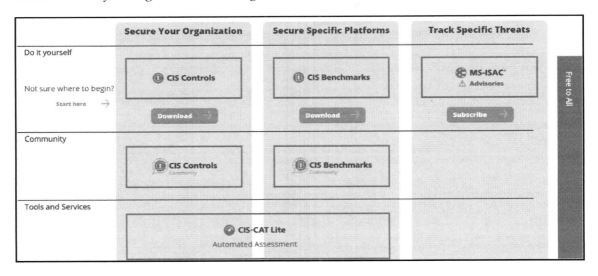

Source: https://www.cisecurity.org/cybersecurity-tools/

National Checklist Program (NCP) repository

The NCP repository provides secure configuration for specific software components. For example, if you are looking for Apache security configuration or the CIS of Apache, you may use the NCP to do the search. The screenshot is from the NIST NCP (National Checklist Program).

National Checklist Program Repository

The National Checklist Program (NCP), defined by the NIST SP 800-70, is the U.S. government repository of publicly available security checklists (or benchmarks) that provide detailed low level guidance on setting the security configuration of operating systems and applications.

NCP provides metadata and links to checklists of various formats including checklists that conform to the Security Content Automation Protocol (SCAP). SCAP enables validated security products to automatically perform configuration checking using NCP checklists. For more information relating to the NCP please visit the information page or the glossary of terms.

Please note that the current search fields have been adjusted to reflect NIST SP 800-70 Revision 4.

Search for Checklists using the fields below. The keyword search will search across the name, and summary.

Checklist Type:	Any............ ▼	Content Type:	Any............ ▼	Search
Authority:	Any............ ▼	Tool Compatibility:	Any............ ▼	Reset
Target:	Any............ ▼	Tested By:	Any............ ▼	
		Keyword:		

Source: https://nvd.nist.gov/ncp/repository

OpenSCAP tools

OpenSCAP is similar to CIS security benchmarks; it also provides a secure configuration baseline. In addition, OpenSCAP also provides different kinds of tool for operation or infrastructure teams to do secure configuration evaluation and scanning. Depending on the requirements, there are four kinds of tool provided, as shown in the following screenshot:

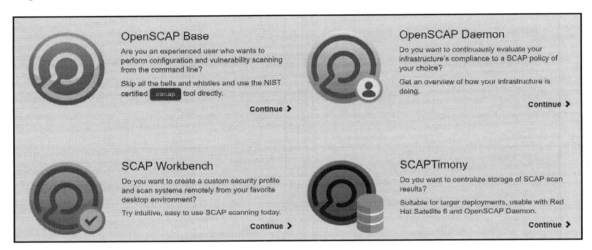

Source: https://www.open-scap.org/tools/

Legal and security compliance

The EU GDPR, which came into force in May 2018, protects all EU citizens from privacy and data breaches. According to the GDPR FAQ:

> *"The GDPR not only applies to organizations located within the EU but it also applies to all companies processing and holding the personal data of data subjects residing in the European Union, regardless of the company's location."*

In other words, if a company is providing services to customers in the European Union, its data handling will need to comply entirely with GDPR. From a DevSecOps point of view, it's related to data collection, handling, storage, backup, modification, transport, and removal—in a secure manner. According to GDPR Article 5, there are six privacy principles:

- Lawfulness, fairness, and transparency
- Purpose limitations

- Data minimization
- Accuracy
- Storage limitations
- Integrity and confidentiality

GDPR, like other security compliance policies, doesn't define the technical approach to achieve it. GDPR can still be too high-level for an engineering team. It needs to translate into software security requirements, design, threat modeling, tools, and so on. The following table summarizes typical security practices for the engineering team:

Stage	Common security practices for privacy or sensitive info handing
Design	**Privacy Impact Assessment (PIA)**
Coding	• Data masking library • Anonymous toolbox • RAPPOR—privacy-preserving reporting algorithms • Encryption storage (RSA, ASE) • Secure erasure • Secure communication protocol (such as TLS v1.2, SSH v2, SFTP, SNMP v3) • Cookie consent • Data Vault • Key management
Testing	OWASP testing for weak cryptography, testing for error handling, testing for configuration, and so on
Deployment	• OWASP configuration and deployment management testing • CIS secure environment configuration • Sensitive information in Git
Monitoring	• ELK for log analysis • Integrity monitoring (IDS/IPS) to monitor any unauthorized changes • CIS secure configuration monitoring • Sensitive information leakage in Git

New technology (third-party, cloud, containers, and virtualization)

New technologies such as virtualization, Docker, and microservices introduce new methods of software delivery and speeds up application deployment, but also brings new security threats and risks. We will briefly discuss how these new technologies change the practices of security and DevOps.

Virtualization

It's very common to install application services on top of a virtualized OS. Virtualization technology helps to make the most physical machine resources such as the CPU, memory, and disks. However, virtualization is a shared OS technology. It also introduces security risks such as VM escape, information leakage, and denial-of-service for applications running on top of virtualization.

Security practices in guest OS virtualization are normally involved with both OS and virtualization hardening. Here are some key security configurations related to virtualization. Refer to CIS Benchmarks for details:

- Limit informative messages from the VM to the VMX file
- Limit sharing console connections
- Disconnect unauthorized devices (USB, DVD, serial devices, and so on)
- Disable **BIOS Boot Specification** (**BBS**)
- Disable guest-host interaction protocol handler
- Disable host guest filesystem server
- Disable VM console paste operations
- Disable virtual disk shrinking
- Do not send host information to guests

The following diagram shows the adoption of virtualization. Virtualization adds a hypervisor layer on top of the physical server so that the virtualized guest OS can run on top of it:

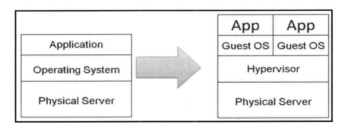

In addition to the secure configuration of virtualization, applying a security patch to virtualization is also a must for operation or IT teams.

In addition, the following resources may help you to search for **Common Vulnerabilities and Exposures (CVE)** in vulnerability databases:

- Exploit Database https://www.exploit-db.com/
- SecLists http://seclists.org/fulldisclosure/
- Vulnerability Notes Database https://www.kb.cert.org/vuls/

To search for the vulnerabilities of a specific product or vendor, refer to the URL search for VMware as following:

- https://cve.mitre.org/cgi-bin/cvekey.cgi?keyword=VMware
- https://www.cvedetails.com/vendor/**252/**Vmware.html

Dockers

The introduction of Docker provides software package delivery and installation with new choices and can be one of the best ways to isolate different applications without using a whole separate OS virtual machine. Software can be packaged into a container by Docker. A container, like a VM image, includes everything needed to run application services such as runtime, system libraries, and settings. The key difference between a virtual machine image and a container is that the container doesn't actually include the whole OS. The container only includes key necessary system libraries and every container shares the same OS kernel during runtime. Therefore, Docker containers can boot up within seconds and use much less memory or far fewer disks than virtualization images.

The use of Docker can also greatly help operation teams to do deployment and secure configuration since a Docker container includes every configuration and the settings you need to run. To understand Docker security practices, check out the **CIS Docker Benchmark** and **Docker security** in the *Further reading* section.

Key secure practices and configurations of Docker are listed here:

- Separate partition for containers
- Updated Linux kernel
- Only allow trusted users to control the Docker daemon
- Audit the Docker daemon, files, and directories
- Restrict network traffic between containers
- TLS authentication for the Docker daemon
- Do not bind Docker to another IP/port or a Unix socket
- Docker daemon configuration files permissions
- Container runtime (Linux Kernel capabilities, SSH, ports, memory, CPU, IPC)

The following diagram shows the key difference between virtualization and Docker. Virtualization is a guest OS level while Docker is actually an application-level isolation and shares the same guest OS:

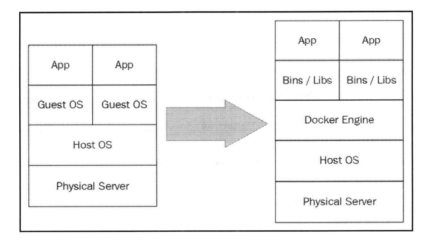

Here is a summary of the known security vulnerabilities identified in Docker.

CVE ID	Related CWE ID	Description
CVE-2014-5282	20	Docker before 1.3 does not properly validate image IDs, which allows remote attackers to redirect to another image through the loading of untrusted images via **Docker load**.
CVE-2017-14992	20	Lack of content verification in Docker-CE (also known as Moby), and earlier allows a remote attacker to launch a Denial of Service attack via a crafted image layer payload; a.k.a Gzip bombing.
CVE-2017-7297	264	Rancher Labs rancher server 1.2.0+ is vulnerable to authenticated users disabling access control via an API call. This is fixed in versions rancher/server:v1.2.4, rancher/server:v1.3.5, rancher/server:v1.4.3, and rancher/server:v1.5.3.
CVE-2016-9962	362	RunC allowed additional container processes via runc exec to be ptraced by the pid 1 of the container. This allows the main processes of the container, if running as root, to gain access to file-descriptors of these new processes during initialization and can lead to container escapes or modification of runC state before the process is fully placed inside the container.
CVE-2014-0047	n/a	Docker before 1.5 allows local users to have an unspecified impact via vectors involving unsafe /tmp usage.

Here is a tip to query a specific vulnerability. Take 'CVE-2014-0047' as an example; just replace the CVE ID number at the end of the following URL.

- `http://cve.mitre.org/cgi-bin/cvename.cgi?name=CVE-2014-0047`
- `https://nvd.nist.gov/vuln/detail/CVE-2014-0047`

Infrastructure as Code (IaC)

Puppet, Chef, Ansible, and SaltStack are tools to apply IaC. The key advantage of using these tools is that any system configuration can be defined in a text file at the design stage and changes can be managed by versions. This will help both operation or development teams to build security configuration baselines such as file permissions, firewall rules, web configurations, or MySQL connections. Once the security configuration baseline is defined, the operation team can monitor any unauthorized changes or roll back the configuration to previous specific versions.

For example, we may have baseline security firewall rules for a web services environment to only allow ports 80 and 443. All an operation team needs to do is to define the firewall rules by using one of the tools (Puppet, Chef, Ansible, SaltStack), and the framework will apply the rules, audit, and even correct changes if other ports are opened by mistake or by other service deployments.

The DevSec Hardening Framework project available at https://github.com/dev-sec provides Ansible, Chef, and Puppet secure configuration baseline template scripts.

The following diagram shows how IaC (for example, Puppet) works:

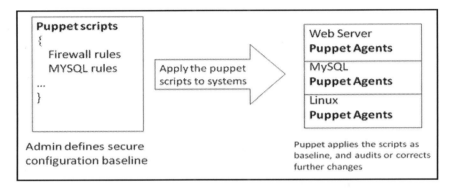

Cloud services hacks/abuse

A CSA survey on the top cloud security concerns has identified the following 12 issues:

- Data breaches
- Weak identity, credentials, and access management
- Insecure APIs
- System and application vulnerabilities
- Account hijacking
- Malicious insiders
- **Advanced Persistent Threats (APTs)**
- Data loss
- Insufficient due diligence

- Abuse and nefarious use of cloud services
- Denial of service
- Shared technology issues

In addition, service abuse has also become a headache for most e-commerce or shopping sites. Let's take one example to understand how hackers or misconduct users can benefit from it.

Case study – products on sale

Assume that one online shopping store is going to have a 50% discount on one new model phone for only the first 100 customers; it will be available at 12:00 on February 1.

What do hackers do?

For this kind of sale with 50 % profit is a great attraction for malicious users to do something. What underground users typically may do involves the massive registration of user accounts. There can be more than 10,000 users accounts registered in a short period of time just before the sales. At the moment of the sale, they will use automated scripts to trigger purchase behaviors and finish the orders within seconds. Once they have ordered or occupied all the phones, they may either sell them at higher prices or even not pay for the orders.

Is this illegal? These behaviors follow the business rules for registration and purchases. Although the behavior may not be against the law, it may be considered misconduct or service abuse. Therefore, this kind of on-sale activity may require additional business rules and regulations. After all, it's not purely hacking behavior. We will discuss this in later chapters. Here, we provide an overview of alleviating measures, which can be by means of business rules or technical approaches:

- The sale is only limited to those customers with a certain period of purchase history
- Apply CAPTCHA to distinguish humans from machines
- Two-factor authentication and registration via phone SMS
- Detection and correlation of IP, phone number, email, account ID, physical address, and GeoIP location
- Unusual page browsing behavior such as skipping products and jumping to the purchase directly
- Unusual massive logins or registration from the same IP or devices

Rapid release

Rapid, frequent, and iterative releases are very common for cloud services. This normally drives the need for DevOps practices. This can be both an opportunity and a challenge to security. The challenge is that a short period of frequent releases may not include enough time to do a full cycle of security testing. There are three maturity levels of DevOps practices:

Maturity level	Achieved	Technology adoption
Continuous integration	• Source code repository and version control • CI workflow with a daily build and unit testing	• Jenkins • Git • Unit testing
Continuous delivery	• Automated deploy to the staging environment • Integration testing on the staging environment • Deployment to production is done manually	• IaC(Puppet) • Docker
Continuous deployment	• Automated deployment and acceptance testing on production • Production changes or configuration management	• IaC (puppet) • Docker • Automated acceptance testing • Configuration monitoring

The adoption of DevOps practices means more collaboration between development, QA, IT, and operation teams, and more in-progress adoption of continuous integration or continuous delivery tools. This provides a good foundation to move to DevSecOps. Depending on the maturity level of the existing CI/CD, security practices or tools can be added on top of the existing CI/CD framework. It's the most effective and least learning curve to introduce security is don't change existing development, QA, IT, operation team the way they work. Building security tools around the existing CI/CD is still the best approach. We will explore this more in upcoming chapters.

The diagram below shows the security involved with development, QA, and operations through the whole CI/CD lifecycle.

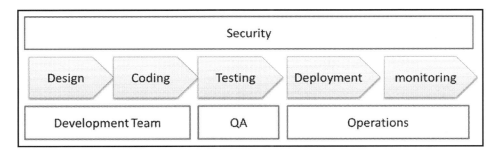

Summary

In this chapter, we discussed external factors that drive the need for security such as security compliance, regulations, and the market. In addition, the adoption of new technologies also brings about new challenges such as Docker, virtualization, cloud services, and IaC.

For security compliance, we briefly discussed ISO 27001 and some security best practices/tools introduced by CSA such as CCM, cloud security guide, CAIQ, and Cloud top threats. FIPS was also discussed for the correct usage of cryptography. In terms of infrastructure security, CIS and OpenSCAP were introduced. Finally, the EU GDPR law regulates and drives the security requirements of data and privacy protection.

Based on all these security challenges and compliance rules, we introduced one small case study for cloud services, which could be hacked and abused. Moreover, what security technologies may apply to DevOps practices. In upcoming chapters, we will further discuss how security goals, metrics, and security assurance programs apply to different kinds of organization and practices.

Questions

1. Does FIPS define the security requirements for cryptography?
2. Which of the following defines the security compliance is primarily focused on personal data privacy?
    1. ISO 27018
    2. FIPS
    3. GDPR
    4. CIS
3. What can be considered cloud service abuse?
    1. Account sharing
    2. Brute-force logins
    3. API abuse
    4. All of the above

4. What is the CIS security benchmark used for?
    1. Anti-virus
    2. Defining secure configuration of the OS, platform, databases, and so on
    3. Firewall
    4. Integrity
5. Which role is involved with security practices during the DevOps cycle?
    1. QA
    2. RD
    3. Operations
    4. All of the above
6. How does the technology Infrastructure as Code help security operation teams?

    1. Virus detection
    2. Secure configuration
    3. Intrusion detection
    4. Encryption
7. Which of the following is not a privacy principle?
    1. Spoofing
    2. Purpose limitations
    3. Storage limitations
    4. Accuracy

Further reading

Read the following links for further readings:

- **CSA (Cloud Security Alliance) Security White Papers:** https://cloudsecurityalliance.org/download/
- **NIST Security Considerations in the System Development Life Cycle**: https://nvlpubs.nist.gov/nistpubs/legacy/sp/nistspecialpublication800-64r2.pdf
- **ISO 29100 information technology security techniques privacy framework**: https://www.iso.org/standard/45123.html
- **NIST National Checklist Program** https://nvd.nist.gov/ncp/repository

- **OWASP Guide to Cryptography** https://www.owasp.org/index.php/Guide_to_Cryptography
- **NVD (National Vulnerability Database)** https://nvd.nist.gov/
- **CVE details** https://cvedetails.com/
- **CIS Cybersecurity Tools** https://www.cisecurity.org/cybersecurity-tools/
- **Security aspects of virtualization by ENISA**: https://www.enisa.europa.eu/publications/security-aspects-of-virtualization/at_download/fullReport
- **CIS Benchmarks also provides a security guide for VMware, Docker, and Kubernetes**: https://www.cisecurity.org/cis-benchmarks/
- **OpenStack's hardening of the virtualization layer provides a secure guide to building the virtualization layer**: https://docs.openstack.org/security-guide/compute/hardening-the-virtualization-layers.html
- **Docker security** at https://docs.docker.com/engine/security/security/

2

Security Goals and Metrics

In the previous chapter, we discussed the challenges and the business drivers for DevSecOps. In this chapter, we will discuss security goals and metrics. The adoption of DevSecOps is a continuous learning journey and takes lots of stakeholder involvement, process optimization, business priority conflict, customization of security tools, and security knowledge learning. This chapter will give you some hands-on tips, challenges, and common practices based on a functional role perspective, and will also look at GDPR as an example to explain how to do a privacy impact assessment.

We will cover the following topics in this chapter:

- Organization goal
- Development goal/metrics
- QA goals/metrics
- Operation goal/metrics

Organization goal

The end goal of security for any organization is to secure customer digital assets. The goal we are going to discuss here is how to define organization-level phased goals for security assurance programs and DevSecOps.

The **Open Web Application Security Project (OWASP)** and **Software Assurance Maturity Model (SAMM)** governance define three key areas when considering an organization security goal:

- **Strategy and metrics**: Establishes the framework for a software security assurance program
- **Policy and compliance**: Focused on ensuring external legal or regulatory compliance (such as GDPR or ISO 27001) is met
- **Education and guidance**: This is for security awareness training and role-specific security capabilities in order to perform DevOps

Here are some typical DevSecOps security practices to be aligned with the business objective. The goal of DevSecOps may be subject to the needs of not only the business objective but also the maturity of the security environment:

- Security compliance with European Union GDPR
- OWASP SAMM self-assessment security maturity to reach level 2
- Security requirement guidelines and baselines ready for each project to follow
- Adoption of secure coding automation tools for a development team
- Threat intelligence security monitoring
- Secure design knowledge-base ready for all developers as a reference
- Security testing tools or platforms ready for QA uses

In addition to OWASP SAMM, NIST 800-160 *Systems Security Engineering* is also a good reference for security engineering methods and practices throughout the life cycle of the software engineering process.

Take the **General Data Protection Regulation (GDPR)** security compliance requirements as an example to review how to implement data privacy during the software engineering life cycle. Whenever a business decides to sell services in European Union markets, the organization will have to comply with GDPR. From an organization-level security management points of view, it's suggested to plan the GDPR compliance in terms of strategy and metrics, security policies, and the security awareness training.

Strategy and metrics

To identify current organization business risk profiles, specific to GDPR compliance, it's suggested you define **Privacy Impact Assessment (PIA)** templates and process to review current data handing risks. The PIA is a tool to identify the privacy risks through the development and operations cycle by the following assessment.

- Whether the information should be collected
- The type of collected information, and related to PII (Personal Identifiable Information)
- Protection and process of handling the information to mitigate any privacy risks.
- Options and explicit consents of the user to collect, handle, edit or remove the information.

Refer to the `https://www.bitkom.org/noindex/Publikationen/2017/Leitfaden/170919-LF-Risk-Assessment-ENG-online-final.pdf` for the PIA resources and templates.

Policy and compliance

Defines general GDPR security requirements and release gates for all projects to follow. In addition, an organization may define security policies as follows:

- Minimum security requirements for the release date
- IAM, privacy, key management, cryptography, and session management
- Security design best practices and templates

It may be a good practice to provide common security requirements as templates or policies for projects teams to follow. Furthermore, it will be more effective to provide or to suggest related implementation frameworks to build into products, which we will discuss in later chapters.

Education and guidance

Education and security awareness training may be subject to the business's needs, culture, roles, and contents. If GDPR compliance is one of the business goals, education should also support the goal. Examples are listed here:

- Privacy and data handling security awareness training
- Deliver role-specific privacy information training to developers, QA, DevOps, or the IT team
- Establish a knowledge-base for a case study, a FAQ, and data-handling templates for employees.

Development goal/metrics

The security goal of a development team is to deliver secure design and implementation. Based on OWASP SAMM practices, there are three key aspects to consider during the construction phase:

- Threat assessment
- Security requirements
- Secure architecture

Although design and implementation review is normally also part of the development team's activities, we will take these into consideration in further discussions.

Threat assessment

To have an effective threat assessment, the following guideline or templates are suggested for the project team:

Threat Modeling tools/templates	Rationale and purpose
Knowledge-base of threats and mitigation	Threat and mitigation knowledge can help the team to decide what's most relevant to the project from the knowledge list instead of starting from zero. For example, CAPEC or ATT&CCK are also good references.
Tools or threat modeling templates	A template or tool can enable the team to deliver consistent quality for threat modeling reports.

In addition, threat modeling analysis won't limit itself to the role of the development team. It also involves the whole team including RD, QA, and DevOps.

If the team is looking for templates or tools, to begin with the followings resources are suggested. We will cover the threat modeling analysis in more detail in `Chapter 7`, *Threat Modeling Practices and Secure Design*.

- **Common Attack Pattern Enumeration and Classification (CAPEC)**: `http://capec.mitre.org/data/definitions/1000.html`
- **Adversarial Tactics, Techniques, and Common Knowledge (ATT&CK)**: `https://attack.mitre.org/wiki/Main_Page`
- **Microsoft SDL threat modeling tool**: `https://www.microsoft.com/en-us/sdl/adopt/threatmodeling.aspx`
- **OWASP threat modeling cheat sheet**: `https://www.owasp.org/index.php/Threat_Modeling_Cheat_Sheet`
- **Elevation of Privilege (EoP) card game**: `https://www.microsoft.com/en-us/sdl/adopt/eop.aspx`
- **OWASP Cornucopia**: `https://www.owasp.org/index.php/OWASP_Cornucopia`

If you are looking for a threat and mitigation knowledge-base, both CAPEC and ATT&CK provide a very good reference. If you need to draw diagrams to do threat analysis, Microsoft's SDL threat modeling tool may help. If you would like to give the team a quick introduction to threat modeling, refer to the OWASP threat modeling cheatsheet. Finally, both the EoP and OWASP Cornucopia provide a card game that makes the threat modeling process more interactive and creates involvement among team members.

Threat assessment for GDPR

Typical threat assessment involves **Spoofing, Tampering, Repudiation, Information Disclosure, Destruction, Escalation (STRIDE)**. When it comes to GDPR compliance assessment, the **Privacy Impact Assessment (PIA)** will focus on how each module collects, handles, and remove Personal Identifiable Information and privacy data. In addition to STRIDE, the PIA focuses on the principles of personal data protection.

Refer to the following diagram of PIA to explore the data flow:

Deliverables and development team self-assessment

The deliverables for a development include threat modeling, design, and coding. The following table summarizes examples of self-assessment metrics for a development team:

Deliverables	Self-assessment checklist
Threat modeling analysis report	Does the threat modeling analysis cover STRIDE six-threat analysis? Does the diagram include all components, data flows, and trust boundaries? Are all the threat mitigations effective and incorporated into the release plan? Does the threat modeling analysis cover all the new features and the previously released risks? Sharing effective threat mitigation as a case study.

Secure coding analysis report	Do any static secure code scanning tools apply to the whole project including legacy parts? Were all the scanning results and false positive warnings reviewed and checked? Secure compiling options have been properly configured. All dangerous or insecure APIs are identified and removed. Knowledge sharing of effective code scanning tools, custom-scanning rules, mitigation approaches, or a common coding issue case study.
Secure architecture	Case study. Delivery of the common security frameworks. Apply an industry best-practice security framework.

Security requirements

Security requirements depend on the business environment, regulations, and security compliance. An organization should define a minimum expected security requirement baseline to be part of the release gate. Based on the severity and impact, the release plan may be a release conditional on the readiness of hotfixes, not released until the issue is fixed, released with mitigation protection, and so on.

To have a security requirement release baseline will also help to build consensus among stakeholders such as IT, development teams, security teams, and so on. Otherwise, it may be that business teams would like to release even though there are security defects, while the security team may not endorse the release.

It's a trade-off between time to market and the level of security maturity. The objective is to build appropriate (not perfect) security controls to protect digital assets with the balance between security quality and time-to-market software releases.

OWASP **Application Security Verification Standard** (**ASVS**) defines three levels of security requirement:

	Application scenario	Threat Protection
ASVS Level 1	This is the minimum required security requirement for all applications.	Simple and easy-to-exploit vulnerabilities.
ASVS Level 2	Application that handles sensitive data.	Specific tools and target attacks to exploit weakness within an application.

| ASVS Level 3 | Applications that require the highest level of security such as e-business, health systems, the Stock Exchange, or critical services. | To attack a Level 3 application will require more in-depth architecture or code analysis. |

In addition, OWASP Secure Software Contract Annex defines a software contract template that covers the security requirements for an outsourcing project: `Https://www.owasp.org/index.php/OWASP_Secure_Software_Contract_Annex/`.

Refer to the following diagram showing OWASP ASVS requirements mapping to a web architecture:

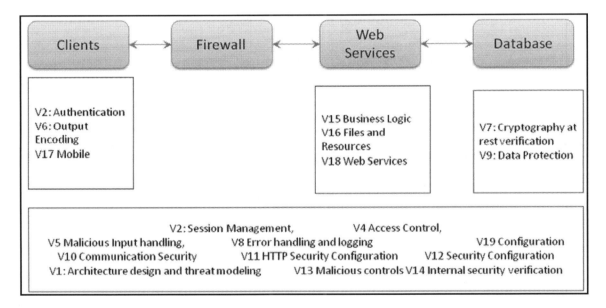

At an organization level, keeping a list of recommended security frameworks or modules can help projects teams not only to build services on top of a mature framework but can also reduce known security risks. Don't reinvent the wheel. An organization should keep these common security modules as part of their security knowledge-base. Here is a common key security module mapping to OWASP ASVS. It's not a comprehensive one; if you are looking for other open source modules, BlackDuck Open Hub may be a good database to search: www.openhub.net.

Security Requirements	Open Source Security Framework
V2: Authentication	OpenSAML2 for Java Central Authentication Service Hostapd
V3: Session Management	Shiro, Spring Security
V4: Access Control	Shiro, Spring Security, OpenSAML OpenLDAP, Apache Directory studio
V5: Malicious Input handling	Apache Jakarta commons validator Bean Validation OWASP Java HTML Sanitizer
V6: Output encoding/escaping	Apache Santuario, Apache XML Security for Java OWASP Java Encoder Project
V7: Cryptography	OpenSSL, BouncyCastle, scrypt, KeyczAr
V8: Error handling and logging	Apache Log4j, Apache Jakarta common logging
V9: Data Protection	Hashicorp Vault, Google Rappor, Private data sharing interface, UTD Anonymization toolbox letsEncrypt, BetterCrypto, mbed TLS
V10: Communication Security	OpenSSL, OpenSSH, JSCH
V11: Http Security configuration	OpenSCAP
V12: Security configuration	OpenSCAP
V13: Malicious controls	VisualCaptcha
V14: Internal Security	This section was incorporated into V13.
V15: Business logic	n/a
V16: Files and resources	ProjectSend, LinShare
V17: Mobile	VisualCaptcha
V18: Web services	Shiro

QA goal/metrics

In this stage of verification, the role of QA is to assess software security-related issues, code-level vulnerabilities, misconfigurations, or logical errors that lead to critical security risks, and so on. OWASP SAMM-defined key security activities in the verification phases include design review, implementation review, and security testing. As we will discuss software security verification details in later chapters, here we highlight some of the key practices in this phase.

Design review

In practice, the security design review can be considered as low-level threat modeling. The following are suggested during design review:

- Security compliance checklist
- Security requirement checklist (OWASP ASVS)
- Top 10 security design issues
- Security issues in the previous release
- Customer or marketing feedback on security issues

When we are doing a design review for the top security issues, we may also refer to industry practices such as OWASP Top 10 and CWE/SANS Top 25 Most Dangerous Software Errors. Meanwhile, the project team may also build its own top security issue based on historical records or customer feedback:

- **OWASP Top 10**: `https://www.owasp.org/index.php/Category:OWASP_Top_Ten_Project`
- **CWE/SANS Top 25 Most Dangerous Software Errors**: `http://cwe.mitre.org/top25/`

In addition, we can review whether the design can effectively mitigate the security risks that we have analyzed in the threat assessment stage. ATT&CK is also a good reference source for design reviews since it lists techniques for threats and also mitigation suggestions:

- **ATT&CK adversarial tactics, techniques and common knowledge**: `https://attack.mitre.org/wiki/Main_Page`

Implementation review

Implementation review involves the following key activities in a development team:

- Secure coding
- Selection of reliable and secure third-party components
- Secure configuration

Since we will discuss secure configuration in a later section, let's focus on third-party components and secure coding in this section. Automated secure code scanning is considered the most efficient way to review. There are some different technical approaches for secure code review.

Third-party components

For third-party component management and review, it's suggested to have the following security guidelines:

- **A third-party software evaluation checklist**:

  This will allow every project to follow consistent criteria to introduce external third-party software components.

- **Recommended third-party software and usage by projects**:

  Having an internal third-party component database allows the project team to cross-reference what projects may have used third-party components and the integration approaches.

- **CVE status of third-party components**:

  Any third-party components may introduce security risks. Track and plan for security patch updates as part of the operation team's routine tasks.

IDE-plugin code review

Having an IDE-plug for code review will help a developer learn and correct a security code issue on the spot even before code submission. It's the most effective way and the least challenging for developers in terms of secure code disciplines. However, due to its line-by-line static code scanning and its inability to analyze the context of the whole source code, the scanning results may give some false positives.

Static code review

Static code scanning tools are used during daily builds or whenever code is submitted for scanning. It's the most effective method to identify security issues at the very beginning of software development. There are various kinds of static code scanning techniques. Refer to the OWASP Benchmark project if you would like to further evaluate these tools (`https://www.owasp.org/index.php/Benchmark`):

Techniques	What is it?	Examples
Static Application Security Testing (SAST)	Static code scanning. Developers can use the tool as part of the IDE plug-in or trigger scanning together with the daily build. It's considered a basic code scanning tool since it's easy for developers to use.	FindSecbugs, Fortify, Coverity, klocwork.
Dynamic Application Security Testing (DAST)	Instead of code review, the DAST identifies security issues by sending an attack payload to the runtime web application.	OWASP ZAP, BurpSuite
Interactive Application Security Testing (IAST)	IAST not only does DAST security testing but also can identify the root/cause at the source code level via a RASP Agent. In simple terms, IAST = RASP Agent + DAST.	CheckMarks Varacode
Run-time Application Security Protection (RASP)	RASP is normally used in web application firewalls since it can detect attacks and take mitigating action in real time.	OpenRASP Refer to `https://github.com/baidu/openrasp`

Target code review

In addition, we can also target and focus on specific security issues by identifying the relevant code patterns. This is also a kind of **Static Application Security Testing (SAST)**, but is more focused on the specific issue. It's the most effective way to review specific kinds of security vulnerability. For example, when it comes to cryptography, the following Java APIs are considered insecure and should not be used:

```
MD5; RC4; SH1; DES; skipjack, SEAL, blowfish, random
```

OWASP Code Review Project and SEI CERT Coding Standards are good references. For other tips on the code review process, please also refer to `Chapter 8`, *Secure Coding Best Practices*.

- OWASP Code Review Project `https://www.owasp.org/index.php/Category:OWASP_Code_Review_Project`
- SEI CERT Coding Standards `https://wiki.sei.cmu.edu/confluence/display/seccode/SEI+CERT+Coding+Standards`

Security testing

The objective of security testing is to ensure the overall application meets security requirements, industry standards, customer expectations, and regulatory controls. At an organizational level, it's suggested to have the following toolkits and knowledge ready in terms of release criteria, testing plan/cases, and automation testing toolkits:

- **Security Release Criteria**:

  The release criteria define the minimum requirement of a quality release gate. They can help business stakeholders to reach consensus decisions about when to release the software. To have such a baseline ready will help to reduce lots of communication issues or arguments between the development, QA, and DevOps teams.

- **Security Testing Plan/Cases**:

  The OWASP testing guide and OWASP ASVS provide a very good reference base for a security testing plan/cases. For mobile security testing, refer to the OWASP Mobile security testing guide. `https://www.owasp.org/index.php/OWASP_Mobile_Security_Testing_Guide`

- **Automation Testing Toolkits**:

  The best approach to security automation is to integrate security tools with existing CI/CD frameworks such as Jenkins. It may require the security tools to have CLI or RESTful API interfaces and also XML/HTML/JSON output reports.

It's important to build in-house toolkits for development and QA teams to do security testing. If your organization has just started to build in-house security testing toolsets, the toolset list in Kali Linux is a good start. The Kali Linux tools listing provides a complete set of security testing tools in many areas. Go here for the list of tools: `https://tools.kali.org/tools-listing`. For mobile testing, refer to the **Mobile Security Testing Guide** (**MSTG**): `https://github.com/OWASP/owasp-mstg/`.

You may consider building an in-house security testing platform with all the security tools ready. Once the software package is deployed, the security testing platform will be triggered to do various kinds of security testing. For example, the **Software Assurance Marketplace (SWAMP)** provides cloud-based source code security analysis with a wide range of programming language and tool support: `https://www.mir-swamp.org/`.

Operation goal/metrics

Based on the SAMM, operational goals can be categorized into three functions: are issue management, environmental hardening, and operational enablement. Let's discuss some of the best practices in each function.

Issue management

Issue management here means how security incidents, vulnerability issues, or security breaches are handled. There should be a vulnerability process in place that involves both the DevOps and Dev team.

In an organization-level security assurance program, it's a must to define security incident and vulnerability response processes and also root cause analysis templates. NIST SP800-61 is a good reference for an organization to establish a security incident response process. It defines an incident handling action checklist in three stages. They are Detection and Analysis; Containment, Eradication, and Recovery, and Post-Incident Activity.

The table lists typical security activities during a security incident handling cycle:

Stage	Development Team	DevOps/IT Team
Vulnerability received	Initially evaluate the received vulnerability. Gives the security issue an initial CVSS rating to understand the level of severity and impact.	
Internal/External Communication	The incident response team (including DevOps, Dev, and IT) discusses the action plan and initial response.	
Root/Cause Analysis	The technical and development teams will look into the security issue, such as which APIs caused the issue, what the data flow may impact, what tools or payload were used for the issue, and come up with a plan to fix it.	IT or DevOps may check if it's a well-known CVE or vulnerability, and any released patches available. If the firewall or virtual patch security controls can be applied to mitigate the issue. Analyze what other cloud services or interface may also have the issue.
Mitigation	Code changes and related impact services. Secure configuration changes.	Firewall security policies Virtual Patch security rules Deployment of security patches Secure configuration changes
Deployment and Verification	Deployment and verification.	

In addition to having an action checklist, it also a good practice to have a vulnerability root cause analysis template. A root cause template will help the incident team to know what to follow, how to collect findings, and what root/cause analysis should be done.

Environment Hardening

The organization-level security policy in environment hardening should at least cover:

- Secure configuration baseline
- Constant monitoring mechanism

The secure configuration baseline defines what is secure and the monitoring mechanism ensures all the configurations are secure all the time.

Secure configuration baseline

Secure configuration guidelines include operating systems, servers, communication protocols, software, web services, databases, virtualization, and so on. It's highly recommended to refer to the CIS benchmarks (`www.cisecurity.org`) as a baseline:

	Common software components
Database	MySQL, SQL Server, Oracle
Web Service	Apache Tomcat, NginX
Virtualization	VMWare, Docker
Operating	Linux (Sent, REdHat, Suse, Ubuntu), Windows Server

Constant monitoring mechanism

In addition to having a secure configuration baseline, there should also be a general policy to define what should be scanned and what tools can apply:

	Purpose	Open source tools
Common vulnerabilities and exposures (CVEs)	To understand if there are any publicly known vulnerabilities in the cloud services. Refer to `https://cve.mitre.org/`.	OpenVAS, NMAP
Integrity monitoring	It determines if major system configuration files have been tampered with.	OSSEC
Secure configuration compliance	Secure configuration to meet industry best practices.	OpenSCAP (`https://www.open-scap.org/`)
Sensitive information exposure	To review whether there is any personally identifiable information, keys, or secret leakage in the configuration files.	No specific open source tool in this area. However, we may define specific regular expression patterns to scan the sensitive info.

Operational enablement

Operational enablement mainly focuses on the interaction between the development team and the DevOps/IT team. Typical activities for an operation team include package deployment to production, ensuring the integrity of every software releases, secure communication protocols, secure configurations and the software updates for the software vulnerabilities. The following three items are considered as a must when a development team delivers a software release to the operation team for production deployment review.

- Code signing for an application deployment
- Application communication ports matrix
- Secure application configurations

Code signing for application deployment

The objective of code signing is to ensure packaged software integrity and authenticity. It ensures the application hasn't been modified and determines the source of the application signed by the specific vendor. The code signing is not only a guideline or process—it's part of the continuous integration build process.

Application communication ports matrix

The purpose of the service communication ports matrix is to allow the IT/DevOps team to know what communication ports/protocols are used. The communication ports list will help the security team to do the necessary firewall configuration adjustment or monitoring. That will also help IT/DevOps to build a networking communication baseline and be able to tell unusual ports or traffic communication. A sample communication ports matrix is listed here:

Source services	Source IP	Source Port	Destination services	Destination port	Protocol	Usage	How to Config
Service A	10.1.1.1	80	Service B	8080	10.1.1.2	REST API	/ect/nginx.conf

Application configurations

The application configuration list defines a list of service or application configurations with change history information The purpose is to allow the DevOps/IT team to manage the secure configuration and monitor any unauthorized changes. The configuration list may cover the OS, virtualization, web services, databases, and frameworks that are specific to the target services. These configurations are often done through Infrastructure as Code, such as Puppet or Chef. Infrastructure as Code makes secure configuration happen even in the implementation phase and allows for easier collaboration between the development and operation teams.

Summary

In this chapter, we discussed security practices from different perspectives based on the OWASP SAMM framework. We discussed security activities in different roles such as security management, development, QA, and operation teams.

First, from the security management perspective, there are organization goals, policies, and education. We use GDPR compliance as an example to show what can be planned in security management.

For a development team, key security activities include threat assessment, security requirements, and secure architecture and coding. Although secure coding is also considered critical in the development stage, we moved the discussion to the secure code verification phase. In terms of threat assessment, we introduced some industry tools, best practices, and even card games. We used GDPR privacy assessment as an example to explain how to execute the PIA. For self-assessment, we listed the key deliverables of a development team. We also discussed the OWASP ASVS security requirements and how the ASVS fits into web framework implementation with suggested open source components.

In terms of verification, there is design review, implementation review, and security testing. We discussed the key considerations of design review and the OWASP Top 10. Different kinds of secure coding review tool were also discussed. Security testing involves release criteria, a testing plan, and automation testing toolkits. After all, automation security testing is the ultimate goal in DevOps.

Operational activities mainly include security issue management, environment hardening, and operation enablement. Moving toward DevSecOps, these activities highly involve not only the operation team itself but also the development and QA teams. We gave examples such as an application communication ports matrix and configuration lists, and analyzed the security incident root/cause.

In the next chapter, we will discuss security assurance programs and organization, and how an organization or culture may execute a security program in an organization.

Questions

1. Does OWASP SAMM stand for Software Assurance Maturity Model?
2. Which of the following are defined in OWASP security governance?
    1. Strategy and metrics
    2. Policy and compliance
    3. Education and guidance
    4. All of the above
3. According to OWASP SAMM, what should be considered during the construction phase?
    1. Security architecture
    2. Threat assessment
    3. Security requirements
    4. All of the above
4. Which of the following is not a tool or technique for threat modeling?
    1. CAPEC
    2. ATT&CK
    3. OWASP Cornucopia
    4. GDPR
5. In GDPR, what security practices may we apply to do a privacy assessment?
    1. PIA Privacy Impact Analysis
    2. Penetration testing
    3. Issue Management
    4. ISO 27001

Further reading

- **GDPR Privacy Impact Assessment**: https://gdpr-info.eu/issues/privacy-impact-assessment/
- **Adversarial Tactics, Techniques & Common Knowledge**: https://attack.mitre.org/wiki/Main_Page
- **SDL Threat Modeling Tool**: https://www.microsoft.com/en-us/sdl/adopt/threatmodeling.aspx
- **Elevation of Privilege (EoP) Card Game**: https://www.microsoft.com/en-us/sdl/adopt/eop.aspx
- **SP 800-100 Information Security Handbook: A Guide for Managers** https://csrc.nist.gov/publications/detail/sp/800-100/final
- **Software assurance marketplace**: https://www.mir-swamp.org/
- **NIST Resources from the Software Assurance Reference Dataset**: https://samate.nist.gov/SARD/around.php
- **NIST Test Suites**: https://samate.nist.gov/SARD/testsuite.php
- **NIST Security Recommendations for Hypervisor Deployment on Servers**: https://nvlpubs.nist.gov/nistpubs/SpecialPublications/NIST.SP.800-125A.pdf
- **NIST Protecting Controlled Unclassified Information in Nonfederal Information Systems and Organizations**: https://www.nist.gov/publications/protecting-controlled-unclassified-information-nonfederal-information-systems-and-3
- **NIST Systems Security Engineering**: https://www.nist.gov/publications/systems-security-engineering-considerations-multidisciplinary-approach-engineering-1
- **OWASP Mobile security testing guide**. https://www.owasp.org/index.php/OWASP_Mobile_Security_Testing_Guide

Security Assurance Program and Organization

3

This chapter will discuss security assurance programs such as **Security Development Lifecycle (SDL)**, OWASP **Software Assurance Maturity Model (SAMM)**, and ISO 27001. Then, we will talk about how security may develop with business growth. Furthermore, there are non-technical parts that matter to the success of any security program, such as the processes, guidelines, training, and roles. A small case study will be discussed to explain how different organization structures may impact the execution of a security assurance program.

The topics to be covered in this chapter are as follows:

- Security assurance programs
- Security growth with business
- Role of a security team in an organization
- Case study—a matrix, functional, or taskforce structure

By the end of the chapter, you will have learned about the following:

- The key parts of a security assurance program, used to rollout DevSecOps
- How security may grow with the business
- The process, roles, and training parts in a security program
- How to plan a security team in an organization across business units

Security assurance program

We will discuss the security assurance program by introducing some industry practices such as SDL, OWASP SAMM, and ISO 27001. SDL lists security activities through the whole development lifecycle. OWASP SAMM explains three levels of maturity to apply security practices in four different functional roles. ISO 27001 is considered the foundation of security certification standards and gives an overview of what a security management program should be.

SDL (Security Development Lifecycle)

Microsoft defines the **SDL (Security Development Lifecycle)** to help developers to build secure software. The security activities in each development phase are shown in the following table:

MS SDL Stages	Security activities
Training	• Core security training
Requirements	• Establish security requirements • Create quality gates/bug bars • Perform security and privacy risk assessments
Design	• Establish design requirements • Perform attack surface analysis reduction • Use threat modeling
Implementation	• Use approved tools • Deprecate unsafe functions • Perform static analysis
Verification	• Perform dynamic analysis • Perform fuzz testing • Conduct attack surface review
Release	• Create an incident response plan • Conduct final security review • Certify, release, and archive
Response	Execute incident response plan

Although there is a mature SDL process that an organization can follow or refer to, the key to these security practices and their execution is how to make these security practices part of developer, QA or development team daily tasks. In addition, for any security program to be successful, it must be tailored to business needs and to support the business's success.

Take a developer's routine daily tasks as an example—he needs to understand the business and functional requirements to do the design, apply appropriate third-party modules, code, debug, troubleshoot, and locally compile/build for verification. It's lots of work just to finish the functions to meet a project deadline. The activity of secure coding takes more than 100+ secure coding rules. It's a big challenge for any developer to be an expert or even be aware of all the coding rules.

Therefore, in most cases, the adoption of proper tools will greatly help. If the developer is using Eclipse as the main source code editor, then it's recommended you have secure coding tools as part of the Eclipse plug-in. Depending on the programming language and IDE, the security and development team may put together a plan involving how security tools can help and be built into the development of daily tasks. A secure coding guideline is still a must; however, the most effective and efficient way to implement secure coding is to provide an easy-to-use tool for every developer—to be parts of his/her daily tasks.

The same situations also apply to QA or IT DevOps teams. It's a challenge to require every QA or IT team to be familiar with all security testing or hardening practices. The best approach is also to provide related automation security tools to do the job.

OWASP SAMM

OWASP SAMM categorizes security practices into four key business functions—governance, construction, verification, and operations. It's a very practical guide for any organization to follow for self-assessment of the security maturity level. Microsoft SDL defines security practices during the development process while OWASP SAMM defines security practices based on business functions and the four levels of security maturity:

Business functions	Security practices
Governance	• Strategy and metrics • Policy and compliance • Education and guidance
Construction	• Threat assessment • Security requirements • Secure architecture
Verification	• Design review • Implementation review • Security testing
Operations	• Issue management • Environment Hardening • Operational enablement

Depending on the organization, the business function or the boundary between construction, verification, and operations may vary; OWASP SAMM 12 security practices are considered the minimum in a DevOps environment. If we map the business organization functions to the OWASP SAMM, it may look like the following diagram. There is a CSO, which manages the whole security program: the development team manages software application construction, the security testing team verification, and the IT or operation team application operations:

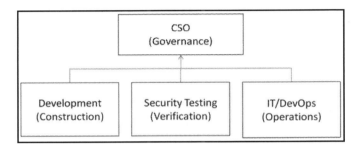

Security guidelines and processes

After looking at the industry practices, SDL, OWASP SAMM, and ISO 27001, it's normally the CSO or CTO security office's job to define the security governance program and the security guidelines. The following table shows an overview of security guidelines. In practice, these security guidelines are templates, suggested centrally and updated in a security knowledge base for every project team to refer to. Again, guidelines won't be effective if these guidelines aren't able to be part of a developer, QA, IT, or DevOps's daily tasks. Providing tools with built-in security practices for DevOps teams is still key to the success of DevSecOps. The following table suggests some industry practices and tools that may apply to security guidelines:

Phases	Guidelines, templates, checklist, toolkits	Industry practice reference
Security training	• Security awareness • Security certification program • Case study knowledge base • Top common issue • Penetration learning environment	• OWASP top 10 • CWE top 25 • OWASP VWAD
Security maturity assessment	• Microsoft SDL, OWASP SAMM self-assessment for maturity level	• Microsoft SDL • OWASP SAMM

Secure design	• Threat modeling templates (risks/mitigation knowledge base) • Security requirements for release gate • Security design case study • Privacy protection	• OWASP ASVS • NIST • Privacy risk assessment
Secure coding	• Coding guidelines (C++, Java, Python, PHP, Shell, Mobile) • Secure coding scanning tools • Common secure coding case study	• CWE • Secure coding CERT • OWASP
Security testing	• Secure compiling options such as Stack Canary, NX, Fortify Source, PIE, and RELRO • Security testing plans • Security testing cases • Known CVE testing • Known secure coding issues • API-level security testing tools • Automation testing tools • Fuzz testing • Mobile testing • Exploitation and penetration • Security compliance	• Kali Linux tools • CIS
Secure deployment	• Configuration checklist • Hardening guide • Communication ports/protocols • Code signing	• CIS Benchmarks • CVE
Incident and vulnerability handling	• Root cause analysis templates • Incident handling process and organization	• NIST SP800-61
Security training	• Security awareness by email • Case study newsletter • Toolkit usage hands-on training • Security certificate and exam	• NIST 800-50 • NIST 800-16 • SAFECode security engineering training

Security growth with business

Depending on the business's development status, the needs and implementation of security may be subject to the business's objectives and environment. A start-up company may leverage external cloud services and out-of-the-box security services to protect services and data. A multi-million dollar cloud service company may self-build and customize security services based on its own business needs, and even share the security technology, making it open source. Let's discuss how business growth in different stages may be related to the scope of security practices.

Stage 1 – basic security control

In this stage, we may be dealing with a start-up company. No dedicated security team is part of the IT team. Most security controls are adopted from cloud services, such as AWS.

Although the cloud service may provide security services, it's still the user's responsibility to protect the application and data. Therefore, the following are critical for the security assurance program at this stage. Take AWS service practices as an example:

- Leverage third-party cloud service provider security mechanisms (for example, AWS provides IAM, KMS, security groups, WAF, Inspector, CloudWatch, and Config)
- Secure configuration replies on external tools such as AWS Config and Inspector
- Service or operation monitoring may apply to AWS Config, Inspector, CloudWatch, WAF, and AWS shield

There may still be no skilled secure coding developers or penetration testers in the organization. Mostly the team still relies on external tools and services for security practices.

Stage 2 – building a security testing team

In this stage, the business is getting stable and mature. The organization may set up a security testing team who is in charge of application security verification before release and continuous environment vulnerability monitoring. The development team may heavily rely on the security testing team for security defects and issues. The development team is only focused on the business's functional development, and not yet involved with the secure design or secure coding.

Dedicated security testing may start to use some security automation testing or open source monitoring tools. Developers are learning secure coding through identified security defects case by case, and still haven't adopted any formal process for threat modeling, design or architecture security review. The team is at the beginning of shifting security to the left.

In this stage, the in-house security team may try to investigate or use parts of open source security tools. The following table shows typical security toolkits that you may consider applying:

Category	Opensource tool name
Vulnerability assessment	• NMAP • OpenVAS
Static security analysis	• FindBugs for Java • Brakeman for Ruby on Rails • Infer for Java, C++, Objective C and C • Cppcheck or Flawfinder for C/C++
Web security	• OWASP dependency check • OWASP ZAP • Archni-Scanner • Burp Suite • SQLMap • w3af
Communication	• Nmap • NCAT • Wireshark • SSLScan • sslyze
Infrastructure security	• OpenSCAP • InSpec
VM Toolset	• Pentest Box for Windows • Kali Linux • Mobile Security Testing Framework
Security monitoring	• ELK • MISP—Open source Threat Intelligence Platform • OSSCE—Open source HIDS Security • Facebook/osquery—performant endpoint visibility • AlienValut OSSIM—opensource SIEM

Stage 3 – SDL activities

As software service delivery becomes more large-scale and frequent, the need for a secure development lifecycle becomes critical. In this stage, the key objective is to build security practices into the development and operation teams.

The key differences and newly introduced security practices in this stage are as follows:

- Security shifts to the left and involves every stakeholder
- Architect and design review is required to do threat modeling
- Developers get secure design and secure coding training
- Operation and development teams are as a closed-loop collaboration
- Adoption of industry best practices such as OWASP SAMM and Microsoft SDL for security maturity assessment

There are be some learning curves or even resistance when applying the SDL. After all, these security practices will bring in additional efforts for the team. In the initial SDL implementation stage, adequate training and communication are necessary. Allow some time for the team to become familiar with security practices and tools. Make it a fun learning journey.

The adoption of tools to bake security into DevOps is critical. Making security tools (threat modeling, secure coding, security framework) easy to use for developers is the key to shifting security to the left in the development cycle.

Stage 4 – self-build security services

In this stage, the company not only has its own security testing and monitoring team but also develops and tailors its own security services such as a **web application firewall (WAF)** and intrusion detection. Furthermore, the company may even contribute some security tools or services to the open source community. The security assurance program covers not only the company itself but also the partners or the ecosystem.

Take Salesforce as an example—the Salesforce Developer Center portal provides security training modules, coding, implementation guidelines, tools such as assessment tools, code scanning, testing or CAPTCHA modules, and also a developer forum. Whether you are building an application on top of salesforce or not, the Salesforce Developer Center is still a good reference not only for security knowledge but also for some open source tools you may consider applying.

Stage 5 – big data security analysis and automation

This stage in security is not only about detection of a known threat but also using the cloud, big data analysis, and machine learning to prevent unknown threats and to enable the system to take proactive protection action. Key characteristics at this stage are:

- Fully or mostly automated security testing through the whole development cycle
- Applying big data analysis and machine learning to identify abnormal behavior or unknown threats
- Proactive security action is taken automatically for security events, for example, the deployment of WAF rules or the deployment of a virtual patch

Typical open source technical components in big data analysis frameworks include the following:

- Flume, Log Logstash, and Rsyslog for log collection
- Kafka, Storm, or Spark for log analysis
- Redis, MySQL, HBase, and HDFS for data storage
- Kibana, ElasticSearch, and Graylog for data indexing, searching, and presentation

The key stages in big data security analysis are explained in the table:

Stage	Description
Data collection	Collects logs from various kinds of sources and systems such as firewalls, web services, Linux, networking gateways, endpoints, and so on.
Data normalization	Sanitizes or transforms data formats into JSON, especially, for critical information such as IP, hostname, email, port, and MAC.
Data enrich/label	In terms of IP address data, it will further be associated with GeoIP and WhoIS information. Furthermore, it may also be labeled if it's a known black IP address.
Correlation	The correlation analyzes the relationship between some key characteristics such as IP, hostname, DNS domain, file hash, email address, and threat knowledge bases.
Storage	There are different kinds of data that will be stored—the raw data from the source, the data with enriched information, the results of correlation, GeoIP mapping, and the threat knowledge base.

| Alerts | Trigger alerts if threats were identified or based on specified alerting rules. |
| Presentation/query | Security dashboards for motoring and queries. ElasticSearch, RESTful API, or third-party SIEM. |

A typical big data security analysis framework is shown in the following diagram, or you can refer to the open source Apache Metron framework: `https://cwiki.apache.org/confluence/display/METRON/Metron+Architecture`.

The big data security analysis conceptual architecture is shown as follows:

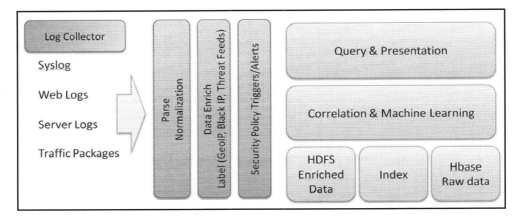

Role of a security team in an organization

The role and job scope of a security team also depend on the stage of the business. It can be part of the IT team at the beginning; a dedicated security team for infrastructure security monitoring, moving toward a specialized security function team for security tool development and security policy management; or a security testing team, and so on.

Let's look at two kinds of typical scenario to discuss the role and the scope that an organization may have. One is the security engineering team under a CTO, and the other is a dedicated CSO with full, specialized functions of a security team.

Security office under a CTO

This is a typical organization structure with the security engineering team under the CTO office. There are some characteristics of this kind of organization structure:

- No dedicated **Chief Security Officer (CSO)**
- The security team may not be big—for example, under 10 members
- The security engineering team serves all projects based on their needs
- The key responsibility of the security engineering team is to provide security guidelines, policies, checklists, templates, or training for all project teams
- It's possible the security engineering team members may be allocated to a different project to be subject matter experts based on the project's needs
- Security engineering provides the guidelines, toolkits, and training, but it's the project team that takes on the main responsibility for daily security activity execution

The disadvantage of this kind of team structure is that the security engineering team may not be able to fully dedicate itself to projects due to limited security members. After all, the security will work the best to tie in with business more closely, and to understand the challenges of the engineering team more deeply.

The following diagram shows how the CTP manages the team on a project basis, and how the security engineering team reports to the CTO directly to support them and ensure security practices for all projects and architecture:

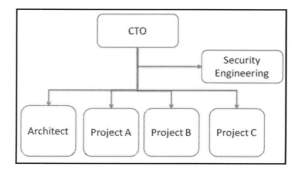

Dedicated security team

As the business grows, the organization may set up an official CSO role with more dedicated security functional teams such as a security management team, security testing, security engineering, security monitoring, and security services:

- **Security management**: The team defines the security guidelines, process, policies, templates, checklist, and requirements. The role of the security management team is the same as the one previously discussed in the *Security office under a CTO* section.
- **Security testing**: The team is performing in-house security testing before application release.
- **Security engineering**: The team provides a common security framework, architecture, SDK, and API for a development team to use.
- **Security monitoring**: This is the security operation team, who monitor the security status for all online services.
- **Security services**: This is the team that develops security services such as WAF and intrusion deference services.

Sometimes, it can be a mixed structure. For example, there is still no dedicated CSO, but the security testing team and security management team report to the CIO. It all depends on the business objective and the stage of the business needs.

This kind of security team structure includes most security functions. However, there is a similar issue to the previous one. We would like security built-in with the project and practices. This will require deep involvement with the project team and a clear understanding of each project business flow. That's why we would like to discuss another matrix style of organization structure in the next section:

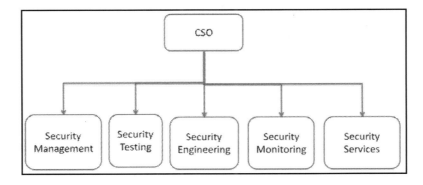

Case study – a matrix, functional, or taskforce structure

John, the CSO of a cloud software application provider, is planning the security team structure in an organization. The existing security team consists of a secure design team, a secure coding team, and a testing team. The secure design team is in charge of threat modeling, the secure framework, and secure design guidelines. The secure coding team is providing secure coding tools and a checklist for development teams. The secure testing team is doing security verification for every service release. On the other hand, the CSO, Peter, manages the software development team (including developers, QA, and operation members).

Both Peter and John know security is an expert knowledge and that is better to have a dedicated security team to allow the security knowledge to apply across projects and also to enable members to increase their security skills. On the other hand, they also know security must tie with business and existing software development teams. Therefore, they are going through two main stages—the security resource pool stage followed by the security technical committee stage.

Security resource pool

The key advantage to keeping security members within one dedicated security team is to allow security knowledge sharing across projects and be able to deliver tools or best practices for the whole organization. However, for security practices to bake into DevOps practices requires a certain level of involvement for DevOps and security teams. Therefore, the CTO lists the all-year project plan for the CSO as a reference to plan the security team's involvement with projects. The CSO allocates security members to participate in different projects. The security members dot line report to the project manager during the period of a project assignment. It works for a while but there are some issues under this kind of organization structure:

- The project team may rely heavily on security team involvement. For example, developers may still have little knowledge of secure coding because the security team has been doing most jobs.
- As the business and project grow, security team members may own several projects at a time, and not be able to handle all the security details for every project.

Therefore, John and Peter realize the situation and would like the existing DevOps team to involve more security tasks, while the role of the security team may be more like security consultants.

Security technical committee (taskforce)

As the project team is getting large, and the number of projects is also rapidly growing. John and Peter decide to form a security technical committee, which is a virtual taskforce team to encourage team involvement in security and also to enable security knowledge sharing across projects. They form three taskforce teams—**secure design, secure coding,** and the **secure testing taskforce team**. Take the secure design taskforce team as an example—the team consists of one or several secure design experts from the security team, and also a developer representative from every project team. The developer representative is like a security champion of the project team. He will join in the security discussion with the task force and take security practices or guidelines back to the project team. The secure design taskforce will have a weekly meeting with all security representatives—from all project teams—and security experts from the security team to discuss the following topics (not an exhaustive list):

- Common secure design issues and mitigation (initiated by security team)
- Secure design patterns for a project to follow (initiated by security team)
- Secure design framework suggestions for projects (initiated by security team)
- Specific secure design issues raised by one project and looking for advice on other projects (initiated by project team)
- Secure design review assessment for one project (initiated by project team)

The structure of the security taskforce team between the developer and security teams is shown in the following diagram:

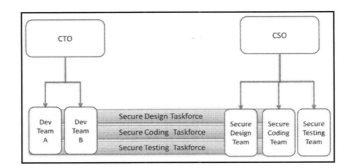

There is no perfect security organization structure. It's a question of a better fit with existing business needs and practices. For any security team structure, the most important thing is to understand the objective of the business goal. Setting up a virtual taskforce team may supplement any existing official team structure since the taskforce allows security knowledge to be shared across projects.

Summary

In this chapter, we discussed three typical security assurance programs. The SDL focused on the security activities in each development stage. The OWASP SAMM defined security activities in four different functions. The ISO 27001 provided an overview of the security management program. These are the foundations on which we can build our own security guidelines, process, checklist, or toolkits.

As a business grows, the need and the scope of security gets complicated. We divided security growth into five stages. In stage one, we began with the basic need for security control. In stage two, an organization may build its own in-house security testing team. In stage three, the security activities apply SDL to the larger scope and shift to the left—to the development team—in the early design stage. In this stage, most security tools or automation are applied not only to testing but also to the development and operation teams. In stage four, instead of purchasing security services, the security team started to build security services, such as WAF, or intrusion detection, that better to fit business needs. In stage five, the team use big data analysis to prevent unknown threats.

Since security ties in with every business stakeholder, the roles and security teams in an organization structure were also discussed. There is no perfect organization structure, only the best fit based on business needs and also the culture. After all, there are critical non-technical things to consider for the adoption of any security program.

Questions

1. Does Microsoft SDL stand for Security Development Lifecycle?
2. According to SDL, what activities should be done during the design stages?
    1. Establishing design requirements
    2. Performing attack surface analysis reduction
    3. User threat modeling
    4. All of the above

3. In OWASP SAMM, what security practice is not part of security governance
    1. Security and metrics
    2. Education and guidance
    3. Secure architecture
    4. Policy and compliance

4. In OWASP SAMM, which security practice is not part of security operations?
    1. Issue Management
    2. Security requirements
    3. Environment hardening
    4. Operational enablement

5. What is not one of the characteristics of the security office under CTO?
    1. Large security team size—over 100 members
    2. No dedicated CSO
    3. The security team serves all projects
    4. The security team may not be able to fully involve project teams

Further reading

- **Microsoft Security Development Lifecycle**: `http://www.microsoft.com/en-us/SDL/`
- **OWASP SAMM Project**: `https://www.owasp.org/index.php/OWASP_SAMM_Project`
- **CWE/SANS Top 25 Most Dangerous Software Errors**: `https://cwe.mitre.org/top25/`
- **OWASP Vulnerable Web Applications Directory Project**: `https://www.owasp.org/index.php/OWASP_Vulnerable_Web_Applications_Directory_Project`
- **CERT Secure Coding Standards**: `https://wiki.sei.cmu.edu/confluence/display/seccode/SEI+CERT+Coding+Standards`
- **NIST Special Publication 800-53**: `https://nvd.nist.gov/800-53`
- **SAFECode Security White Papers**: `https://safecode.org/publications/`
- **Microsoft Threat Modeling tool 2016**: `https://aka.ms/tmt2016/`
- **Salesforce Developer Center**: `https://developer.salesforce.com/devcenter/security`
- **Apache Metron for real-time big data security**: `http://metron.apache.org/documentation/`

- **Introducing OCTAVE Allegro: Improving the Information Security Risk Assessment Process**: https://resources.sei.cmu.edu/asset_files/ TechnicalReport/2007_005_001_14885.pdf

- **NIST 800-18 Guide for Developing Security Plans for Federal Information Systems**: http://nvlpubs.nist.gov/nistpubs/legacy/sp/ nistspecialpublication800-18r1.pdf

- **ITU-T X.805 (10/2003) Security architecture for systems providing end-to-end communications**: https://www.itu.int/rec/dologin_pub.asp?lang=eid=T-REC-X.805-200310-I!!PDF-Etype=items

- **ETSI TS 102 165-1 V4.2.1 (2006-12) : Method and proforma for Threat, Risk, Vulnerability Analysis**: http://www.etsi.org/deliver/etsi_ts/102100_ 102199/10216501/04.02.01_60/ts_10216501v040201p.pdf

- **SAFECode Fundamental Practices for Secure Software Development**: https:// safecode.org/wp-content/uploads/2018/03/SAFECode_Fundamental_ Practices_for_Secure_Software_Development_March_2018.pdf

- **NIST 800-64 Security Considerations in the System Development Life Cycle**: https://nvlpubs.nist.gov/nistpubs/legacy/sp/ nistspecialpublication800-64r2.pdfhttps://csrc.nist.gov/publications/ detail/sp/800-64/rev-2/final

- **NIST 800-50 Building an information technology security awareness and training program**: https://nvlpubs.nist.gov/nistpubs/legacy/sp/ nistspecialpublication800-50.pdf

- **CIS Security Benchmark**: https://www.cisecurity.org/cis-benchmarks/

- **NIST 800-16 Information Technology Security Training Requirements**: https://csrc.nist.gov/publications/detail/sp/800-16/ final

- **SAFECode Security Engineering Training**: http://safecode.org/publication/ SAFECode_Training0409.pdf

- **A Hybrid Threat Modeling Method**: https://resources.sei.cmu.edu/ library/asset-view.cfm?assetid=516617

- **Microsoft SDL tools** https://www.microsoft.com/en-us/SDL/adopt/tools. aspx

4
Security Requirements and Compliance

We previously discussed a security assurance program in an organization, and we will explore security requirements and compliance in this chapter. We all agree that security and privacy are essential to software release. However, it can be a challenge for a product manager to plan security or privacy features into product releases.

In this chapter, we will discuss security requirements covering four aspects: the security requirements for each release quality gate, the security requirements for general web applications, the security requirements for big data, and the security requirements for compliance with **General Data Protection Regulation** (**GDPR**). Some security requirements are engineering-driven, such as release gates, and some are marketing-driven, such as GDPR. This chapter provides security requirements planning guidelines by looking into different angles of security requirements.

We will cover the following topics in this chapter:

- Security requirements for the release gate
- Security requirements for web applications
- Security requirements for big data
- Privacy requirements for GDPR

Security requirements for the release gate

It's important to set up security quality criteria for each release stage, such as threat modeling, design, coding, testing, and deployment. The objective of the release gate is to improve the quality of security releases in each stage. When you start defining release gates, it's suggested to start with a few major or high-priority security issues, since a long checklist will result not only in overhead but also in resistance from the development or QA teams.

For the introduction of security release gates, allow the team to learn, to become familiar with the security practices, and also to make mistakes. Try to be a coach to support and help the team to meet a higher standard of security quality instead of acting like the police and inspecting deliverables.

Release gate examples

When all teams are familiar with security practices and have performed some security automation, additional security checklists can be added for higher security standards. A typical security release gate example for each stage is shown in the following table:

Stage	Examples of release Gate
Design	• Threat modeling activities were performed for high-risk modules. • The uses of third-party component versions was reviewed without major vulnerability. • The top common secure design issues were reviewed without major issues.
Coding	• The static code analysis tool was used to identify major security risks. • High severity issues in the code scanning results were all checked. • No sensitive information was found in the source code (such as password, IP, email, encryption key).
Build	• Toolchain (compiler and linker) hardening configurations such as **Position Independent Executables (PIE)**, or **Address Space Layout Randomization (ASLR)**, or **Data Execution Prevention (DEP)** were correctly configured.
Testing	• No high-severity security issue. The severity is measured by the **Common Vulnerability Scoring System (CVSS)** version 3.0. • OWASP testing cases were followed and executed. • All protocols were tested with a fuzzer.
Production delivery	• The secure configuration definition was delivered. • The communication ports, interface, and protocols were documented.
Monitoring	• The readiness of services and the configuration list for security scanning. • The readiness of service logs for security analysis.

Common Vulnerability Scoring System (CVSS)

When it comes to the point-of-release review, it's very common to have arguments over the decision to move to the next stage or not among different stakeholders. For example, a development team may think it's a minor issue to proceed to the next stage, while the operation team may consider it a high-risk issue.

Therefore, to get a more objective standpoint on the severity and impact of a security issue, it's suggested to apply CVSS 3.0. CVSS 3.0, `https://www.first.org/cvss/calculator/3.0`, evaluates a security issue by answering the following eight questions:

- **Attack Vector (AV)**: Does the attack require physical access, or can it be done through a network?
- **Attack Complexity (AC)**: Can the attack be done at any time, or at only under specific conditions?
- **Privileges Required (PP)**: Does the attack require administrator privileges?
- **User Interaction (UI)**: Does the attack require user interaction (such as a click) to be successful?
- **Scope (S)**: Does the attack only impact the vulnerable component, or all other components and the whole system?
- **Confidentiality (C)**: Will any confidential information be stolen?
- **Integrity (I)**: Will there be any integrity impact, such as tampering or changes to system information?
- **Availability (A)**: Will there be any availability impact, such as a performance impact or services unavailable?

In addition to the preceding base score as mentioned, we may also go further by reviewing the **Temporal Score** and **Environmental Score**. The Temporal Score reviews the maturity of the exploit code, the level of remediation (hotfix, workaround, or none), and report confidence. The **Environmental Score** mainly evaluates the required network, or host modification for a successful exploitation such as privileges, user interaction, integrity, availability and confidentiality. These two additional vectors may help to give us an insight into the complete severity and impact of a security issue.

Security requirements for web applications

The OWASP **Application Security Verification Standard (ASVS)** not only provides a list of security requirements that a development team should follow but can also be used as a checklist for a QA team to do verification and assess the security level of the application. Please refer to the project source at `https://www.owasp.org/index.php/Category:OWASP_Application_Security_Verification_Standard_Project`.

OWASP Application Security Verification Standard (ASVS)

The OWASP ASVS defines the following security requirements at the time of writing, in 2018. Some section numbers were skipped because they were incorporated into other sections:

- ASVS V1 Architecture
- ASVS V2 Authentication
- ASVS V3 Session Management
- ASVS V4 Access Control
- ASVS V5 Input Validation and Output Encoding
- ASVS V7 Cryptography
- ASVS V8 Error Handling
- ASVS V9 Data Protection
- ASVS V10 Communications
- ASVS V13 Malicious Code
- ASVS V15 Business Logic Flaws
- ASVS V16 Files and Resources
- ASVS V17 Mobile
- ASVS V18 API
- ASVS V19 Configuration
- ASVS V20 Internet of Things

The OWASP ASVS defines three levels of security requirements. Take *V7: Cryptography at rest* as examples; in level-1 applications, it may only require that cryptographic modules fail securely. For level 2/3 applications, whose security requirements surpass level 1, additionally requires the use of an approved random number generator in the application.

In practice, the product manager may use ASVS to plan the required security features for coming releases, a development team refers to ASVS for the right implementation of a secure application, and a QA team uses it as a checklist to evaluate the application, or as release gate. Customize the ASVS checklist and build the checklist into your security practices to make it more effective. For example, make the security requirements baseline part of product feature-planning templates, or list a security check as the release gate in the process. After all, we don't expect the ASVS will be just a checklist document. It takes awareness, process, and consensus to make it into practice.

Security knowledge portal

You may also consider building an internal security knowledge portal, which includes the security requirements, case study, guideline or template and so on. An in-house security portal not only helps to deliver the organization-level related security policies, but also to build an internal knowledge base. The project team can also share their best practices or tools on the portal, to increase experience sharing across business units. An ideal security knowledge portal may cover the following areas, as shown in the following figure:

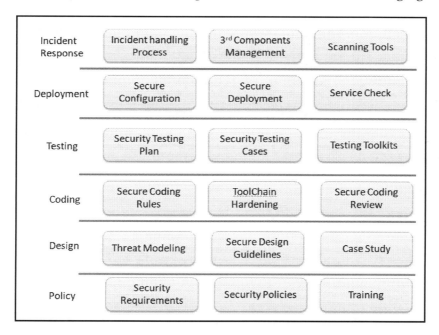

If your organization is new or just planning to build an in-house security knowledge portal, OWASP **Security Knowledge Framework (SKF)** is highly recommended. OWASP SKF provides the OWASP ASVS checklist, security knowledge base, and also security code examples. The following is the URL from which to download the OWASP SKF: `https://github.com/blabla1337/skf-flask`.

Security requirements for big data

Security requirements for big data consist not only the security for the whole big data framework but also the protection of the data itself. Protecting data takes more than just encryption. According to CSA Top 10 challenges in big data security and privacy, the security and privacy of big data are classified into four areas:

- Infrastructure security
- Data privacy
- Data management
- Integrity and reactive security

We will further discuss security requirements based on these four security categories.

Big data security requirements

The following table lists examples of security requirements in each category. It's not an exhaustive list, but some key security requirements you should consider for big data:

Big data security classifications	Examples of security requirements
Infrastructure Security	• Database and service availability • Protection against DDOS and a huge volume of data • Secure data transmission, such as TLS 1.2
Data Privacy	• Data classification and protection • Unauthorized access auditing and logging • Data masking for sensitive or personal information • Compliance with privacy laws or regulations
Data Management	• Secure database storage, such as secure configurations, encryption, and hardening • Data governance during data life cycle processes • Tell the users how the data is collected and used • Explicit user consent for any collection of personal data • Allow a user to edit, update, or delete the collected data

Integrity and Reactive Security	• Security analysis of logs to identify abnormal data access • Prevent data from being tampered with • Inform users when a security incident occurs

Big data technical security frameworks

On the other hand, if we look into the big data infrastructure, we understand that it typically includes HDFS, Hive, HBase, Storm, Knox, Solr, Kafka, ZooKeeper, and YARN. These bring new security challenges, such as how to secure a distributed data environment, granular data access control, secure storage, privacy data protection, and data governance. From a big data security framework point of view, the following table lists big data security requirements mapping to suggested technical control components:

Security requirements	Technical implementation components
• Centralized security administration and management • Authorization and permissions control • Centralized audits and reports	• Apache Ranger • Apache Sentry
• Operation monitoring and audits	• Apache Ambari
• Enforcement of REST API security • Perimeter security	• Apache Knox
• Secure transmission	• TLS v1.2 instead of HTTP • SSH v2 instead of Telnet • SFTP instead of FTP
• Authentication	• Kerberos
• Secure configuration and deployment	• Kerberos, and Knox secure configuration such as file permissions, daemon users, NTP, certificates, and TLS
• Data governance • Data life-cycle management • Data classification such as PII, classified • authorization/data-masking based on classifications	• Apache Atlas

The following are some further recommended references for big data privacy and security:

- SP.1500-4 big data interoperability framework: Volume 4, Security and Privacy
- ENISA: Privacy by design in big data
- CSA Expanded top ten big data security and privacy challenges
- Information Commissioner's office *Guide to data protection*
- ENISA: Big data security

Privacy requirements for GDPR

The GDPR is a regulation in EU law on privacy data protection that came into effect in May 2018. We need to be aware of and also plan for it, since the GDPR defines Data Privacy regulation. It's not just a guideline or best practice. The GDPR is an official regulation that must be followed across the EU.

Here we will walk through some key steps for GDPR self-assessment and security requirements related to software applications. There are four major steps, as follows:

Key step	Checklist
• GDPR compliance	GDPR compliance is a must if one of the following conditions is met: • Firms located in the EU • Firms offer free or paid goods or services to EU residents (firms not located in EU) • Firms monitor the behavior of EU residents (firms not located in, or offering goods or services to, the EU) The GDPR official site includes lots of resources that are worth reading such as 'who must comply' and the 'FAQ'.
• Privacy Impact Analysis	This step mainly refers to a contact **Privacy Impact Assessment (PIA)**. A PIA includes the following steps: • Identify the need for a PIA • Describe the information flow • Identify privacy and related risks • Identify and evaluate privacy solutions • Sign off and record the PIA outcomes • Make an action plan with stakeholders Refer here for the PIA assessment template. https://gdpr-info.eu/issues/privacy-impact-assessment/
• Data controller or Data processor	• Execute GDPR compliance based on the role of the data controller or data processor
• Verification	• It's suggested to have a checklist for a development team to do self-assessment and evaluation • Alternatively, an organization may consider having privacy-related security certification, such as EuroPrise for the EU or TRUSTe for the US

Privacy Impact Assessment (PIA)

The objective of a PIA is to perform an initial self-assessment of what business modules may involve privacy data handling and readiness for GDPR compliance. the data privacy impact analysis is required by the GDPR article 35. It's highly suggested to apply a PIA assessment template for all project team to follow, or you may customize the templates for your organization. The key deliverables of the PIA are a list of privacy data attributes and data flow. A typical PIA assessment report may include the following agenda.

1. Introduction
2. The scope of the PIA
3. Data Attributes Identification
4. Data Flow Assessment
5. Planned actions and existing gap
6. Results of data protection impact assessment

The following sections show how to identify the privacy data and the data flow risk assessment.

Privacy data attributes

For privacy data, we must also further identify its attributes. The list of the attributes (purpose, ways of the collection, storage, format, retention period and so on.) will help to determine and review how to handle the privacy data. For example, some of the privacy data may be identified not a must to collect or no legal basis for collection, and the privacy data should never be collected.

Attributes	Describe related business flow or applications
Privacy data type	Describe collected or processed privacy data, such as name, address, phone
Purpose of collection	Describe the objective of the data collection and the business
Is it a must?	Is the data collection essential to keep the business application running?
Ways of collection	How the personal data is collected, such as API, email, or web form registration
Lawful basis	Is the data collection based on user agreement, contract, or legal compliance?
Rights of data subject	Can the data subject edit or delete the data?
Transmission	How the data is transmitted, such as FTP, email, or API

Storage country	Which country is the data stored in?
Storage format	In what format is the data stored, such as big data, relational database, or paper-based?
Expiration period	Any specified expiration period of the data usage?
Cross-border transfer	Will the data be transferred out of or into the EU?
Third-party involvement	Is any third party involved with the data processing?
Owner	Who/which team is the owner of the data?

Example of a data flow assessment

The following diagram shows a typical troubleshooting data flow between the customer, service, and RD team. For the data flow, it must identify if there is any private data, data handling operations, and the goal of the data processing:

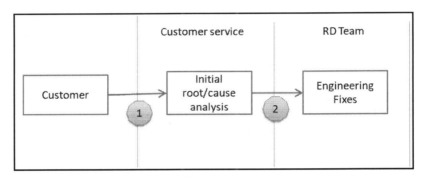

The table describes data privacy handing operations in the relevant business scenario flagged in the diagram:

#	Business Scenario	Data Privacy	Operations	Objective
1	The customer sends his PC to customer services for fixes	The customer's contact info and personal data are stored on the PC	Customer services receive the PC	Initially test the functionality of the PC
2	The PC is delivered to the engineering team for further inspection	Customer contact info and personal data are stored on the PC	The engineering team performs more deep analysis	Deliver engineering fixes for the PC

GDPR security requirements for data processor and controller

According to the GDPR FAQ, *A controller is the entity that determines the purposes, conditions and means of processing of personal data, while the processor is an entity which processes personal data on behalf of the controller.*

For example, an e-commerce website that sells services to EU customers (data subjects). The e-commerce website is the data controller, which should comply with GDPR requirements. The software vendors who are data processors provide software services to the e-commerce website.

As compared with the data processor, the data controller will have more GDPR requirements to meet. That's why it's necessary to identify its role in the privacy data handing lifecycle. The following table lists the GDPR security requirements for a software/service in respect of the Data processor and Data controller.

GDPR requirements	Data processor	Data controller
Provide Data Privacy Declaration	Must	Must
Data collection requires a user's explicit consent to data collection and allows a user to disable data collection	Must	Must
For the purpose of error troubleshooting, the user must be informed if the collection of logs includes personal information	Must	Must
Collection of a user's cookies requires the user's consent	MUST	MUST
If the data is collected for marketing analysis purposes, the application must allow users to disable the analysis	Recommended	Must
Provide a secure data removal capability after the data expires	Must	Must
If the data will be provided to third-party partners, it must have the user's explicit consent	Recommended	Must
Provide the capability for a user to query and update the data	Recommended	Must
Delete any temporary data which is no longer in use	Recommended	Must
Provide the capability to export the data	Recommended	Must
Secure data transmission	Must	Must
Secure local data storage with encryption, access control, and logging security controls	Must	Must

Summary

We discussed security requirements in four areas. We provided samples of how to define security release gates for each development stage, such as design, coding, build, testing, delivery, and monitoring. CVSS evaluation is also suggested whenever there is a dilemma: whether to go for the next release or not.

For a product manager to plan security features, we recommend OWASP ASVS. Depending on the business scenario, there are three levels of security. Based on the OWASP ASVS, an open source OWASP Security Knowledge Framework was introduced to help an organization to set up an in-house security knowledge portal.

For data security and privacy, we discussed the security requirements for big data.

For big data requirements, the CSA defines four security categories: such as Infrastructure Security, Data Privacy, Data Management and Integrity, and Reactive Security. In addition, we also gave a list of suggested big data security frameworks, such as Apache Ranger and Atlas. Further reading with NIST SP 1500-4 and ENISA big data security were also suggested.

Last but not least, we discussed the security requirements for GDPR. The security requirements may vary depending on the role of a data controller or data processor. We also reviewed an example to see how to use the PIA template as a self-assessment for GDPR.

We discussed security requirements with industry practices (OWASP ASVS, CSA big data), tools (OWASP SKF, Apache Ranger), and templates (CVSS, PIA). In the next chapter, we will look at a case study on how security practices are executed during DevOps.

Questions

1. Which of the following can be security requirements for the release gate of the design stage?
    1. Threat modeling activities should be performed
    2. Review the uses of third-party components
    3. Review the top common secure design issues
    4. All of the above

2. Which of the following is not the security gate for the coding stage?
   1. Source codes were scanned by one static code analysis tool
   2. No sensitive information was found in the source code
   3. Service logs were ready for security analysis
   4. High-severity issues in the code scanning results were all checked

3. Does CVSS stand for Common Vulnerability Scoring System?

4. Which of the following technologies is commonly used to do authorization for a big data framework?
   1. Apache Ranger
   2. Apache Ambari
   3. TLS
   4. NTP

5. GDPR does not apply to those organizations which are not located in EU, true or false?

6. Is the key difference between the data controller and data processor the ability to determine the purpose of data processing?

Further reading

Visit the following URL for more information:

- **NIST 1500-4 Big Data Interoperability Framework: Security and Privacy**: https://bigdatawg.nist.gov/_uploadfiles/NIST.SP.1500-4.pdf
- **ENISA Privacy by design in big data**: https://www.enisa.europa.eu/publications/big-data-protection
- **SAFE Practical Security Stories and Security Tasks for Agile Development Environments**: http://safecode.org/publication/SAFECode_Agile_Dev_Security0712.pdf

- **Big data, artificial intelligence, machine learning and data protection**: https:/
  /ico.org.uk/media/for-organisations/documents/2013559/big-data-ai-ml-
  and-data-protection.pdf
- **PCI DSS Prioritized Approach for PCI DSS 3.2**: https://www.
  pcisecuritystandards.org/documents/Prioritized-Approach-for-PCI_DSS-
  v3_2.pdf
- **Open Reference Architecture for Security and Privacy**: http://security-and-
  privacy-reference-architecture.readthedocs.io/en/latest/
- **National Checklist Program for IT Products – Guidelines for Checklist Users
  and Developers**: https://nvlpubs.nist.gov/nistpubs/SpecialPublications/
  NIST.SP.800-70r3.pdf
- **CSA Expanded Top Ten Big Data Security and Privacy Challenges**: https://
  cloudsecurityalliance.org/download/expanded-top-ten-big-data-security-
  and-privacy-challenges/
- **Information Commissioner's office 'Guide to data protection'**: https://ico.
  org.uk/for-organisations/guide-to-data-protection/
- **SANS A Security Checklist for Web Application Design**: https://www.sans.
  org/reading-room/whitepapers/securecode/security-checklist-web-
  application-design-1389
- **GDPR Who must comply:** https://www.gdpreu.org/the-regulation/who-
  must-comply/
- **GDPR FAQ:** https://www.eugdpr.org/gdpr-faqs.html
- **GDPR Privacy Impact Assessment:** https://gdpr-info.eu/issues/privacy-
  impact-assessment/
- **CookieLaw:** https://www.cookielaw.org/the-cookie-law/

- **ISO/IEC 29151:2017 Code of practice for personally identifiable information
  protection:** https://www.iso.org/standard/62726.html

Case Study - Security Assurance Program

5

Since we have covered the security requirements and security assurance program in previous chapters, in this chapter, we will discuss two case studies looking at the security assurance program and security practices in the DevOps process. Microsoft SDL and SAMM were introduced to apply to the security assurance program. In addition to the process, the non-technical parts, security training, and culture are also critical to the success of the security program. We will also give an example of how security tools and web security framework can help during the whole DevOps process.

In this chapter, we will learn about the following topics:

- Microsoft SDL and SAMM
- Security training and awareness
- Security culture
- Baking security tools into DevOps
- Web security frameworks

Security assurance program case study

Let's take two typical business scenarios to discuss the adoption of a security assurance program. One concerns services built on top of a third-party cloud service provider, and the other concerns building your own, complete cloud services, including **Software as a Service (SaaS)**, **Platform as a Service (PaaS)**, and **Infrastructure as a Service (IaaS)**:

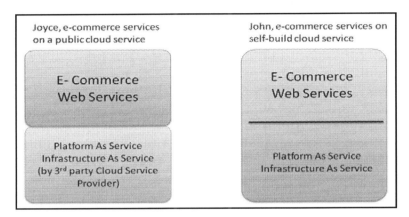

- **Scenario 1: Joyce, e-commerce services on a public cloud service:** Joyce is a security leader at an e-commerce company. The company has an in-house software development, IT, and security team. They deploy an e-commerce service based on a third-party cloud service provider, and apply most security services provided by the IaaS/PaaS cloud service provider. Due to the payment and handling of credit card information, compliance with PCI DSS is a must for e-commerce services.

- **Scenario 2: John, e-commerce services on self-build cloud service:** John is a CSO of e-commerce services. The key difference in John's case is that there is a well-established security organization team, and lots of security services, such as WAF, IDS, or security monitoring, were self-built and tailored to the business's needs. Furthermore, the e-commerce was built on their own self-operated cloud services. PCI DSS compliance is also a minimum requirement in this case.

For these two scenarios, let's discuss how the adoption of a security assurance program might be different, by reference to Microsoft SDL and OWASP SAMM practices.

Microsoft SDL and SAMM

The adoption of Microsoft SDL and SAMM in Joyce's case may apply security on top of the framework provided by the cloud service provider. It's always suggested we build security practices based on existing business processes, or to have the security tools integrated to the existing CI or CD framework.

Most cloud service providers provide related cloud security services. In Joyce's case, familiarity with the security services provided by the cloud service provider, as well as how they apply to her e-commerce applications, will help to build a security foundation. In addition, most cloud service providers have been certified with security standards for IaaS and PaaS. This means that Joyce only needs to focus on the data and software security which were built on top of the IaaS and PaaS. In John's case, he will need to self-build or purchase those security services to protect the IaaS, PaaS, and software applications. The following table shows a typical security service provided by a cloud service provider:

Security area	Cloud security services
Security management	• Threat intelligence • Cloud connector • Outsourcing security services
Content security	• Spam prevention • Machine brute-force attack prevention • Accounts abuses detection
Infrastructure	• CA certificate manager • Key management • HTTPS service • Secure configuration monitoring and checking
Data protection	• Encryption • Database auditing • Integrity monitoring • Granular access control
Networking	• HTTPS service • Web application firewall • Anti-DDOS services

Building software applications on top of third-party cloud services may reduce the effort involved in securing a cloud infrastructure and platform. Since Joyce's business requires PCI DSS compliance, security practices are also recommended tied to be the business needs. The following are examples of security practices that Joyce may plan:

Security area	Examples of security activities in Joyce's case
Strategy and metrics	• Define release gates depending on the PCI compliance levels
Policy and compliance	• Compliance with PCI DSS
Education	• Security training and exams for the team
Security requirements	• Security requirements may be based on the six categories of PCI DSS • Secure network and systems • Protect cardholder data • Vulnerability management program • Strong access control measures • Monitor and test networks • Maintain an information security policy
Threat assessment	• The threat assessment focuses on software applications
Secure architecture	• Assess the external dependencies used in application-level components
Design review	• Secure API interface with external vendors • Secure data storage and transmission
Implementation review	• Secure coding scanning tool adoption, such as flawfinder, FindSecbugs, OWASP Dependency Check. . • The web service implementation is based on the Java security framework and Apache Shiro, for authentication, authorization, cryptography, and session management.
Security testing	• Apply security scanning services provided by cloud service providers, such as secure configuration scanning, web service security, or vulnerability scanning
Issue management	• The cloud services provide security events monitoring or alerts, but Joyce still needs to set up a security incident handling process for the company
Environment hardening	• The cloud service may provide mechanisms to secure configurations, and to apply the latest patches automatically
Operation enablement	• Apply the service monitoring tools provided by the cloud service provider; in addition, keeping the operation team and development team together to handle issues fed back by customers is the most important thing here

In John's case, the security assurance program coverage extends to the cloud platform and infrastructure. It means John will need to additionally consider these security controls: security testing, issue management, environment hardening, and operation enablement. Other aspects, such as strategy, policy, education, threat assessment, secure architecture, design review, and implementation review, will be similar to Joyce's case.

Self-build or buy? The question may be raised whenever we plan tools for security practices. One of the key advantages to using commercial products is to win the customer's trust. It's like the services are tested and certified by third-party commercial tools. On the other hand, self-build security tools enable closer integration with the existing framework, and can be customized to its needs. If you are in such a dilemma due to budget constraints, using open source tools may be a good alternative. Open source tools may provide built-in security rules and knowledge, while also giving you the flexibility to customize to your needs.

Security training and awareness

In both John's and Joyce's cases, the theme of security awareness may be focused on PCI DSS compliance. There are many ways to deliver security training, such as posters, newsletters, e-learning or teleconferencing, in-person workshops, or hands-on tutorials. NIST SP 800-50 **Building an Information Technology Security Awareness and Training Program** and PCI DSS **Best Practices for implementing a Security Awareness Program** are two good references for building a security awareness program. Here, we discuss some of the key points to consider when delivering a security awareness and training program with an organization.

Sending newsletters is considered to be one of the most cost-effective and common practices to target all employees across business units. What can be even more effective is to look at a real example or case study that relates to that role or the business. For example, HR may be more interested in stories or case studies about employment related to access control or the required security knowledge certificates for each job grade, rather than security technology or threat introduction. Try to use a case study specific to each role, such as HR, Developers, Testers, or the operations team to explain how security relates to and impacts their jobs. In addition, newsletters are no different than other emails, and may be easily ignored. A simple follow-up online quiz or required email-reply with comments is also suggested. For managers, leaders, and specific roles, the purpose of security awareness is to win their support. The content requires not only security awareness but also that you call them to action. Sometimes, it's not just a one-way message delivery; it can be a forum discussion or the process of seeking consensus to achieve security goals. Whenever possible, face-to-face communication or a forum discussion is recommended for this group.

For the development or operations team, the most effective way to apply security practices is still to have hands-on tutorials and workshops. Engineers love to build and to take part in hands-on exercises. In-person, hands-on exercises take time and require physical involvement. However, they are much more effective than posters, newsletters, e-learning, or teleconferencing sessions.

For a large, geographically distributed organization, it's common to have online self-study e-learning courses. These e-learning courses have exams with required passing scores. Some organizations may require you to pass a security knowledge certification annually. For the adoption of any new security compliance such as GDPR, integrating security practices into existing processes or training programs is still the recommended approach.

Security culture

The organization's culture may impact security practices and execution. The term *culture* may be quite vague, but generally speaking, there are two kinds of security culture. One is the **strict process** type, and the other is **empowering the team**. In the strict process, there is almost no room for flexibility. Once the expected security baselines are defined, they are all compulsory. Detailed security checklists are defined for every project to follow. No violation is allowed. On the other hand, the empowering the team type means the organization only defines general security guidelines, while project teams may define their own security checklists based on project needs.

A strict-process culture fits an environment that requires high-level controls, such as the military or banking. There are defined **Standard Operating Procedures** (**SOPs**) and checklists for every security control. The SOP or checklist will greatly reduce the chances of human error. In addition, any exception or failure to meet the security checklist will require the team to submit a formal review. From a security management point of view, this may reduce the need to check with each project team, since the project team will need to initiate a formal review for any security requirements it fails to meet. There is little room for project teams to make any judgment call, which must be done by the security management team. One disadvantage is that project team members may just follow the SOP, and don't know the rationale behind the checklist.

In an empowering-the-team culture, security management only defines guidelines, while each project team may develop a checklist based on the project's needs. The checklists we refer to here are software security requirement features for a development team. It also means an organization-level security policy only defines a few compulsory requirements, without detailed instructions, and allows the team to figure out how to achieve them. It may take time for each project in the beginning and may suffer some trial-and-error mistakes for new start-up teams, but the project team will learn from mistakes, which may still be identified in the testing phase, instead of the design phase. After all, making mistakes and trying different methods of execution are the roots of innovation and creativity.

In addition, the team may decide on its training needs, instead of a compulsory course list defined by the security management team. Again, the security training decided by the team may not be comprehensive enough, but the team will learn through experience.

There is nothing wrong or right between these two cultures. It all depends on the business status, the needs for compliance, the organizational culture, existing processes, and so on. Some organizations may have a very strict security program, with specific roles, but maybe flexible with other roles. Some organizations may still have a detailed security checklist for every business unit, but allow each project team to judge whether to follow it strictly or not. In the end, fitting into the organizational culture and aligning with business objectives are key to the success of a security assurance program.

Web security frameworks

Applying a mature web security framework will help developers to reduce a lot of the design and coding effort required to meet security requirements, since the web security framework itself provides the necessary security controls, such as authentication, authorization, logging, validation, encryption, and session management. To build web services, the followings are some popular open-source Java security frameworks under Apache 2.0 license:

- Spring Security
- Apache Shiro
- PicketLink
- **Object Access Control (OACC)** Framework

Some large organizations may prefer to build or to customize a web security framework for every project to use. No matter what security framework is used, it normally includes the following common security modules.

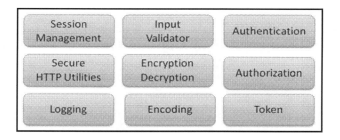

An organization-level security assurance program may suggest a list of mature security frameworks, or even provide a common one for a project team to use. After all, one working security framework is always much more effective than a list of security requirement documents.

Baking security into DevOps

We have discussed the culture aspect of how security fits into an organization. Let's now discuss the technical aspect. When it comes to fitting security into DevOps, we are mostly talking about integration with an existing **Continuous Integration (CI)** or **Continuous Delivery (CD)** framework. There are various kinds of CI/CD framework. We may focus on how to integrate security with Jenkins, since Jenkins is the hub of the whole CI/CD ecosystem, such as code and commit, build, scan and test, release, and deployment. One typical CI/CD process with security tools integration is shown in the following diagram. Please be aware that security requirements, threat modeling, secure design, and architecture design are not in the diagram, since the security practices of these activities normally tie with the team process, and not directly with a tool, such as Jenkins.

In Joyce's case, she may build security based on the framework provided by the cloud service provider. In John's case, he builds security based on the existing in-house CI/CD framework. No matter which approach is used, the security in the CI/CD process will be similar to one of the examples in the following diagram:

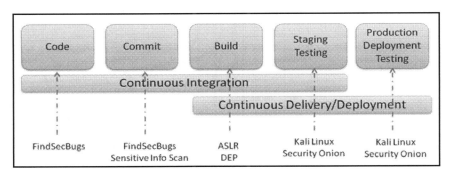

CI/CD process with security tools

Avoiding reinventing the wheel, and fitting security into the existing process or framework, are critical success factors for a security assurance program at any stage. A checklist of security requirements helps us understand what is needed. Furthermore, a tool set and framework can help to implement the security of the products. The following table shows another example of how the tools and framework support security in DevOps:

Types of security tools	Key activity in DevOps	Example of tools and framework
Security framework	Architecture design	• Shiro • Spring Security
Secure coding	Implementation and coding	• FindSecBugs for Java Code scanning • Java HTML Sanitizer
Security testing	Verification	• Kali Linux Toolkits
Security monitoring	Operational monitoring	• Security Onions (IDS/IPS, security monitoring and log analysis) • OpenSCAP

Summary

In this chapter, we discussed two typical business scenarios for security assurance program. One is building software on top of a third-party cloud service provider, and the other is building complete cloud services on top of your own cloud. Cloud service providers may allow security services to protect the platform and infrastructure, but it's still the cloud service tenant's responsibility to protect the web application and customer data in the cloud. Then, we discussed the adoption of Microsoft SDL and SAMM into security activities in different development and operations phases. For security training, we recommend delivering training based on roles and needs. How security culture impacts the security assurance program was also discussed.

Finally, we took security tool integration with CI/CD and the adoption of a web security framework as examples to explain how tools and framework are critical to the success of any security program. In the following chapters, we will look further into how to build a secure architecture, common module, and design principles.

Questions

1. Does the cloud services provider take all the responsibility for security, including the software application and customer data?
2. What security services are provided by cloud service providers?
    1. Data encryption
    2. Security monitoring
    3. Anti-DDOS
    4. All of the above
3. What are the most cost-effective ways to raise security awareness?
    1. Newsletter
    2. Workshop
    3. Teleconferencing
    4. Tutorials
4. Does CI stand for Continuous integration?
5. Does CD stand for Continuous Delivery and Continuous Development?
6. Which activities are considered to be within a CI cycle?
    1. Code
    2. Commit
    3. Build
    4. Testing
7. The FindSecBugs tool is used in which kinds of security practices?
    1. Secure code scanning
    2. Security monitoring
    3. Intrusion prevention
    4. Authentication
8. Which of the following is not a Java web security framework?
    1. Passport
    2. Spring Security
    3. Apache Shiro
    4. PicketLink

Further reading

- **PCI DSS**: https://www.pcisecuritystandards.org/pci_security/
- **Microsoft SDL**: https://www.microsoft.com/en-us/sdl
- **SAMM**: https://www.owasp.org/index.php/OWASP_SAMM_Project
- **flawfinder**: https://www.dwheeler.com/flawfinder/
- **FindSecbugs**: https://find-sec-bugs.github.io/
- **OWASP dependency Check**: https://www.owasp.org/index.php/OWASP_Dependency_Check
- **NIST SP 800-50 Building an Information Technology Security Awareness and Training Program**: https://nvlpubs.nist.gov/nistpubs/legacy/sp/nistspecialpublication800-50.pdf
- **Best Practices for implementing a Security Awareness Program**: https://www.pcisecuritystandards.org/documents/PCI_DSS_V1.0_Best_Practices_for_Implementing_Security_Awareness_Program.pdf
- **Spring Security**: https://projects.spring.io/spring-security/
- **Apache Shiro**: https://shiro.apache.org/
- **PicketLink**: http://picketlink.org/
- **OACC (Object Access Control) Framework**: http://oaccframework.org/
- **Static Security Analysis** https://github.com/mre/awesome-static-analysis/

6
Security Architecture and Design Principles

Security management, including its goals, security assurance program, and security requirements, were explained in previous chapters. This chapter will discuss security architecture and design principles. For security architects and developers, building software on a mature security framework will greatly reduce not only security risks with industry best practices but also implementation efforts. Therefore, this chapter introduces the key security elements of a cloud service architecture and some mature security frameworks, which can be applied based on the scenario. We will also discuss GDPR and data protection techniques in this chapter.

We will cover the following topics in this chapter:

- Security architecture design principles
- Cloud service security architecture reference (ESAPI)
- Security framework (Shiro, encryption, validation, data masking)
- GDPR and data governance

Security architecture design principles

In this section, we would like to discuss two key concepts, which are security by design and privacy by design. When we discuss security, it's more about the security controls of the whole system such as authentication, authorization, availability, accountability, integrity, and confidentiality. For privacy, it focuses specifically on privacy data or PII (personal identifiable information). Privacy protection is focused on the authorized data handling life cycle and governance.

If we categorize some security controls in general terms, you may find some differences, although there are some overlapping areas in terms of security and privacy:

	Security by design	Privacy by design
Primary concerns	Unauthorized access to the system.	Authorized process of privacy data.
Principles	According to OWASP, security by design principles are the following: • Minimize attack surface area • Establish secure defaults • Principle of least privilege • Principle of defense in depth • Fail securely • Don't trust services • Separation of duties • Avoid security by obscurity • Keep security simple • Fix security issues correctly	Referring to OECD Privacy Principles, the term privacy by design is defined by eight principles: • Collection Limitation Principle • Data Quality Principle • Purpose Specification Principle • Use Limitation Principle • Security Safeguards Principle • Openness Principle • Individual Participation Principle • Accountability Principle
Examples of controls	• Access control • Unsuccessful login attempts • Session control • Timestamps • Non-repudiation • Configuration change control • Audit security events • Cryptographic module • Incident monitoring • Error handling	• Cookie • Anonymity • Consent • Obfuscation • Restrict • Notify and inform • Authentication • Minimization • Separation • Encryption • Data masking

The following industry references may help you to build a secure architecture:

- **Open Security Architecture (OSA) Patterns**: `http://www.opensecurityarchitecture.org/`

- **CSA CAIQ (Consensus Assessment Initiative Questionnaire)**: `https://cloudsecurityalliance.org/group/consensus-assessments`

- **Google VSAQ (Vendor Security Assessment Questionnaires)**: `https://github.com/google/vsaq`

- **PCI Self-Assessment Questionnaire (SAQ)**: `https://www.pcisecuritystandards.org/pci_security/completing_self_assessment`

- **NIST 1500-4 v4 Big Data Interoperability Framework Security and Privacy**: `https://www.nist.gov/publications/nist-big-data-interoperability-framework-volume-4-security-and-privacy`

- **NIST 800-122 Guide to Protecting the Confidentiality of Personally Identifiable Information (PII)**: `https://csrc.nist.gov/publications/detail/sp/800-122/final`

We have understood the concepts and principles of security and privacy. However, the challenges for most organizations are how to build these into applications or services. Therefore, we will discuss some design patterns and also open source framework implementations in upcoming sections.

Cloud service security architecture reference

The **Open Security Architecture (OSA)** Patterns **SP-011: Cloud Computing Pattern** and **SP-008: Public Web Server Pattern** provide an overview diagram of the whole system. In addition, **SP-001: client module** and **SP-002 Server module** are also a good reference. Take a look at the components of the cloud computing pattern in the following link: http://www. opensecurityarchitecture.org/cms/library/patternlandscape/251-pattern-cloud-computing

In addition, if you are looking for a questionnaire or checklist for self-assessment or for partner security evaluation, here are some suggested references. CSA CAIQ consolidated most security standards (including ISO 27001, FedRAMP, NIST 800-53 R3, and PCI DSS) into a self-assessment questionnaire. VSAQ is mainly for external vendor assessment with the aspects of web application security, security and privacy programs, infrastructure security, and physical and data center security.

- **CSA CAIQ (Consensus Assessment Initiative Questionnaire)**: https://cloudsecurityalliance.org/group/consensus-assessments/
- **Google VSAQ (Vendor Security Assessment Questionnaires)**: https://vsaq-demo.withgoogle.com/
- **PCI Data Security Standard Self-Assessment Questionnaire (SQA)**: https://www.pcisecuritystandards.org/documents/SAQ-InstrGuidelines-v3_2.pdf

Security framework

Architecture principles may still be too high-level for most developers. Therefore, in this section, we will discuss some key open source security frameworks. Depending on the purposes of the security objective and programming languages, there are various kinds of open source security framework. We will only discuss some major or widely used security frameworks.

Adoption of a security framework is the best approach to achieve *secure by design*. A mature security framework provides security controls such as authentication, access control, session management, HTTP security, cryptography, and logging. It also enables a junior developer who has little knowledge of security to build secure software.

Just remember that the security frameworks we will introduce are third-party security components built with our applications. Security applications such as anti-virus software, web application firewalls, and intrusion detection will not be discussed in this section but will be discussed in a later chapter.

Java web security framework

As discussed earlier, the adoption of a web security framework will help us to handle lots of security controls. Take Spring Security as an example—a few edits of the XML configuration will not only provide login/logout form authentication but also CSRF attack, session, and HTTP security header (HSTS, X-content-type, XSS, X-Frame-Options) protection:

Java security framework	Key characteristics
Spring Security	• The Spring Security framework is only for Java- and Spring-based applications. It provides lots of out-of-box security controls such as user authentication, CSRF attack protection, session fixation protection, a HTTP security header, and URL access control. Also, it supports various kinds of authentication such as Oauth2.0, CAS, and OpenID.
Shiro	• Shiro is a more lightweight and simple framework compared to Spring Security. The key difference between Shiro and Spring Security is that Shiro doesn't require a Spring-based application, and it can run standalone without tying into any web framework or a non-web environment.
Object Access Control (OACC)	• OACC primarily provides authentication and authorization. The key characteristic of OACC is that it provides a security relationship with application resources while Spring Security defines authorization by URL, methods, and roles. • A security relationship example definition in OACC may be: (Sara) has (READ, EDIT) permissions on (`TimeSheet.xls`). Being able to establish the application resource (`TimeSheet.xls`) in a security relationship is a unique authorization model in OACC.

For a Java development team, which one is recommended? If the web is built purely on Java Spring, Spring Security is still the best choice due to its powerful security features and complete technical documents. However, if your web applications are running with non-web or non-Spring applications, Shiro is recommended. If your application may need resource access control models, try the OACC.

Non-Java web security frameworks

For non-Java programming, here are some recommendations:

Programming language	Authentication framework
Node.JS	• **Passport framework** is an authentication module for Node.JS.
Ruby on Rails	• **Devise Security:** This is a security module for Ruby. It provides security features such as password complexity, CAPTCHA, user account inactivity checks, verification code, and session control for the web.
ASP.NET	• **ASP.NET Core** provides security features such as authentication, authorization, anti-XSS, SSL enforcement, anti-request forgery, encryption, and also APIs to support GDPR.
Python	• **Yosai** is a security framework for Python applications • **Flask Security:** It provides common security controls to Flask applications such as authentication, password hashing, and role management.

Web readiness for privacy protection

To evaluate the privacy protection readiness for a website, include not only general web security controls but also the following major areas:

- **TLS for secure data transmission**: The misconfiguration of TLS may result in insecure data transmission or man-in-the-middle attacks.
- **Referrer Policy**: The Referrer Policy defines how the browser should handle Referrer information, which reveals the user's original visiting web site. The website visiting history is also considered to be personal privacy information.
- **Cookie Consent Disclaimer**: To comply with the GDPR, the collection of cookie information and the use of any third-party cookies will require explicit cookie consent.
- **HTTP Security Headers**: The HTTP protocol itself provides web security controls. Please also refer to the following table for the suggested HTTP security header configurations.

The following table summarizes the technical parts of privacy security requirements and suggested tools to assess and build the web:

Privacy technical requirements	Tools
Secure Communication: HTTPS by default and secure configuration of TLS.	• SSLyze, SSLScan, and TestSSLServer included in Pentest Box or Kali Linux
The origins of a visiting website source should not be leaked to other websites by the referrer header.	• Referrer Policy defines how the referrer can be used. The configuration of the Referrer Policy depends on the requirements. • no-referrer will ensure the browser never sends the referer header. • If the information is needed, it's suggested to configure sending information over HTTPS by using 'strict-origin'.
If Google Analytics is used, enable privacy extension to anonymize IPs.	• Enable IP masking for Google Analytics
Third-party cookies or embeds services (such as Google Analytics), with user consent.	• Cookie Consent • Cookie Consent JavaScript plug-in: `https://github.com/insites/cookieconsent`
HTTP Security Headers	The following are the suggested mandatory examples of secure http headers. • Content-Security Policy (CSP) "default-src 'self' " • Referrer-Policy "no-referrer" • Strict-Transport-Security "max-age=31536000" • X-content-Type-options "nosniff" • X-Frame-Options "SAMEORGIN" • X-Xss-Protection "1;mode=block" • Cookie "Secure" Refer to OWASP Secure Headers Project for details of each security headers definition.

It's also suggested to build in-house privacy scanning tools for your websites. The following resources provide online scanning services for the privacy requirements mentioned:

 Privacy Score Assessment: `https://privacyscore.org`.

Login protection

Login protection can be seen as the first defense layer of the application. Hackers may use tools or APIs to do brute-force login attacks. CAPTCHA is one of the approaches to distinguishing human from machine input. A CAPTCHA requires the client to complete visual-perception tasks. However, the CAPTCHA may be defeated by OCR or unwitting human labor. In addition to CAPTCHA, we can also have another layer of security defense to monitor the number of login failures. If the number of login failures reaches a certain threshold level, the system should take action, such as banning the IP source:

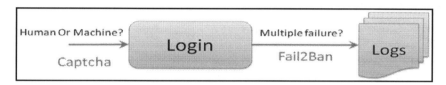

Tools/modules for login protection are summarized in the table:

Login protection techniques	Tools/Modules
Detect the number of login failures in logs and take action	• Fail2Ban
CAPTCHA solution to prevent machine brute-force login attacks	• VisualCaptcha to build your own CAPTCHA service • Google reCAPTCHA

Cryptographic modules

Typical use case cases for cryptographic modules are not only data encryption/decryption, but also SSL/TLS secure communication, key exchange, X509 certificate handling, one-way hashing for message integrity, and random number generation. The recommended encryption modules that the development team may need are shown here:

Encryption module	Adoption scenario
OpenSSL	• Full-featured and most widely used cryptography and SSL/TLS toolkit
Bouncy Castle Crypto APIs	• Lightweight cryptography Java API
mbed TLS	• OpenSSL alternative • Cryptographic and SSL/TLS in embedded products • Cryptography C API
SSLyze	• Verify the secure TLS configuration of the web server

In addition, an operation team may care more about the configuration of encryption on servers such as web servers, SSH, Mail, VPNs, database, proxy, and Kerberos.

 Refer to Applied Crypto Hardening: `https://betterCrypto.org/static/applied-crypto-hardening.pdf`.

Input validation and sanitization

Input validation is like the perimeter security control of the whole application. The input not only includes data input from users but also covers the parameters passing between function calls, methods, APIs, or systems. The concept of validation covers various kinds of technical approaches:

Techniques	Purpose	Example
Canonicalization Normalization	Process input data into known or expected form.	• URL decode/encode • File path or names handling
Sanitization	Sanitization is to remove illegal characters or make potentially risky data safe. Always sanitize an output to avoid XSS.	• Escape: replace < > ' " & with HTML entities.
Validation	To check if the input is valid or within the constraint data type, length, and so on.	• IsAlpha, isCreditCard, isDecimal, isIP

The right order of implementation also matters and reduces the chances of malicious data bypassing the validation. Secure coding requires the following:

- Normalize strings before validating them
- Canonicalize path names before validating them
- Perform any string modifications before validation
- Canonicalize a URL before it is used

When the data is received, the data should be canonicalized first to transform it into expected forms, then the data will be sanitized to remove illegal characters, and the validation may check if it's acceptable based on business rules. Finally, if the data requires output, it always needs to do output sanitization to prevent XSS:

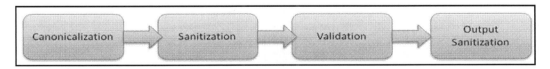

For general canonicalization, sanitization, and validation, we can apply the APIs provided by the mature security framework, while the development team can focus more on business logic validation:

Programming languages	Validation and Sanitization Framework
Java	• OWASP Java HTML Sanitizer
Ruby on Rails	• Active Record Validations
Node.js/JavaScript	• Validators
JavaScript	• DOMPurity to sanitize HTML and prevents XSS attacks
Python	• Cerberus

Data masking

Data masking is the process of obfuscating original/sensitive data to protect it. There are five typical key scenarios that require data masking. Different tools are required based on different roles or usage scenarios:

Scenario	Involved roles	Required tools/modules
• The application receives data and will do data masking based on defined policies	Developer	• Data masking modules • Data masking policies
• Define the PII data tag and access policies	DBA	• PII metadata definition • PII access policies
• Query results with data masking based on defined PII tags and access policies	Data query users	• Dynamic data masking
• The operation team may monitor and check if there is any PII in data, files, configuration, or any unstructured data	Operation team	• PII data discovery
• Any PII in the logs or files must be masked before further processing.	Support team	• Data Anonymizer tools

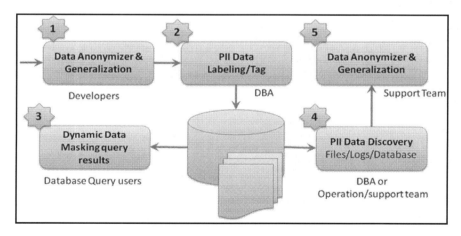

For data masking techniques, anonymization and pseudonymization are two common categories.

	Anonymization	Pseudonymization
Key Difference	Anonymous data cannot be re-identified.	Pseudonymous data is a data substitution which allows for some form of re-identification. Encryption or hashing are the most common techniques in this category.
Data	Anonymization is mainly used for sensitive personal information such as: • Names • IDs (Credit Cards, Social Security numbers and so on.) • Postal addresses • Telephones • Postal codes + cities	• Any data

The table lists common techniques used for data masking, anonymization, and pseudonymization:

Category	Sub-Category	Techniques	Application Scenario
Anonymisation	Randomization	Noise Addition	Numeric data
		Permutation	Numeric data needs to be reversible
		Differential privacy	Big Data statistics
	Generalization	Aggregation	Big Data statistics
		K-anonymity	
		L-diversity	
		T-closeness	
Pseudonymisation		Encryption (AES256)	data needs to be reversible
		Hash (HMAC-SHA256)	Fixed length value
		Tokenization	Keep data format such as ID.

Let's take a telephone number as an example to tell the key differences between anonymization and pseudonymization. If the original value of a telephone number is 12345678, then the anonymization of the number will be 123***** and the pseudonymization of the phone number will be the hash or encrypted value ADF231DADEF. It also means it's impossible for users to know the original value if its anonymization is similar to 123*****. However, it is still likely that the hash or encrypted value can be reversed to the original value if the algorithm is known or enough data samples are collected.

- For the implementation of anonymization and pseudonymization, please also refer to the ARX Data Anonymization Tool: http://arx.deidentifier.org/.
- Reference to data masking techniques: https://www.pdpjournals.com/docs/88197.pdf

Data governance – Apache Ranger and Atlas

When it comes to data privacy governance, we will need more than just **role-based access control (RBAC)** or **attribute-based access control (ABAC)** which are common in securing access control. Data governance requires additional metadata or tags to define the data classification, and also row-level attribute-based access control for data masking or row filtering. Take data centers in both the EU and US as an example—we would like to have granular access control policies, as follows:

- US support team can only query US data, and cannot view EU data
- EU support team can only query EU data, and cannot view US data
- The age is considered PII and can only be displayed as a range for the US support team
- The age cannot be displayed to the EU support team
- The ID is PII and will be applied with data masking

This example shows privacy by data is more about the authorized access control of privacy data. The need for techniques such as data governance, data masking, encryption, data classification, and granular ABAC is on the rise due to the usage of big data with cloud services, GDPR compliance, and also the awareness of personal privacy:

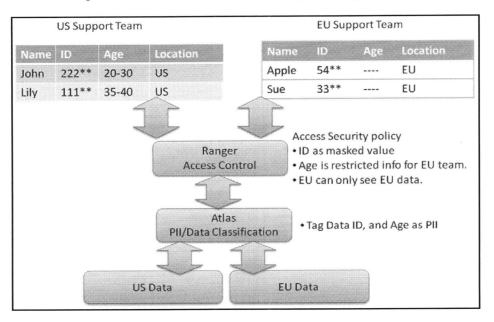

You may consider building data privacy governance based on the Apache Ranger and Atlas frameworks. Apache Ranger is mainly for ABAC while Atlas is for data classification.

Third-party open source management

An organization should set up its own internal open source and third-party software database and selection criteria. The database keeps records of open source or in-house developed components adopted in projects. It will provide a good framework selection reference for similar projects such as the web security framework we discussed earlier. If you are looking for an open source component search database, try Open Hub. You may search open source projects and find what you need for the project: `https://www.openhub.net/`. Furthermore, the open source selection criteria help to reduce legal and quality risks.

A typical criteria checklist is listed in the following table:

Selection criteria	Example and description
Does the open source community fix the security issue in a timely manner?	• High-security risks fixed within 1 month.
Adoption of latest and stable releases	• Official and stable release by the community.
Availability of technical support?	• The open source community provides official technical support and issues feedback.
Software licenses with GPL and LGPL are less preferred.	• Licenses with GPL and LGPL are not preferred. If any GPL software components are used, custom-developed source code may also need to be available as open source. • The **binary analysis tool** (**BAT**) is suggested for license scanning based on binary files: `http://www.binaryanalysis.org/`.
Vulnerability status and fixes	• Search for the vulnerability status of the components. For more details, please visit `https://nvd.nist.gov/vuln/search`.
Software release or update frequency	• Was the latest version released within 6 months or several years ago?
Software architecture	• Is it using the latest software technologies or legacy framework?

For the security of open source components, the recommended security practices and tools during the DevOps stages are summarized in the table:

Stage	Activities	Recommended Tools/Practices
Design and Selection	Selection of Open Source.	• `www.openHub.Net` • Open Source selection checklist • In-house Open source database
Package Delivery	Identify all the dependencies in the project and check known vulnerabilities.	• OWASP dependency check • OWASP dependency Track
Package Deployment	On-line services monitoring and scanning of CVE.	• CVE database (`https://nvd.nist.gov/vuln/search`) • NMAP or OpenVAS scanning

 Also, refer to SAFECode Managing Security Risks Inherent in the Use of Third-party Components: `https://www.safecode.org/wp-content/uploads/2017/05/SAFECode_TPC_Whitepaper.pdf`.

Summary

We discussed security architecture design principles including the clarification of security by design and privacy by design. Security by design is focused on **confidentiality, integrity, and availability (CIA)** and design by privacy is more about the protection of privacy data. The industry-standard CSA, Google, PCI, or NIST provide good references. We can also refer to the OSA cloud computing pattern to understand the whole security architecture of a cloud service.

To build a security framework, we list some open source security frameworks to achieve some security controls instead of reinventing the wheel. For example, there is Spring Security and Shiro for web security frameworks in Java, and the Password Framework for NodeJS.

When it comes to website privacy protection, we discussed what is required legally, such as copyright notices, cookies, disclaimers, and data protection notices. We listed key security technical controls for web privacy.

We also discussed login protection modules such as Fail2Ban and reCAPTCHA, and cryptographic modules (OpenSSL, SSLyze). We explained the concept of input validation including normalization, sanitization, and validation. To protect sensitive data, the scenario of data masking and techniques (anonymization, pseudonymization) were explained. Data governance with Apache Ranger and Atlas frameworks was explained to classify and mask sensitive data. With lots of third-party components and security framework components introduced, we also suggested how an organization should manage third-party open source software.

In the next chapter, we will discuss threat modeling and secure design security practices in more detail.

Questions

1. Which of the following is one of the security by design principles?
   1. Establish secure defaults
   2. Least Privilege
   3. Fail securely
   4. All of the above

2. Which one of the following references consolidated most security standards such as ISO, FedRAMP, and NIST?

    1. CSA CAIQ
    2. Google VSAQ
    3. PCI DSS
    4. (OSA) Open Security Architecture Patterns

3. What security protection does a Spring Security framework provide?

    1. Authentication
    2. CSRF attack protection
    3. HTTP security headers
    4. All of the above

4. What's the key difference between Shiro and Spring Security?

    1. Shiro doesn't require a Java Spring framework
    2. Logging
    3. Encryption
    4. Intrusion defense

5. Which one of the followings may apply to the Passport Framework?

    1. ASP .NET
    2. Node.JS
    3. Ruby on Rails
    4. Python

6. Which one of the following cryptographic modules is specially used for embedded applications?

    1. OpenSSL
    2. Mbed TLS
    3. SSLyze
    4. Fail2Ban

7. Which one of these is an example of sanitization?

    1. Process input data into known or expected form
    2. Check if the input is valid
    3. Remove illegal characters
    4. Check the data type

Further reading

- **Privacy by Design, the 7 Foundational Principles**: `https://ipc.on.ca/wp-content/uploads/Resources/7foundationalprinciples.pdf`
- **NIST 800-53 Rev.4 Security and Privacy Controls for Federal Information Systems and Organizations**: `https://www.nist.gov/publications/security-and-privacy-controls-federal-information-systems-and-organizations-including-0`
- **NIST SP800-30 Rev 1 Guide for Conducting Risk Assessments**: `https://csrc.nist.gov/publications/detail/sp/800-30/rev-1/final`
- **NIST SP 800-12 Rev 1 An introduction to Information Security**: `https://csrc.nist.gov/publications/detail/sp/800-12/rev-1/final`
- **SP 800-39 Managing Information Security Risk: Organization, Mission and Information System View**: `https://csrc.nist.gov/publications/detail/sp/800-39/final`
- **SP 800-37 Rev 1 Guide for Applying the Risk Management Framework to Federal Information Systems: a Security life Cycle Approach**: `https://csrc.nist.gov/publications/detail/sp/800-37/rev-1/final`
- **Privacy Pattern**: `https://privacypatterns.org/patterns`
- **Open Reference Architecture for Security and Privacy**: `https://media.readthedocs.org/pdf/security-and-privacy-reference-architecture/latest/security-and-privacy-reference-architecture.pdf`
- **OSA (Open Security Architecture) Patterns**: `www.opensecurityarchitecture.org/cms/library/patternlandscape`
- **Google VSAQ Vendor Security Assessment Questionnaires**: `https://github.com/google/vsaq`
- **Hadoop Data security**: `https://docs.hortonworks.com/HDPDocuments/HDP2/HDP-2.6.4/bk_security/content/ch_hdp-security-guide-overview.html`
- **Cryptographic Key Length Recommendation**: `www.keylength.com/`
- **SAFECode Managing Security Risks Inherent in the Use of Third-party Components**: `https://www.safecode.org/wp-content/uploads/2017/05/SAFECode_TPC_Whitepaper.pdf`
- **Practices for Secure Development of Cloud Applications**: `https://safecode.org/wp-content/uploads/2018/01/SAFECode_CSA_Cloud_Final1213.pdf`
- **OECD Privacy Principles** `http://oecdprivacy.org/`

7
Threat Modeling Practices and Secure Design

After discussing security architecture and design principles, we will now introduce threat modeling security practices and tools. The adoption of threat modeling practices can help to reduce major security risks in the design phase. In addition, once the risks are identified, we will introduce how to apply OWASP secure design best practices to mitigate security risks.

The topics to be covered in this chapter are the following:

- Threat modeling practices
- Threat modeling with STRIDE
- Diagram designer tool
- Card game
- Threat library references
- Case study: formal documents or not?
- Secure design

Threat modeling practices

Threat modeling is a security practice for the team to identify threats, attacks, and risks based on the existing architecture design, and also to mitigate these potential security risks. There are a few key points to clarify in threat modeling before we discuss them further:

- It's a team activity. It's not just the developer's job. It will be more effective with QA, operation, architect, and security team involvement.
- Threat modeling may be the only security practice that is not recommended to be done by automation. It's a team exercise.

- The purpose of threat modeling is not to offer a comprehensive threat list, but to identify high-risk threats with key modules such as authentication, authorization, purchases, or customer info handling.
- It's suggested to do threat modeling when the architecture design is done or before the detailed design and coding stages, although it's also common to apply threat modeling to existing applications.

A typical threat modeling process includes a DFD diagram or architecture review, threat analysis, risk impact assessment, mitigations, and product implementation action review. A Threat modeling normally begins with an analysis of the architecture. DFD diagrams may commonly be used in threat modeling activity. However, as long as the team can understand the whole architecture design and information flow, UML or other existing architecture designs may also do the job. The objective of threat modeling is to discuss the most relevant and high-priority security risks with mitigations. Don't let the process or tools limit the team's learning and innovation.

Depending on the complexity of the applications, we may do threat modeling with architecture or high-level design. If it's a very large project, and most of the modules serve similar functions, it's suggested you perform the threat modeling with high-risk parts or the one which can mostly represent the business functions. Here are the recommended modules for threat modeling. These also apply to coding review:

- Modules with security controls such as authentication, authorization, session management, encryption, data validation, error handling, or logging, administration, and database handlers.
- Legacy modules with vulnerable CVE.
- Modules that may externally interact with unknown users or third-party APIs.
- Modules that handle sensitive information.

Threat modeling with STRIDE

The STRIDE threat model defines threats in six categories, which are spoofing, tampering, repudiation, information disclosure, denial of service, and elevation of privilege. It's normally used to assess the architecture design.

The threat STRIDE model and general security mitigation are summarized in the following table. In addition to STRIDE, it's also suggested to include privacy in the analysis:

STRIDE threats	Mitigation
Spoofing	Authentication such as credentials, certificates, and SSH
Tampering	Integrity (HASH256, digital signature)
Repudiation	Authentication, logging
Information Disclosure	Confidentiality (encryption, ACL)
Denial of Service	Availability (load balance, buffer, message queue)
Elevation of Privilege	Authorization (ACL)
Privacy (additionally included)	Data masking, access control, user consent, removal

The analysis of STRIDE analysis normally involves the entity (user, admin, external application), the process (web server, FTP, service), the data store (database or file), the dataflow (parameters or information between modules, processes, systems, or users), and the trust boundary. Here are some examples of STRIDE analysis mapping:

STRIDE and privacy threats	Examples
Spoofing	The entity (user or client side) may spoof its identity. The process may spoof its source.
Tampering	The process may be tampered with, such as in a DLL injection attack. The data store can be tampered with. The information flow may be tampered with, such as MITM.
Repudiation	The entity (client side) may deny what has been done. The process may tamper with logs to deny what has been done. The data store of audit logs can be tampered with.
Information disclosure	The process itself may include an encryption key and can be reversed. The data store keeps clear-text copies of passwords. The data flow transmits the password without an encryption channel.
Denial of service	The process may be connected to too many clients, and be overloaded. The data store is damaged or full. The data flow is disconnected and can't reach the destination.

Elevation of Privilege	The process should be in user-mode but can execute a kernel-mode command. The process is running with additional permissions.
Privacy	The external entity (client app) may collect PII but doesn't inform the user. The data store keeps PII in logs without anonymization.

Refer to OWASP *Application Threat Modeling* for more examples based on the DFD diagram: `https://www.owasp.org/index.php/Application_Threat_Modeling`.

In practice, STRIDE may still be too general for the team to proceed with the threat discussion. It's highly suggested to use a checklist or threat library lists, such as a CWE list (`https://cwe.mitre.org/data/index.html`), **Common Attack Pattern Enumeration and Classification (CAPEC)**, or **Adversarial Tactics, Techniques and Common Knowledge (ATT&CK)**, which we will discuss in the next section.

Tools and templates are there to help the team to do threat modeling more efficiently. On the other hand, the use of tools may introduce a learning curve or overhead to the team. We will introduce some tools to apply to threat modeling practices.

Diagram designer tool

These kinds of tool help you to draw the application diagrams (DFD), to mark the trust boundaries, and to label the threat attributes. The tools also include a threat library for users to select a threat from the library. It's an ideal tool to document the threat modeling analysis report. Normally, the application architecture and system diagram DFD were presented followed by the threat identification.

If your team is geographically distributed across several regions, or the threat modeling requires offline feedback with several roles across different time zones, using of the tool to produce the threat modeling analysis report is highly recommended.

The Microsoft Threat Modeling tool, OWASP Threat Dragon, and Mozilla SeaSponge are the tools in this category that allow you to draw DFD diagrams with threat analysis:

- Microsoft Threat Modeling Tool: `https://www.microsoft.com/en-us/download/details.aspx?id=49168`
- OWASP Threat Dragon: `https://www.owasp.org/index.php/OWASP_Threat_Dragon`
- Mozilla SeaSponge: `http://mozilla.github.io/seasponge/`

Card games

Card games makes threat modeling a team-building game. All team members are gathered together with a deck of cards and the data flow diagram of the application. Each card represents one common threat. Take OWASP Cornucopia as an example. The threats are also mapped to industry practices such as OWASP SCP, OWASP ASVS, CAPEC, and SAFECode.

The OWASP Cornucopia defines six suits for the key security areas:

- **Data validation and encoding (VE)**
- **Authentication (AT)**
- **Session management (SM)**
- **Authorization (AZ)**
- **Cryptography (CR)**
- **Cornucopia (C)**

Refer to this link for a DOC or PDF version of the cards: `https://www.owasp.org/index.php/OWASP_Cornucopia#tab=Get_the_Cards`.

For example, in the **Data Validation & Encoding** suit card 2, which follows, shows the attack scenario, and the mapping security best practices with OWASP SCP, ASVS, AppSensor, CAPEC, and SAFECode:

2
Brian can gather information about the underlying configurations, schemas, logic, code, software, services, and infrastructure due to the content of error messages, poor configuration, or the presence of default installation files or old, test, backup, or copies of resources, or exposure of source code
OWASP SCP 69, 107-109, 136, 137, 153, 156, 158, 162
OWASP ASVS 1.10, 4.5, 8.1, 11.5, 19.1, 19.5
OWASP AppSensor HT1-3
CAPEC 54, 541
SAFECode 4, 23
OWASP Cornucopia Ecommerce Website Edition v1.20-EN

This card game can also be an effective tool even with just one developer. A developer or tester can draw a card randomly to reflect the security issue of the existing application. Use the cards to think about whether the existing design will be vulnerable to threats or any missing security considerations. This card game can make threat modeling a lot of fun. There is no doubt that F2F discussion is always the most effective method of communication.

There are two issues we need to be aware of. First, for a team to be able to play the card game together, the F2F team must be sitting together. Secondly, a project team that is distributed across several regions may not be able to play the card game together. To address these two issues, an official documentation of discussion results is still needed. The documentation, which includes identified risks and mitigation actions, is not only for the team that can't join the card game for review but also for the purposes of tracking.

References of the card games are as follows:

- Microsft EOP card game: `https://www.microsoft.com/en-us/sdl/adopt/eop.aspx`
- OWASP Cornucopia card game: `https://www.owasp.org/index.php/OWASP_Cornucopia`

Threat library references

Sometimes, it's just difficult to brainstorm threats during threat modeling analysis. It will be easier to pick up and select threats from the threat list library that fit the existing application design. Card games do help, but they may only present the most common threats. If you find the threats do not fit your projects or you need additional threat libraries to refer to, here are some suggested industry threat libraries:

Threat library	Characteristics
CAPEC	It lists 508 attack patterns in a tree view. The attack patterns are also available in CSV and XML format. Each attack pattern is labeled with a CAPEC-ID number.
ATT&CK	The threats are categorized by platform (Linux, Windows, Mac, mobile) with specific attack techniques. Each threat is also discussed with technical mitigation and detection approaches. It includes lots of practical hacker and malware attack techniques.
CWE	CWE is a list of software weaknesses. Each CWE is categorized into a threat tree view and presented with both insecure and secure source code implementations. It's also a very good reference for secure coding.

Case study – formal documents or not?

Let's look at a case study to discuss the different approaches of threat modeling practices. Peter and Linda, who are security leads, plan to do threat modeling with a project team. Peter is in a very large organization. The project team is distributed across the Globe. The security process requires a formal threat modeling analysis report as parts of the criteria to move on to the next step. On the other hand, Linda is working with a small software company. Team members are all in the same location. Linda thinks using a whiteboard and card game discussion will be more interactive and efficient instead of detailed documents. As a result, Peter and Linda decided on different approaches to run the threat modeling as summarized in the following table:

	Formal process (Peter)	Group discussion (Linda)
Characteristics	Required formal document delivery Follow templates and tools to generate the required output Documents may accumulate knowledge	No formal document delivery Apply card games that focus on the process of team interaction and discussion.
Tools	Checklist and templates Threat modeling and diagram designer	Card games White board
Disadvantages	Documents may be an overhead for the team	Lack of documents during the discussion It may only fit a team whose members are geographically located together

There is no perfect process. It's just a case of which approach works best for the team. There is no constraint that Peter should not use card games or Linda should not apply the formal process. The most important part of any process's adoption is to understand the objective and the rationale of the process. For example, Linda may consider documenting the final card game discussion results for stakeholders' reference. Peter may consider using card games for a small module/team to reduce the documentation overhead. Considering a mixed approach may be a good idea. Just don't let the process limit the team's creativity and innovation.

Secure design

Secure design can be a very broad topic to discuss. In this section, we are going to focus on the discussion with seven key security controls: authentication, authorization, session management, data validation, error handling, logging, and encryption. Refer to the following diagram:

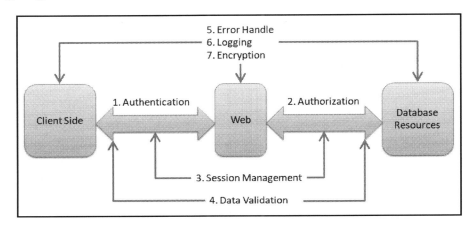

A secure design may be related to several factors including security requirements, the adoption of the security framework, the logic flow, and the right implementation. Take authentication as an example—market security requirements may add two-factor authentication or **one-time password** (OTP). A security framework, such as Spring Security or Shiro itself, provides authentication, authorization, and session management security controls. However, the wrong logic flow and incorrect implementation may result in its authentication bypassing security issues. Although an organization can define secure design policies and guidelines, it's still the most effective by showing the security framework, CWE case studies, and implementation samples.

Secure design training or newsletters can include the industry-common CWE and also in-house projects' common issues followed by secure design suggestions. It's also suggested to introduce a security framework with the common incorrect implementations that result in security risks. Here, we only list a sample for Java implementation. In addition, the following links are suggested for further reading:

- OWASP Cheat Sheet: `https://www.owasp.org/index.php/OWASP_Cheat_Sheet_Series`

- OWASP Secure Coding Practices: `https://www.owasp.org/index.php/OWASP_Secure_Coding_Practices_-_Quick_Reference_Guide`
- SAFECode Security in Agile: `http://safecode.org/publication/SAFECode_Agile_Dev_Security0712.pdf`
- OWASP Top 10 Proactive Control: `https://www.owasp.org/images/b/bc/OWASP_Top_10_Proactive_Controls_V3.pdf`

Just remember that the adoption of a security framework doesn't mean the application will be secured. It still requires the right implementation of the framework:

	Common CWE	**Open-source framework**
Authentication	CWE-294: Authentication Bypass by Capture-replay CWE-306: Missing Authentication for Critical Function CWE-307: Improper Restriction of Excessive Authentication Attempts CWE-640 Weak Password Recovery Mechanism for Forgotten Password	Spring Security Shiro KeyCloak VisualCaptcha privacyIDEA
Authorization	CWE-639: Authorization Bypass Through User-Controlled Key CWE-647: Use of Non-Canonical URL Paths for Authorization Decisions CWE-425: Direct Request ('Forced Browsing')	Spring Security Shiro
Session Management	CWE-384: Session Fixation CWE-613: Insufficient Session Expiration CWE-6: J2EE Misconfiguration: Insufficient Session-ID Length CWE-488: Exposure of Data Element to the Wrong Session	Spring Security Shiro Jetty
Data validation	CWE-89 Improper Neutralization of Special Elements used in an SQL Command CWE-77: Improper Neutralization of Special Elements used in a Command CWE-120: Buffer Copy without Checking Size of Input ('Classic Buffer Overflow')	Java Commons Validator

Error handling	CWE-200: Information Exposure CWE-460: Improper Cleanup on Thrown Exception	N/A. It normally requires secure coding practices and proper configurations.
Logging	CWE-532: Information Exposure Through Log Files CWE-117: Improper Output Neutralization for Logs CWE-779: Logging of Excessive Data	SLF4F (Simple Logging Façade for Java) OWASP Security Logging
Encryption	CWE-759: Use of a One-Way Hash without a Salt CWE-523: Unprotected Transport of Credentials CWE-330: Use of Insufficiently Random Values	OpenSSL BouncyCastle

Here are other practical secure software implementation frameworks suggested by OWASP Proactive Controls:

OWASP top 10 proactive controls	Open source tools and frameworks
C1: Define Security Requirements	• OWASP **Application Security Verification Standard** (ASVS) • OWASP **Mobile Application Security Verification Standard** (MASVS)
C2: Leverage Security Frameworks and Libraries	• OWASP Dependency Check • OWASP Dependency Track • Retire.JS
C3: Secure Database Access	• CIS Database Hardening Standards
C4: Encode and Escape Data	• OWASP Java Encoder Project Examples • OWASP Java Encoder Project • AntiXSSEncoder • Zend/Escaper
C5: Validate All Inputs	• OWASP Java HTML Sanitizer Project • Java JSR-303/JSR-349 Bean Validation • Java Hibernate Validator • JEP-290 Filter Incoming Serialization Data • Apache Commons Validator • PHP's filter functions
C6: Implement Digital Identity	• LinOTP OTP Authentication: https://www.linotp.org/ • Gluu Server: https://www.gluu.org/gluu-server/overview/
C7: Enforce Access Controls	• OWASP ZAP with the optional access control testing add-on
C8: Protect Data Everywhere	• **SSLyze**: SSL configuration scanning library and CLI tool • **SSLLabs**: free service for scanning and checking TLS/SSL configuration • **OWASP O-Saft TLS Tool**: TLS connection testing tool • **TLS Observatory** • **SSL Config generator** • **GitRob**: Command-line tool to find sensitive information in publicly available files on GitHub • **TruffleHog**: Searches for secrets accidentally committed • **KeyWhiz**: Secrets manager • **Hashicorp Vault**: Secrets manager
C9: Implement Security Logging and Monitoring	• OWASP Security Logging Project • Apache Logging Services
C10: Handle All Errors and Exceptions	• Error Prone • Chaos Monkey

When it comes to the root/cause analysis of a security issue, sometimes it's very difficult to identify if the issue was caused by insecure design or insecure coding. Whenever it's possible, it's suggested to document the secure design as a detailed specific implementation. For example, the security design document may define the uses of a secure random number to do encryption. However, without the specific definition of a secure random number, the development team is still unable to achieve a secure implementation. Please also refer to the OWASP Cryptographic Storage Cheat Sheet for advice on strong random numbers.

An organization may consider building an internal secure design knowledge portal, which includes the following resources:

- **Secure design case studies**: Every case study includes the scenario, the security issue, and the design to mitigate risks.
- **Suggested implementation framework**: Adoption of a mature security framework to solve common security issues.
- **Security Assistant as part of the IDE plugin**: All secure coding rules can still be an overhead for developers. It's suggested to provide developers with an IDE plugin to do a secure coding check and to complement other secure coding scanning tools.

  Implementation review toolkit such as code review and dependency review tools. We will discuss this in the next chapter.

If you still find difficulties in building a secure design knowledge portal, the following are good reference sources. The objective of the knowledge portal is to provide a developer with all the knowledge, tools, tutorials, and best practices to achieve a secure design:

- OWASP Security Knowledge Framework: `https://www.securityknowledgeframework.org/demo.php`
- Open Reference Architecture for Security and Privacy: `http://security-and-privacy-reference-architecture.readthedocs.io/en/latest/index.html`
- Mobile Threat Catalogue: `https://pages.nist.gov/mobile-threat-catalogue/`
- OWASP Cheat Sheet Series: `https://www.owasp.org/index.php/OWASP_Cheat_Sheet_Series`

In practice, the adoption of a secure framework can help you to achieve secure architecture, design, and implementation since those security frameworks are built with security by default. In addition, the adoption of a secure framework still requires the secure coding and implementation. In the next chapter, we will explore more secure coding and implementation in more detail.

Summary

We discussed the importance of the whole team's involvement with threat modeling practices and the STRIDE examples (spoofing, tampering, repudiation, information disclosure, denial of service, and elevation of privilege).

There are several tools and methodologies to do threat modeling. If you would like to have a DFD/threat diagram designer, you can use the Microsoft threat modeling tool, OWASP Threat Dragon, or Mozilla SeaSponge. If you have a small team and would like to do threat modeling via a card game team activity, the Microsoft EOP card game and OWASP Cornucopia are recommended.

We also introduced some threat libraries such as CAPEC, ATT&CK, and CWE, which can also support threat identification during threat modeling. We also discussed a threat modeling case study, and we understood the pros and cons of using threat modeling designers and card games.

On the topic of secure design, we discussed the major key security controls, authentication, authorization, session management, data validation, error handling, logging, and encryption. We suggested some references on CWE and open source security frameworks in each security control category. Furthermore, building a secure design knowledge portal is recommended. OWASP SKF and Open Reference Architecture for security and privacy are good reference sources.

In the coming chapters, we will discuss secure implementation and coding in detail.

Questions

1. Threat modeling is only related to developers. QAs, architects, or operation teams don't need to get involved. True or false?
2. Which of the following modules should apply threat modeling?
    1. Legacy modules
    2. Modules with external interaction with third-party vendors
    3. Modules that handle personal information
    4. All of the above

3. Which of the following is a security mitigation for Repudiation?
    1. Hash
    2. Authentication logging
    3. Load balance
    4. Encryption

4. Which one of the following is not mainly used for threat library references?
    1. CAPE
    2. ATTCK
    3. SeaSponge
    4. CWE

5. Which one of the following is not related to the authentication security framework?
    1. Shiro
    2. Spring Security
    3. VisualCaptcha
    4. Java Commons Validator

Further reading

- **ETSI TS 102 165-1 V4.2.1 (2006-12): Method and proforma for Threat, Risk, Vulnerability Analysis**: http://www.etsi.org/deliver/etsi_ts/102100_102199/10216501/04.02.03_60/ts_10216501v040203p.pdf
- **NIST 800-18 Guide for Developing Security Plans for Federal Information Systems:** https://csrc.nist.gov/publications/detail/sp/800-18/rev-1/final
- **ITU-T X.805 (10/2003) Security architecture for systems providing end-to-end communications:** https://www.itu.int/rec/T-REC-X.805-200310-I/en
- **Oauth2.0 Threat Model and Security Considerations:** https://tools.ietf.org/html/rfc6819
- **SafeCode Tactical Threat Modeling:** https://safecode.org/safecodepublications/tactical-threat-modeling/
- **OWASP Threat Risk Modeling:** https://www.owasp.org/index.php/Threat_Risk_Modeling

- **OCTAVE Allegro: Improving the Information Security Risk Assessment Process:** https://resources.sei.cmu.edu/library/asset-view.cfm?assetid=8419
- **NIST 800-30 Guide for Conducting Risk Assessments:** https://csrc.nist.gov/publications/detail/sp/800-30/rev-1/final
- **SAFECode Fundamental Practices for Secure Software Development:** https://www.safecode.org/publication/SAFECode_Dev_Practices0211.pdf
- **MSDN Threat Modeling:** Https://msdn.microsoft.com/en-us/library/ff648644.aspx
- **Threat Assessment & Remediation Analysis (TARA):** https://www.mitre.org/sites/default/files/pdf/11_4982.pdf
- **SAFECode Practical Security Stories and Security Tasks for Agile Development Environments:** http://safecode.org/publication/SAFECode_Agile_Dev_Security0712.pdf
- **SAFECode Fundamental Practices for Secure Software Development:** https://safecode.org/wp-content/uploads/2018/03/SAFECode_Fundamental_Practices_for_Secure_Software_Development_March_2018.pdf
- **SAFECode Managing Security Risks Inherent in the Use of Third-party:** https://www.safecode.org/wp-content/uploads/2017/05/SAFECode_TPC_Whitepaper.pdf
- **SEI Secure Design Patterns:** https://resources.sei.cmu.edu/asset_files/TechnicalReport/2009_005_001_15110.pdf
- **Secure Design Patterns, Carnegie Mellon University:** https://resources.sei.cmu.edu/library/asset-view.cfm?assetid=9115
- **MITRE Attack Matrix:** https://attack.mitre.org/wiki/ATT%26CK_Matrix
- **SAFECode practical security stories and tasks in Agile:** http://safecode.org/publication/SAFECode_Agile_Dev_Security0712.pdf
- **NIST 800-63 Digital Identity Guidelines:** https://nvlpubs.nist.gov/nistpubs/SpecialPublications/NIST.SP.800-63-3.pdf
- **The Java Exception Handling Tutorials:** https://docs.oracle.com/javase/tutorial/essential/exceptions/index.html

Secure Coding Best Practices 8

Secure architecture design and threat modeling are followed by the secure coding phase. In the coding phase, we would like to avoid the use of unsafe APIs, buffer overflow, sensitive information leakage, and so on. It's difficult for every developer to be familiar with all secure coding rules. Therefore, how to apply secure coding tools and tips to spot major security issue will be discussed in this chapter.

We will cover the following topics in this chapter:

- Secure coding industry best practices
- Establishing secure coding baselines
- Secure coding awareness training
- Tool evaluation
- Tool optimization
- High-risk module review
- Manual code review tools
- Secure code scanning tools
- Secure compiling
- Common issues in practice

Secure coding industry best practices

Secure coding is the foundation of secure software. We have done threat modeling and secure architecture design. These require secure coding to make them happen. Secure coding can be a challenge for the development team since developers are occupied with working on new features, and there may be hundreds of secure coding rules to learn. Before we discuss secure coding practices in more detail, we will review existing secure coding standards we can refer to.

Depending on programming languages, secure coding standards are summarized in the following table:

Reference standards	Description and reference
CERT Secure Coding	• This provides secure coding standards for C, C++, Java, Perl, and Android.
Find Security Bugs	• This provides bug patterns with samples of vulnerable code and solution for Java.
CWE	• This provides vulnerable source code samples from the perspective of common software weaknesses. The coding samples cover C, C++, Java, and PHP.
Android	• Android Application Secure Design and Secure Coding Guidebook
OWASP SKF	• OWASP Security Knowledge Framework. • It can be used as an internal security knowledge base, which includes OWASP ASVS and secure coding knowledge.
PHP Security	• OWASP PHP Security Cheat Sheet
OWASP Code Review	• OWASP Code Review Project
Apple Secure Coding Guide	• Apple Secure Coding Guide
Go	• Secure Coding Practices for GO language
JavaScript	• JavaScript Secure Coding Practices
Python	• OWASP Python Security Project

We understand the secure coding baseline and standards. Furthermore, the key challenge is how to apply these secure coding rules to developers' daily coding activities. The following are the recommended approaches to proceed with the secure coding practices.

Establishing secure coding baselines

Secure coding baselines are the minimum secure coding requirements and a checklist for the project team to move to the next stage. Secure coding baselines are also part of the release criteria. It's always suggested you use secure coding guidelines based on industry best practices or standards, such as **CERT Secure Coding**, as described in the preceding table.

Define secure coding baselines based on each programming language, such as PHP, Python, JavaScript, Android, and iOS. The secure coding baseline is better to include the information not only secure coding rules but also examples of security risks, vulnerable code examples, and suggested ones. Here is an example.

Secure code issue – predictable random numbers:

The use of a predictable random number can result in vulnerabilities in the session ID, token, or encryption initialization vector. It's suggested to use `java.security.SecureRandom` instead of `java.util.Random`:

```
// Vulnerable Code
Random rnd = New Random ();

// Suggested Code
SecureRandom rnd = SecureRandom();
```

All projects must be scanned with specified code scanning tools before releases. Some organizations may also define release criteria for secure coding practices. Here are some examples:

- All the warnings from scanning results that were generated by scanning tools must be checked
- All compiler warnings (not just errors) should be checked and cleared
- The number of open defects in the scanning results cannot exceed a certain percentage per line of code

In addition, the secure coding baselines require related developer tools and training in practice; otherwise, those secure coding rules will be just documents.

Secure coding awareness training

The purpose of secure coding training is to inform the development team of the forthcoming secure coding practices we are going to perform. At the initial stage of the secure coding awareness training, the focus will be mainly on the following:

- What are secure coding standards or baselines?
- What are common industry secure coding issues?
- How will they impact on a developer's daily tasks?
- Release criteria for secure code scanning

A case study or scenario-based vulnerable source code example will have better training effects than simply secure coding rules. The following are good references in this area and provide a lot of vulnerable and secure best practice code samples:

- **OWASP Security Knowledge Framework**: `https://www.securityknowledgeframework.org/`
- **Android Application Secure Design and Secure Coding Guidebook**: `http://www.jssec.org/dl/android_securecoding_en.pdf`
- **Find Security Bugs Patterns for Java**: `https://find-sec-bugs.github.io/`
- **OWASP Teammentor**: `https://owasp.teammentor.net/angular/user/index`

Tool evaluation

Once the team realizes the importance and the challenge of secure coding, it will look for some tools to make the secure coding easier. The evaluation of a scanning tool may include the following considerations:

Considerations	Description
Usability	• The target users of the code scanning tools are developers. The usability includes the capability to scan parts of the source code, differential scans, scanning reports, tracing back to original source code, and so on.
Budget	• If it's an IDE plugin commercial tool, we need to consider how many concurrent users' licenses it will need.
Programming languages support	• Most tools support C/C++ and Java, but do not support script languages, such as Python, JavaScript, or PHP. • Do a survey of the programming languages used by in-house projects and prioritize the programming languages that are going to be supported.
Detection rate and false positive rates	• It's common for any scanning tools to have false positive rates, depending on the scanning engine and rules. A high false positive is not a bad thing, and it can also mean the scanner takes a more conservative approach. Find the tool that best fits the projects instead of the most well-known. • To evaluate the detection rate, we may use known vulnerable projects.
Scanning rules update	• It's important that the tool is constantly updated with rules and scanners. One of the key advantages of a commercial tool is that the tool will have up-to-date scanning rules.

Generally, there are two approaches for code scanning. One is static code scanning with IDE plugin. It works like a spellcheck and is more intuitive for a developer to learn and correct security issues. The other one is to do code scanning with a daily build that generates a daily scanning report. Developers will need to look into the daily scanning report to fix or to comment on security issues by batch. This approach may not be that intuitive for developers, but the compiled security scanning may provide better accuracy. To promote adoption of these two kinds of scanning tool, starting with a small-scale pilot team is suggested. There are some commercial and open source tools available in these two kinds of scanning approach.

	Pros	Cons
IDE plugin static code scanning	Intuitive to developers (works like a spellcheck).	• It may have higher false positives. • It requires every developer to install the plugin • The detection capability is limited. • The license costs for every developer. • Requires enforcement uses of the tool for every developer.
Daily complied scanning	• Security scanning accuracy based on the project integration and compiled scan. • Centrally manages the scanning rules and results. • It is easy to build security metrics and monitor the results for every project.	• Fully buildable source code is required. • The scanning results need further assignment for developers to check. When a developer is assigned to check the reports, he may not be familiar with other modules.

Evaluation of code scanning tools consists of a detection rate, false positive rate, potential overhead, and usability for the development team. The vulnerable code projects for the evaluation of static code scanning tools are listed in the following table:

Vulnerable projects	Description	Programming languages
NIST Software Assurance Reference Dataset Project	The project provides on-purpose insecure code examples which can be used to test the detection rate of secure code scanning tools	Java, C/C++, C#, PHP
OWASP Node JS Goat	It's a vulnerable website to practice OWASP top 10 security testing and is built by NodeJS.	Node JS
OWASP WebGoat .Net	It's a vulnerable website to practice OWASP top 10 security testing and is built by .NET.	.NET
OWASP WebGoat PHP	It's a vulnerable website to practice OWASP top 10 security testing and is built by PHP.	PHP
OWASP RailsGoat	It's a vulnerable website to practice OWASP top 10 security testing and is built by Ruby.	Ruby on Rails

Once the security team has selected scanning tools after testing the results, the security team may engage with more development teams to discuss adoption of the tools. Before the adoption of the tools, it's suggested to conduct hands-on training via demo usage of the results, handling the scanning results, and using the scanning tools.

This stage of training is focused more on *how* instead of *what*. Examples of hands-on tutorials are how to use scanning tools, how to review security issues, how to fix based on the scanning results, how to disable some scanning rules, and so on.

Tool optimization

Once the teams have been using the code scanning tools for a while, the security team may help to optimize the tools, processes, or rules based on user feedback. Here are some key factors to be optimized for a large-scale code scanning adoption:

Key factors	Suggestions
Scanning rules customization	The purpose of rules customization is to help the project team reduce false positives. The security team may help to disable some rules that don't apply to the projects or change rules that always result in false positives.
Recommendation fixes	Ideally, IDE plugins will present not only security warnings but also suggested fixes. However, if the tools you are using don't support the team, using the OWASP Security Knowledge Framework can be an alternative.
Integration	Integrate code scanning tools into Jenkins, and developers' IDE plugins. Automation framework. Integration with Jenkins is one of the basics of CI/CD.
Reporting	The team may request further quality metrics reports, such as incremental scanning reports based on previous checked results or top common issue cross-projects.
Automation platform	Moving to the next level of secure coding automation involves integrating several tools together on an automation platform. Try the following open source tools to build your own secure coding automation platform: • **SWAMP-in-a-Box**: • **JackHammer**:

High-risk module review

The automation code scanning tool can help to detect most source code security issues. However, there is still a need for high-risk modules. In addition to source code scanning tools, we will also apply blackbox or **Dynamic Application Security Testing (DAST)**, which will be discussed in later chapters. Think like a hacker. Which modules will a hacker be interested in? What information can be most valuable to a hacker? What might be the weakest link in the whole application? The following table lists high-risk modules that require further review:

High-risk modules	Security Review Focuses
Authentication	• Accounts registration • Login and CAPTCHA • Password recovery or reset • Password changes • Identity and password storage and access control • Account lockout control after multiple failures
Authorization	• Sensitive resource access • Administration management

Configuration	• There are two kinds of review in the configuration:
	  ○ Secure configurations of the applications, such as turning off debug mode and enabling TLS communication.
	  ○ The impact of the configuration for each software release.

Finance	• Payment functions • Order and shopping carts
File handling	• File upload • File download
Database	• Database query • Database add, update, and delete
API interface	• Restful API interfaces • Third-party integration interfaces
Legacy	• Modules that don't support secure communication • Modules that may still use weak encryption algorithms • Uses of banned or dangerous APIs
Encryption	• Uses of banned encryption algorithms • Hardcoded sensitive information or comments in the source code during development, such as IP, email, password, or hidden hotkey
Session	• Concurrent session control and detection • The randomness of the session ID and expiration period

Manual code review tools

A manual code review may take some time. A manual code review without proper tools and strategies can be like looking for a needle in a haystack. As previously discussed, we only do a manual code review for specific high-risk modules, not for whole projects. In addition to the selection of target scopes, tools can also help us to do a manual code review more efficiently. Here are some open source recommended tools that will help make source code reviews more efficient, although these are not specialized for this purpose:

Tools	Usage scenario
AndroGuard	• This includes lots of Python analysis modules to do a reverse-engineering analysis of Android applications. • The generated graph can be viewed by Gephi.
Doxygen	• This supports a wide range of program languages to generate online HTML or PDF documentation. It can also generate a functions call graph that can be viewed by Graphviz. • It's useful to give us an overview of the program and to identify the modules with high-risk that we should focus on.
Kscope	• This tool can analyze C source code with a tree of calling functions and a call graph.
OpenGrok	• This provides Google-like syntax and a RegExp full-text source code search. It can also do cross-referencing based on the search results.

WinMerge	• This can compare the differences between two files and folders. The comparison results are presented in visual colors. It's useful when we are looking for code changes between different releases.
	• For non-Windows platforms, KDiff3 or Meld are alternative open source options:
	  ○ `http://kdiff3.sourceforge.net/`
	  ○ `http://meldmerge.org/`

NCC Code Navi	• The key advantage of the NCC Code Navi tool is the capability to do a keywords search across source code files. Right-clicking to launch a CERT search coding search is also useful.

Secure code scanning tools

In terms of source code scanning, there is no-one-size-fits-all solution. There are also no scanning tools that can find zero false positives with a 100% accurate detection rate. Therefore, for the same programming language, it's common that we may apply at least two scanning tools for a cross-reference check.

Here are some commonly used open-source secure coding analysis tools, as in 2018. Note that we only list open source tools here:

Tools	Background and key characteristics of the scanning tool
Retire.JS	• Detection of vulnerable JavaScript libraries, such as jQuery, AngularJS, Node, and so on. • It provides the command line, grunt plugin, and also OWASP ZAP plugin for integration scanning.
Clang Static Analyzer	This provides standalone command line analysis for C, C++, and Objective C.
Flawfinder	A simple C/C++ code scanning tool. It's a Python command line scanning tool and can be easily customized based on the needs.
DREK	• This acts like GREP to search specific security issue by regular expressions, but it can generate scanning results in PDF or HTML format. • It's easy to extend any scanning rules by regular expressions. It can be used to scan any programming languages.
Pylint	Pylint is a source code checker for the Python programming language.
PHPMD	• PHP Mess Detector is a PHP source code scanner.
DawnScanner	Security scanner for Ruby Web applications.
SpotBugs	• This provides a standalone GUI and command line. • SpotBugs can also be used as an Eclipse plugin. It's the successor of FindBugs.
CPP Check	This is a static code analysis tool for C/C++.
Mobile Security Framework (MobSF)	The Mobile Security Framework is a fully automated scanning tool for Android apps. A developer can just upload the APK to the MSF, and the MSF will do all the analysis automatically.
Clang Static Analyzer	This is a code analysis tool for C/C++ and Objective C.
ESLint	• This provides command-line code scanning with JavaScript. • Refer here for the secure code scanning rules: `https://eslint.org/docs/rules/`.
JSHint	This is for JavaScript code scanning, and also provides command line tools by NodeJS.
Infer	This is a static code analyzer for Java, C/C++, and Objective C, provided by Facebook.
Phan	Phan is a static analyzer for PHP.
PHP Security Checker	This checks PHP project dependencies for known security issues.

OWASP Dependency check	This supports a wide range of programming frameworks and checks the disclosed vulnerabilities with updated NVD data feeds. The tool can run as a command line or via integration with Jenkins.
VisualCodeGrepper (VCG)	VCG is a language-independent scanning tool. The scanning rules can also be easily customized by regular expressions. There are also default rules for commonly banned APIs. It provides a GUI and command line to scan any piece of source code.
PMD	This is a source code analyzer for Java and JavaScript. It's mainly for common programming flaws.
Graudit	This is a simple script to find potential security issues by using GREP to search for specific code patterns. The signatures database templates provide clues for what to look for.
SonarQube	This provides support for more than 20 languages and can integrate with CI frameworks. It is also UI-friendly for quality code scanning results.
Brakeman	Static analysis security scanner for Ruby on Rails.
bandit	Security analysis for Python source code.
Error Prone	Error Prone detects potential Java errors during compile time.
Dawn	Dawn is a static analysis security scanner for Ruby web applications.

Here is another categorization by language:

Programming language	Scanning tools
C/C++	• Infer • CPP Check • Flawfinder • Clang Static Analyzer
Java	• Infer • SpotBugs • PMD
Android	• MobSF
PHP	• Phan • PHPMD
Ruby	• DawnScanner

Python	• Pylint
JavaScript	• ESLint • JSHint • Retire.JS • PMD
Dependencies vulnerabilities	• OWASP Dependency check • PHP Security Checker • Retire.JS
Language-independent	• SonarQube • DREK • Graudit • VisualCodeGrepper

Due to rules and detection engine capabilities, the scanning results may vary for the same programming language. Using two scanning tools for the same language is recommended. For example, one commercial tool for daily compiled scanning and another open source tool for developers' IDE plugins. The use of commercial scanning tools helps to tell customers how the services are tested while open source scanning tools give flexibility for further customization and large-scale deployment without budget constraints.

Secure compiling

Memory corruption and buffer overflow may result in exploit code injection attacks. For the C/C++ programming language, these can be protected by compiler options. By a properly secured configuration of a C/C++ compiler (GCC, MS Visual Studio), the application will be able to add an additional layer of runtime defenses against exploit code injection attacks. These are also mostly ignored by a development team. The common secure options are summarized in the following table:

Protection techniques	Secure options	OS/Compiler
Address Space Layout Randomization (ASLR)	`echo 1 >/proc/sys/kernel/randomize_va_space`	Android, Linux OS
Stack-based buffer overrun protection	`-fstack-protector` `-fstack-protector-all`	gcc
GOT Table Protection	`-Wl,-z,relro`	gcc
Dynamic link path	`-Wl,--disable-new-dtags,--rpath [path]`	gcc

Non-executable stack	`-Wl,-z,noexecstack`	gcc
Image randomization	`-fpie -pie`	gcc
Insecure C runtime function detection	`-D_FORTIFY_SOURCE=2` `-Wformat-security`	gcc
Stack-based buffer overrun defenses (Canary)	`/GS`	MS (Microsoft)Visual C++
Address Space Layout Randomization (ASLR)	`/DYNAMICBASE`	MS Visual C++
CPU-level No-eXecute (NX) support. Data Execution Prevention (DEP)	`/NXCOMPAT`	MS Visual C++
Safe-structured exception handling	`/SAFESEH`	MS Visual C++
Enable additional security check	`/SDL`	MS Visual C++

For further reference and a description of each protection technique, here are some references:

- **SAFECode Development Practices**: `https://www.safecode.org/publication/SAFECode_Dev_Practices0211.pdf`
- **OWASP C-based ToolChain Hardening**: `https://www.owasp.org/index.php/C-Based_Toolchain_Hardening`
- **Linux Audit ASLR**: `https://linux-audit.com/linux-aslr-and-kernelrandomize_va_space-setting/`
- **MS Security Best Practice for C++**: `https://msdn.microsoft.com/en-us/library/k3a3hzw7.aspx`
- **Secure Compiler and linker flags for GCC**: `https://developers.redhat.com/blog/2018/03/21/compiler-and-linker-flags-gcc/`

To verify whether the application or the environment has been configured with secure options, the following tools are useful:

- **CheckSec**: http://www.trapkit.de/tools/checksec.html
- **BinScope**: https://www.microsoft.com/en-us/download/details.aspx?id=44995

Common issues in practice

There are many commercial and open source secure coding tools. Does any tool offer a low false positive rate with a high detection rate?

Answer: There are no perfect or outstanding tools that offer high detection rates with low false positive rates. Every tool offers a different scanning results. The high positive rate can also mean more conservative scanning, which identifies more potential or suspicious code issues. You will find the detection rate and scanning results also vary with different tools. Tool A may be able to detect an issue that tool B can't, and vice versa. In practice, it's also suggested to use at least two tools for code scanning as a cross-reference review.

The scanning results may list over 1,000 issues. Is there any advice on how to handle these issues?

Answer: For a large-scale project, it's very common to have such issues. It can be overwhelming for the developer team to check all of the issues identified by the scanning tool. Here are some possible approaches to consider:

- Filter and evaluate those issues scored as high-risk first.
- Customize the scanning rules for the project to filter those rules that are irrelevant to the project.
- Do an incremental scan for the scopes of source code that were newly added or recently changed. This may depend on whether the scanning tool provides incremental scanning capability.
- Categorize common issues for the same root/cause. Maybe 50% of issues are caused by the same root/cause, such as the use of the same module.

Summary

We have discussed secure coding industry best practices, such as CERT, CWE, Android secure coding, OWASP Code Review, and the Apple secure coding guide. Based on those secure coding rules, we established secure coding baselines as part of the security policy and release criteria. To allow the team to be familiar with secure coding, a training portal was prepared. It was suggested that the secure coding knowledge portal should provide not only coding rules but also case studies.

To apply secure coding to developers' daily tasks, secure coding tools must be adopted. We evaluated secure coding tools, taking into account usability, budget, programming language support, detection rates, and scanning rule maintenance. To evaluate the detection rate of a scanning tool, we also introduced some vulnerable projects that can be used as testing projects.

Secure coding rules and best practices are guidelines. They require the right secure coding tools to make them happen, and also the right approaches to make them more effective and efficient. Therefore, we discussed code review approaches and also examples of high-risk modules. For a more efficient manual code review for high-risk modules, we also listed some tools that can help. Finally, we listed some common open source secure code scanning tools for different programming languages.

In the next chapter, we will present a case study to walk through security requirements, threat modeling, secure architecture, design, and implementation for the development stage.

Questions

1. Which one of the following is not included in CERT Secure Coding standards?
    1. C/C++
    2. Java
    3. Android
    4. PHP

2. Find Security Bugs is mainly used for which of the following programming language?

    1. C/C++

    2. Python

    3. Java

    4. Go

3. Which one of the following can be a release criterion for secure coding?

    1. All source code must be reviewed with specified code scanning tools.

    2. All of the compiler warnings should be checked and cleared.

    3. All the warnings in scanning results which were generated by scanning tools must be checked

    4. All of above

4. What's the main purpose of using vulnerable projects to evaluate code scanning tools?

    1. Detection rate and false positive rates

    2. Budget

    3. Licenses

    4. Performance

5. Which one of the following does not mitigate against buffer overflow exploit code injection?

    1. Address Space Layout Randomization (ASLR)

    2. CSRF Token

    3. Stack-based buffer overrun protection

    4. Non-Executable Stack

6. Which one of the following is not used to scan dependency vulnerabilities?

    1. OWASP Dependency check

    2. PHP Security Checker

    3. Retire.JS

    4. VisualCodeGrepper

7. Which one is an automated mobile security testing framework?

    1. MobSF

    2. OpenGrok

    3. Retire.JS

    4. SonarQube

8. Which of the following tools is not used for the Android security assessment?
    1. AndroGuard
    2. MobSF (Mobile Security Framework)
    3. Flawfinder
    4. SpotBugs

Further reading

- **NIST 500-297 Report on the Static Analysis Tool**: `https://nvlpubs.nist.gov/nistpubs/SpecialPublications/NIST.SP.500-297.pdf`
- **Android Secure Coding**: `https://www.jssec.org/dl/android_securecoding_en.pdf`
- **OWASP PHP Security Cheat Sheet**: `https://www.owasp.org/index.php/PHP_Security_Cheat_Sheet`
- **PHP Security Manual**: `https://php.net/manual/en/security.php`
- **OWASP Code Review**: `https://www.owasp.org/index.php/Category:OWASP_Code_Review_Project`
- **OWASP Secure Coding Practices**: `https://www.owasp.org/index.php/OWASP_Secure_Coding_Practices_-_Quick_Reference_Guide`
- **Apple Secure Coding Guide**: `https://developer.apple.com/library/content/documentation/Security/Conceptual/SecureCodingGuide/Introduction.html`
- **Salesforce Security**: `https://developer.salesforce.com/devcenter/security`
- **OWASP Python Security**: `http://www.pythonsecurity.org/`
- **SAFE Practices for Secure Development of Cloud Applications**: `https://safecode.org/wp-content/uploads/2018/01/SAFECode_CSA_Cloud_Final1213.pdf`
- **C/C++ Banned API**: `https://github.com/Microsoft/ChakraCore/blob/master/lib/Common/Banned.h`
- **Awesome Static Code Analysis**: `https://github.com/mre/awesome-static-analysis`
- **Oracle Secure Coding Guidelines for Java**: `http://www.oracle.com/technetwork/java/seccodeguide-139067.html`

- **FindSecBugs Java Bugs Patterns**: `https://Find-sec-bugs.github.io/bugs.htm`
- **SEI CERT Secure Coding Standards**: `https://wiki.sei.cmu.edu/confluence/display/seccode/SEI+CERT+Coding+Standards`
- **MITRE CWE White Paper V3.1**: `https://cwe.mitre.org/data/published/cwe_v3.1.pdf`

- **CheckMarx Go Secure Coding:** `https://checkmarx.gitbooks.io/go-scp/`

- **CheckMarx JavaScript Secure Coding:** `https://checkmarx.gitbooks.io/js-scp/`

Case Study - Security and Privacy by Design

9

We have discussed secure architecture and design principles, threat modeling, and secure coding practices. In this chapter, we will examine a case study to discuss the implementation of security by design and privacy by design. The case study will show us the common challenges a DevOps team may have to face when applying security practices, and how the security team may help to provide best practices, tools, a security framework, and a training kit.

The case study will begin with a security assessment by OWASP ASVS, and will further identify the required security improvements, such as authentication, authorization, session management, data input/output controls, and privacy by design. We will look at some of the suggested tools and open source security framework implementations. In addition, the third-party components will also introduce vulnerabilities and security risks. We will also discuss the processes and tools that are used to review and manage the open source frameworks and dependencies.

We will cover the following topics in this chapter:

- Secure architecture review
- Privacy by design
- Summary of security and privacy frameworks
- Third-party component management

Case study background

Richard is the CTO of an online bookstore and manages around 500 developers. Richard would like to work with the security team to apply standard security practices during the architecture review, design review, and third-party framework review, and also apply secure coding. Both Richard and the security team reached the consensus that they should have the following in order to prepare for the next stage of their business development:

- Secure design checklist
- Recommended secure design pattern
- A list of reusable third-party components

Let's look at how the security team helps Richard through the stages of development.

Secure architecture review

To evaluate the existing security architecture of the e-commerce site, the security team decides to work with architects to do an initial architecture review based on OWASP ASVS practices. To do the assessment, the project team can either use an online portal or EXCEL. In this case, the project security architecture review was done by using EXCEL checklist before an in-house security assessment portal was used. The following table contains some resources and documentation concerning these two tools that you may find useful:

OWASP assessment tool	Reference of resources
On-line Demo	• OWASP ASVS Assessment Generator ○ Demo site: `http://ibuildingsnl.github.io/owasp-asvs-report-generator/index.html` ○ Source: `https://github.com/ibuildingsnl/owasp-asvs-report-generator` • OWASP Security Knowledge Framework ○ Demo site: `https://demo.securityknowledgeframework.org/project-new` ○ username: admin password: test-skf. ○ Source: `https://github.com/blabla1337/skf-flask`
Off-line EXCEL	• `https://github.com/shenril/owasp-asvs-checklist`

The result of the OWASP ASVS assessment can be presented as a diagram to show you which security areas need further improvements:

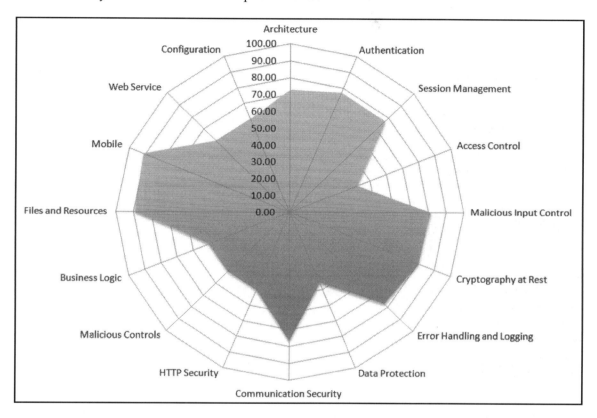

After some of the pilot projects, the security teams grew more familiar with the OWASP ASVS assessment, and there are more projects that require a security assessment. For ease of project data management and cross-reference review, the security team decided to build and customize an in-house assessment portal based on one of the following open source frameworks instead of EXCEL:

- `https://github.com/ibuildingsnl/owasp-asvs-report-generator`
- `https://github.com/blabla1337/skf-flask`

In order to establish a **secure design checklist**, the security team introduced the OWASP ASVS practices, built an in-house knowledge base, and went through a self-assessment with the project teams. To establish the secure design pattern and a list of reusable security frameworks, the security team decided to propose an open source security framework based on the assessment results of the OWASP ASVS. This is because some of the security frameworks also included security best practices, such as web security frameworks, Spring security, and Shiro.

Authentication

Based on the OWASP ASVS assessment of the project, the security team identified that they were not meeting one of the authentication security requirements.

OWASP ASVS authentication:

OWASP ASVS authentication verifies that secrets, API keys, and passwords are not included in the source code, or in online source code repositories.

The security team further investigated the existing practices of secrets management. The CTO, Richard, clarified that the issue was becoming a headache for both the development and operation team. In the development and testing environment, developers may keep the password or keys in a separate configuration file. However, to filter these files and to separate them in a different version controls repository really take lots of communication, and creates collaboration overhead.

To mitigate the risks, the security team proposed some security practices. They advised that the sensitive information should be encrypted when source codes are committed into a repository. Both the testing and operation teams will do regular scanning on the source code repository for any sensitive information. The following diagram shows the revised development workflow model:

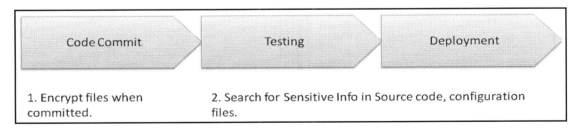

The security team also suggested some tools to integrate into the existing practices of the development, testing, and operation teams' daily usage. Here are some of the open source tools that may be used in secret management:

Tools	Scenario and tools
Git Secret	Developers may need a tool that can handle sensitive files that are to be encrypted when committed and decrypted when checked out transparently. If your development team is using Git as the primary source code repository, the following tools can be applied to reduce the leakage of secrets such as API key, passwords, or encryption key. • Git-Secret • BlackBox • Git-Crypt • Git-Remote-gcrypt
Truffle DumpsterDiver	Developers, QA, or operations teams prefer to search source code or configuration files regularly to identify whether there is any potential secret leakage in the files. The TruffleHog can do the secrets search on the GIT repository, and DumpsterDiver searches for the secrets on the local files.

Once the security team evaluates the tools, the next stage is to perform pilot testing with some of the development and operations teams before large-scale deployment. The purpose of the pilot testing was to make the process smooth and to customize the tools for better usability.

Authorization

The authorization security requirements can refer to the 'OWASP ASVS V4: Access control verification requirements'. For example, the OWASP ASVS self-assessment results showed the need for centralized mechanism protection.

 Centralized Mechanism Protection: You should verify that there is a centralized mechanism (including libraries that call external authorization services) for protecting access to each type of protected resource.

To achieve the centralized mechanism protection, the security team decided to introduce the API gateway architecture that was designed so that all the API interfaces were controlled by the API gateway/manager, such as authentication, the API key, monitoring, ACL, logging, and rate limiting. The security team discussed this with the CTO, Richard, and realized that the existing security controls were implemented by each service, and the implementation was also subject to change for each service. Richard would like to have a common security framework for the purposes of not only consistent access control behaviors, but also the central management of security policies.

A central security policies management is critical for those services that need to interact with external partners:

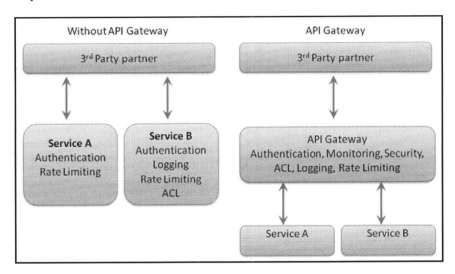

There are a number of API manager options in the market. The following table lists some open source API manager solutions. One of the key advantages of adopting open source frameworks or tools is that you are able to make further customizations based on your business needs:

API manager	Open source reference
Kong	• https://github.com/Kong/kong • https://getkong.org/
API umbrella	• https://github.com/NREL/api-umbrella
WSO2 API Manager	• https://github.com/wso2/product-apim

Session management

The CTO also pointed out some existing challenges to the session management implementation. The existing session management needs to tie with specific container technology and does not support various kinds of client application access, such as standalone or non-web application. The CTO would like to have the session management support heterogeneous client access, and wants it to be container-independent. In addition, the team wants to implement the CSRF token in different ways, and this could result in potential risks and extra effort. The CTO expects the team to provide a common library to have consistent CSRF protection.

After assessing the challenges and needs of session management, the security team works on the evaluation of feasible security frameworks and prepares a security kit that may include the information in the following table. The purpose of the security kit is to help the development team to apply related security practices and tools during the development process:

Stage	Security references and tools
Threats analysis	• CWE-6 Insufficient Session-ID Length • CWE-352 Cross-Site Request Forgery (CSRF) • CWE-384 Session Fixation • CWE-488 Exposure of Data Element to the Wrong Session • CWE-613 Insufficient Session Expiration: Tips to query a specific CWE. Just specify the CWE ID number at the end of the URL below. For example, the CWE-613 will be `https://` `cwe.mitre.org/data/definitions/613.html`.
Secure design	• OWASP ASVS V3 Session Management • OWASP Top 10 A2 Broken Authentication • OWASP Session Management Cheat Sheet
Secure architecture	• Apache Shiro Session Management • OWASP CSRFGuard: `https://www.owasp.org/index.php/` `Category:OWASP_CSRFGuard_Project`

Data input/output

Each project team implements the data input validation differently. Some project teams may miss filtering certain illegal characters, some may not know how to encode the output correctly, and some may neglect to do path or URL canonicalization before validation. These data input/output handling issues could cause some security problems. Therefore, the CTO wants the security team to help provide the appropriate security framework and also create hands-on tutorials for their staff members.

The security team proposes a security training kit that includes coding rules, the coding framework, scanning tools, and some case studies.

Data input/output training kit:

The purpose of the training kit is to provide security best practices, tools, and implementation guides for data input validation and also data output encoding to avoid XSS attacks.

General secure coding rules:

Canonicalization and normalization must occur before validation.
Output encoding should be used to avoid XSS attacks.

The following table shows the preliminary agenda of the security training kit:

Security Framework/tools	Security Controls
OWASP HTML Sanitizer Project (`https://www.owasp.org/index.php/OWASP_Java_HTML_Sanitizer_Project`)	This is for Java to perform HTML sanitization to protect against XSS attacks.
Commons Validator (`https://commons.apache.org/proper/commons-validator/`)	This is a general data validator that provides data format validation, such as email, credit card, date, URL, and so on.
ValidateJS (`https://validatejs.org/`)	This is a frontend JavaScript data validator.
OWASP Java Encoder (`https://www.owasp.org/index.php/OWASP_Java_Encoder_Project`)	This works in a similar way to the HTML sanitizer. It's used to perform output encoding to avoid XSS attacks.

Secure coding scanning tools

- The Checker Framework: `https://checkerframework.org/`
- Find security bugs: `https://find-sec-bugs.github.io`

Examples of security risks:

- FIO16-J: Canonicalizes path names before validating them
- IDS07-J: Sanitizes untrusted data passed to the `Runtime.exec()` method
- IDS00-J: Prevents SQL injection
- IDS16-J: Prevents XML injection
- IDS08-J: Sanitizes untrusted data included in a regular expression
- IDS06-J: Excludes unsanitized user input from format strings

More can be found at `https://wiki.sei.cmu.edu/confluence/display/java/2+Rules`.

Privacy by design

The team realizes the importance of privacy and also receives some awareness training related to privacy laws. However, there is still a gap between translating the legal languages into technical security requirements. The CTO would like the security team to help to provide common privacy design solutions and to make *privacy by design* manifest in technical guidelines for the software engineering team. As well as having the existing data tasking implementation being done by each project team, the CTO plans to have common libraries for consistent data-masking behaviors and to reduce implementation efforts across the teams. There are also other issues raised by the operation, such as sensitive information classification and privacy assessment scanning. The role of the security team is not only to introduce industry best practices but also to evaluate feasible tools or frameworks that support the privacy by design during the DevOps process. Some resources to help you in this stage of the process are listed in the following table:

Challenges of privacy by design	Suggestions by the security team
How do you translate 'privacy by design' into technical security requirements?	• Privacy design patterns: `https://privacypatterns.org/patterns/` • NIST SP 800-122 Guide to Protecting the Confidentiality of PII
Developers need a data-masking implementation API to handle the sensitive information.	The ARX De-Identifier Data anonymization tool.
The operations team needs to classify PII attributes with the existing database and configure the access security policies.	Evaluate the Apache Atlas framework for the data governance and access control.
The DevOps team needs an automatic privacy-scanning tool to evaluate the privacy status of all web services.	Try to apply the Web privacy assessment by 'PrivacyScore'.
The developer team needs a common library to implement the consistent Cookie Consent behaviors for all the web services.	The open source CookieConsent library may be a good candidate to evaluate.

Summary of security and privacy frameworks

The adoption of any security framework requires not only the consideration of business needs but also the fit into the existing architecture. Here is the summary of the industry practices, tools, and frameworks that we discussed in this case study:

Security improvement area	Open source security and privacy framework
Authentication	• Gluu: it's for multiple-factor authentication and social login. • CAPTCHA is commonly used to prevent machine logins. The HCaptcha, ReCaptcha, Patcha are the open source solutions to be considered. • Git-Secret: For the protection of sensitive information in source code repositories, consider using the tool for the development team.
Authorization	• Gluu: It also provides the user consent management • Apache Shiro Session Management • OWASP CSRF Guard can generate a secure token to protect the CSRF attack.
API manager	The following open source frameworks can be considered to apply the API manager to secure the external restful API interfaces. • Kong • API umbrella • WSO2 API Manager
Data input/output	Depends on the programming language, there may be various kinds of data validator framework. • OWASP Java HTML Sanitizer Project: It's a HTML Sanitizer written in Java to protect against XSS. • Commons validator: It's a Java validator library • ValidateJS: It's a JavaScript validator library. • OWASP Java Encoder: It's a Java encoder library which is mainly used to prevent XSS.
Privacy	• Data anonymization tool: `http://arx.deidentifier.org/` • Data governance: `https://atlas.apache.org/index.html` • Web privacy assessment: `http://privacyscore.org/` • Cookie Consent: `https://github.com/insites/cookieconsent`

Third-party component management

To mitigate the security risks of third-party components, the team defines a process to evaluate the third-party components. However, the CTO identified that the manual inspection of open source licenses to collect related information really took a lot of effort, and, in doing so, the team also made some mistakes, such as allowing information to go missing or incorrectly inputting data. The CTO met with the security team, discussing such matters as the feasibility of automating the process of scanning the whole project and creating an identity license for each component, and other such related information. The stages and key activities of this review are shown in the following table:

Stages	Key activities of the third-party component review
Requirements	• Evaluate open source framework components from legal, license, security, and support perspectives
Design	• Keep the open source information in a central database, including details such as the open source name, version, sources, and licenses • Threat and security analysis of the components, ensuring that there is no backdoor, no hard-coded encryption key, and no hidden malware • Ensure that a channel is provided for software updates and patches
Implementation	• The third-party components must be verified with secure code-scanning tools • All the security updates and changes should be documented as part of the change management
Verification	• The scope of security testing includes all the third-party components • License declaration should be implemented in the project • The licenses' compliance should be confirmed with the legal department
Release	• Known CVE or vulnerabilities must be uncovered • Ensure the integrity of all the binary files
Maintenance	• A security update plan must be drawn up and implemented

Without a proper tool or automation tool, security practices can be a big overhead to the development team. After understanding the challenges of the execution, the security team identified three key areas:

- Code scanning for license information
- Binary scan for known vulnerabilities
- Binary scan and runtime behavior monitoring for potential backdoors and malicious behaviors

Here are some recommended scanning tools for the third-party components:

Purposes	Suggested Open Source tools
Open source licenses check	The following projects help to identify and retrieve critical information from the open source components such as vulnerabilities, license, and copyright status. • AboutCode • FOSSology • Ninka • Linux Foundation open source scanning
Known vulnerabilities check	OWASP Dependency Check, OWASP Dependency Track, and OpenVAS are the suggested open source tools to scan software vulnerabilities.
Malware and suspicious behaviors analysis	Cuckoo: It's a sandbox used to analyze static and dynamic behaviors of an unknown file.

Summary

In this case study, we reviewed a typical e-commerce website's adoption of security practices for the requirement, architecture, security framework, design review, and threat-modeling stages. We discussed the role of the security team and also the challenges for the DevOps team in adopting the security practices.

The team did an architecture assessment by applying OWASP ASVS. The team identified that there are some security areas that can be improved, including authentication, authorization, session management, and data-input validation. In addition, the team was also looking for advice on the implementation of privacy by design.

For the authentication process, they discovered that some of the sensitive information, such as the encryption key, password, or secrets, may accidentally be committed in the source code repositories. The security team suggested applying monitoring or encryption tools (Git-Secret) to prevent developers from committing credentials into Git repositories in plain text.

For the authorization process, because of the REST API's open interface with third-party partners, the architecture requires a central security access control. The API manager was introduced to manage all the API's ACL, logging, authorization, and rate limiting. Open source solutions, such as Kong and WSO2 API Manager, were introduced to the team for further evaluation. In addition to the API access control, the team was also looking for a secure session management framework to handle various kinds of client technologies and to secure the system against a CSRF attack. To address the problem of the secure session management, the security team proposed a security kit that included threat analysis with examples of CWE, OWASP cheat sheets for secure design, and open source frameworks with Shiro and CSRF Guard for implementation.

When it comes to data-input validation and output encoding, the security team prepared a training kit that included the secure coding rules, security framework, and code-scanning tools. For the implementation, some of the open source frameworks were suggested based on their security needs, such as HTTP Sanitizer, common validator, ValidateJS, and Java Encoder.

Privacy by design is critical not only for legal compliance but also for personal data protection. The project team was confused about how to translate those legal requirements into software engineering technical requirements. The security team suggested some industry best practices and tools based on the likely scenarios. For example, the developers needed their API to correctly implement data masking. The operations team needed to classify the data classification of the PII attributes with the existing database and configure the access security policies. The DevOps team needed an automatic privacy-scanning tool to evaluate the privacy status of all web services. The developer team needed a common library to implement the consistent Cookie Consent behaviors for all the web services. Privacy by design will put our requirements into practice more easily if we apply the right tools and framework.

Last but not least, we discussed third-party component management. There were lots of open source frameworks and tools applied to the security practices. The third party components also introduced legal and security risks. We introduced some practices and tools to mitigate those risks.

We have looked in great detail at threat modeling, security requirements, secure architecture, framework, security by design, and security by privacy, in the development stage. In the coming chapters, we will begin to explore security testing in greater detail.

Questions

1. Which of the following are secrets that we don't want to be included in the source code?
    1. API keys
    2. Passwords
    3. Encryption key
    4. All of the above

2. What can't an API gateway do?
    1. Access the control list
    2. Rate limiting
    3. Antivirus
    4. API key authentication

3. Which one of the following is related to the security of the session management?
    1. Insufficient session ID length
    2. Cross-Site Request Forgery (CSRF)
    3. Session fixation
    4. All of the above

4. True or False: For the data validation, does the canonicalization and normalization occur after validation?

5. What is data anonymization used for?
    1. It's to perform the data masking of sensitive information
    2. It's for data governance
    3. Web privacy assessment
    4. Cookie Consent

6. What can the AboutCode, FOSSology, and Ninka tools do?
    1. Open source licenses check
    2. Known vulnerabilities check
    3. Suspicious behaviors analysis
    4. Intrusion defense

Further reading

- **OWASP Secure Application Design**: https://www.owasp.org/index.php/OWASP_Secure_Application_Design_Project
- **Microsoft MSDN Security Checklist: Architecture and Design Review**: https://msdn.microsoft.com/en-us/library/ff647464.aspx
- **SANS Web Application Security Design Checklist**: https://www.sans.org/reading-room/whitepapers/securecode/security-checklist-web-application-design-1389
- **Microsoft Design Guidelines for Secure Web Applications**: https://msdn.microsoft.com/en-us/library/ff648647.aspx
- **Core Security Patterns**: http://coresecuritypatterns.com/downloads/patterns.pdf
- **OWASP ASVS Assessment Tool**: https://www.owasp.org/index.php/OWASP_ASVS_Assessment_tool
- **Microsoft's guide for data classification (PDF)**: https://download.microsoft.com/download/0/A/3/0A3BE969-85C5-4DD2-83B6-366AA71D1FE3/Data-Classification-for-Cloud-Readiness.pdf
- **Carnegie Mellon University: Guidelines for Data Classification**: https://www.cmu.edu/iso/governance/guidelines/data-classification.html#classification
- **OVIC Privacy and Data Protection Checklists and Tools**: https://www.cpdp.vic.gov.au/menu-resources/resources-privacy/resources-privacy-checklists-and-tools
- **Microsoft GDPR Compliance Assessment**: https://assessment.microsoft.com/gdpr-compliance
- **ENISA Privacy and Data Protection by Design**: https://www.enisa.europa.eu/publications/privacy-and-data-protection-by-design/
- **SP 800-122 Guide to protecting the confidentiality of personally identifiable information (PII)**: https://csrc.nist.gov/publications/detail/sp/800-122/final
- **Data Anonymization for production data dumps**: https://github.com/sunitparekh/data-anonymization
- **CSA Code of Conduct for GDPR Compliance**: https://cloudsecurityalliance.org/media/press-releases/cloud-security-alliance-issues-code-of-conduct-self-assessment-and-certification-tools-for-gdpr-compliance/

10
Security-Testing Plan and Practices

We have already discussed the security practices involved in development, which included phases such as securing architecture, securing design, threat modeling, and securing coding. We will now discuss the security-testing plan and practices in the testing phase.

The objective of this chapter is to give an overview of what a security-testing plan, security-testing domains, and the minimum set of security-testing scope. We will discuss a security testing plan, testing approaches, risk analysis, security domains, and industry practices, to build your security-testing knowledge base. In addition, we will introduce some industry best practices, testing approaches, and security tools, for security testing.

We will cover the following topics in this chapter:

- Security-testing knowledge kit
- Security-testing plan templates
- Web security testing
- Privacy
- Security-testing domains
- Thinking like a hacker
- Security-training environment

Security-testing knowledge kit

Security-testing, also called *penetration testing,* is a very specialized profession. The testing results and the quality of the security testing may vary without proper guidance, training, and tools. It's suggested to have an internal security-testing knowledge portal, which can include the security-testing guidelines, best practices, instructions, tools, and the training environment. An **Open Web Application Security Project (OWASP)** security-testing knowledge kit can be used to build such a knowledge portal. The following table gives an overview example of what the whole security-testing knowledge kit should cover:

Security-testing kit	Purpose
Security-testing plan templates	The testing plan defines the security baselines to achieve the business objective, testing approach, tools, and risk analysis. Depending on the business of the application, it's also suggested to adapt it to suit the technical domain.
Privacy or security checklist	The checklist can be a basic set of testing cases. Security is more focused on the CIA of the application, and privacy is more about protecting personal information.
Security-testing toolkits	The toolkits provide commonly suggested security-testing tools for the project teams.
Training environment	The training environment uses vulnerable applications for the security team to do hands-on security-testing practice.

To build your own in-house security testing knowledge portal, consider the adoption of the OWASP Security Knowledge Framework, which provides the OWASP ASVS, Security Knowledge, and Code Examples as shown in the following screenshot:

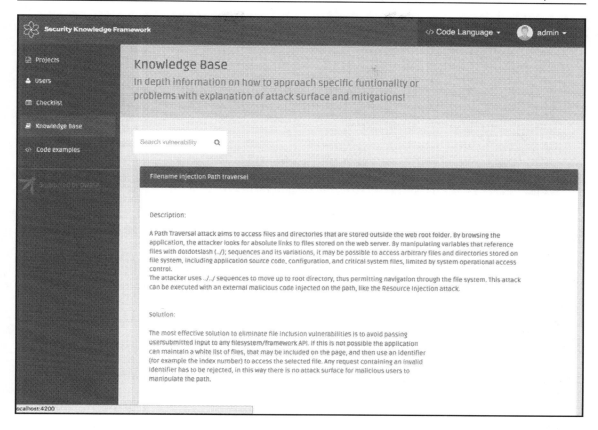

Source: https://skf.readme.io/docs/knowledge-base

Security-testing plan templates

The key difference between hacking and security testing is that security testing requires a comprehensive security quality assurance of the whole application, while hacking is looking for specific security issues or vulnerabilities. Creating a security-testing template will help the project team to plan security testing and maintain the quality of security testing. The following are the well-known industry best practices to build a security testing plan:

- **OWASP Testing Guide**: The OWASP testing guide provides the what, why, when, where, and how of the web applications security testing.

- **PCI Penetration Testing Guidance**: Instead of listing detailed testing cases and tools, the PCI penetration testing guide includes four key agenda of the testing such as Penetration Testing Components, Qualifications of a Penetration Tester, Penetration Testing Methodologies, Penetration Testing Reporting Guidelines.
- **NIST 800-115 Technical Guide to Information Security Testing and Assessment:** It provides practical recommendations for planning and conducting penetration testing activities.
- **Mobile Security Testing Guide (MSTG)**: It's focused on the mobile security testing which includes the testing approaches, techniques, and tools.

The following is a sample of the security testing template that includes major sections only.

Security-testing objective

This section should clearly define the business objective of security testing. For example, the most important part of the business objective can be GDPR compliance, PCI DSS compliance, customers' expectations, or a regular or major release security check. Tying the security testing to the business objective will help to manage the focus and scope of the security testing.

Security-testing baseline

The security-testing baseline defines the minimum expectation of the testing scope and criteria. OWASP ASVS and the OWASP MSTG are good references for organizations that are just beginning to build security-testing baselines. In addition to software application security, it also includes the following areas, which are often neglected:

- Platform secure configuration, such as OS, database, virtualization, web services (nginX, Apache)
- The secure communication protocol, such as SFTP, SSH v2, or TLS v1.2
- Known vulnerabilities for third-party software components
- Sensitive information, or the PII data handling, storage, and removal
- Documentation or on-line help instructions related to access management, changes of password, authentication, and usages of external communication interfaces
- Secure channels of software patch update and integrity check
- The complexity of password policies
- Logging files access control and logging for all non-query actions

Security-testing environment

The testing environment lists all software components, including the application, all dependencies, and the platform. When preparing a security-testing environment, it's recommended to have a staging environment that is exactly the same as the production one. In most cases, the security issue may not be caused by the software application itself but by the dependencies or the insecure configuration of the platform.

Testing strategy

The testing strategy highlights the testing approaches for certain high-risk functions. The testing strategies can be a manual review, automation, or whitebox or blackbox testing. The whitebox testing primarily focuses on the source-code-level inspection, and the blackbox testing reviews the while application from end users' and hackers' perspectives. These testing strategies are normally executed using a mixed approach. The following table shows an example of testing strategies for the platform and the authentication function:

Testing strategy	Platform	Authentication
Manual review	NA	Design review
Automation	Fully automated scanning	Brute force attack
WhiteBox	Review configuration files	Code review for encryption
BlackBox	Port or services scanning	Brute force attack

High-risk modules

The purpose of this section, *High-risk modules*, is to list the functions that hackers may be most interested to attack or those that may have a bigger security impact. The following table lists some of the high-risk modules' risks and testing approaches:

Module or functions	Security risks	Testing approaches
Authentication	Accounts compromised Brute-force attack.	Bruce-force account attacks Password attacks
Administration management	Privilege escalation.	The same function tested with different roles. List of admin URLs to be tested with operator or guest accounts. Files ACL check.

Files upload	Malicious license files uploaded or files injection attacks.	Illegal file type, size, name, and contents.
Software update	The software may be updated or injected with malicious code.	The software package integrity check, signature check, and file size check.
Password reset	The accounts may be compromised or under the accounts enumeration bruteforce attacks.	The password can't be sent in plain text. The password reset flow requires the original email, security questions, or mobile phone verification.

Recommended security-testing tools

This can be a very broad area. Here is a typical set of security-testing tools, and we will discuss this further in later chapters. A minimum security testing scope includes the vulnerability scan, port scan, web security, fuzz testing, secure configuration, and so on. Each security testing area is suggested to use at least two security tools to cover more testing scenarios. Take a look at this table:

Security-testing area	Suggested security-testing tools
Vulnerability scan	**Nessus, OpenVAS, Retina:** These are common open source tools to scan vulnerabilities of the applications, web services, and all the software dependencies.
Port scan	**Nmap:** Nmap is widely used for network security scanning. The common network security scanning scenarios include port scanning, hosts, and services discovery.
Web security	**OWASP ZAP, Arachni, Burp:** These are the most popular open source and free web security testing tools that can execute OWASP Top 10 security testing.
Code scanning	**FindBugs, SonarQube:** The tools are used for static secure coding scanning. FindBugs is mainly for Java. SonarQube supports over 20 programming languages for the code quality issues.

Fuzz testing	**Peach, FuzzDB, API-fuzzer:** The objective of the fuzzing testing is to give a massive amount of dynamic and random data input to verify the target application behaviors under the unexpected input.
Secure configuration	**OpenSCAP:** The tool performs the security assessment and enforcement of the secure configuration baseline of the OS, software, and services configurations
Secrets or sensitive information	**TruffleHog or GittyLeaks:** These tools scan any potential secrets, API key, or passwords on the GIT source code repository.
Mobile	**Mobile Security Testing Framework (MSTF):** The MSTF provides a fully automated static and dynamic analysis of an APK file.
SSL	**SSLScan, SSLyze:** These tools scan and detect the insecure SSL/TLS configuration of a website.
Denial-of-Service (DoS) attack	**Hping:** Hping can do TCP packet manipulation. **HTTPSlow:** HTTPSlow is used to generate HTTP SLOW DoS attack.
Injection	**SQLMap**: SQLMap is a common tool used for the SQL injection attack. **Commix**: Commix is used for command injection attack.
Login brute force	**THC Hydra**: The tool is famous for the brute force login attack. It supports a wide range of protocols such as SNMP, SMTP, Cisco AAA, HTTP, MySQL, and so on.
Android testing	**APKtool**, **dex2Jar**, **JD-Gui**, **Appie**: These are common open source tools to do Android security testing. Appie is a portable Android security testing toolkit that includes all of the tools and can be executed on Windows without the need of a virtual machine.
SQL Injection Testing	**SQLMap, Sqlninja** SQL injection is also a very common attack to allow hackers to steal or manipulate the website backend database. Both SQLMap and the Sqlninjia can help do various kinds of SQL injection testing.

Web security testing

As we have discussed the general security-testing plan, it's also suggested to prepare security-testing instructions based on the specific domain. Each domain requires different kinds of security-testing tools and approaches. Generally, there are the web, virtualization, firmware, big data, privacy, and IoT security domains.

Web services are the most common presentation of applications and cloud services. Almost all the cloud services are presented with Web UI, which can be easily managed by any browser without installing a client application. Besides, the restful API communication that is used for inter-services communication is also built on top of HTTPS. The web security can be seen as the foundation of cloud services. When it speaks to web security, we have to be familiar with the **Open Web Application Security Project (OWASP) Top 10**, which lists the most common web security issues by an **Industry-Ranked Survey**. Take a look at the following:

- **A1:2017-Injection**: Any source of data input can cause an injection attack, the common attacks include SQL injection, command injection, XML injection, and so on.
- **A2:2017-Broken Authentication**: Weak password policy, authentication controls, or session management may allow the attackers to gain unauthorized accounts access.
- **A3:2017-Sensitive Data Exposure**: Insecure data transmission, or weak encryption or access control of the data storage may result in personal data exposure.
- **A4:2017-XML External Entities (XXE)**: The uses of XML processor vulnerability to do XXE injection to achieve remote control, steal data, or denial-of-service attack.
- **A5:2017-Broken Access Control**: It's the weak or missing access control with privileged functions, URLs, or critical resources.
- **A6:2017-Security Misconfiguration**: The attack may use default accounts, enabled services, error message, directory listing, default permissions or known vulnerabilities to attack the system. The security configurations include application services, network services, web server, application server, database, frameworks.
- **A7:2017-Cross-Site Scripting (XSS)**: The uses of Cross-Site Scripting (XSS) allow the attacker to execute arbitrary HTML and JavaScript in the victim's browser or stores attacker-controllable data on the web server.

- **A8:2017-Insecure Deserialization**: The serialization is the common process of converting an object into a stream of bytes in order to transmit it to memory, a database, or a file. The attacks may tamper with the object or data to achieve remote code injection attacks.
- **A9:2017-Using Components with Known Vulnerabilities**: It includes any vulnerable dependencies or unused libraries in the OS, web/application server, database management system (DBMS), applications, APIs and all components, runtime environments, and libraries.
- **A10:2017-Insufficient Logging and Monitoring**: The lacks of logging or monitoring may allow the attacks or unauthorized users to steal sensitive information without being detected or audited.

OWASP also suggests that security testers consider using **Open Web Application Security Project (OWASP)**, **Application Security Verification Standard (ASVS)**, OWASP Testing Guide, and OWASP Security Knowledge Framework as an input, and don't just depend on specific security tools to do all the security assurance. There is no one-size-fits-all solution. Don't just copy and apply all those OWASP projects. Review the needs of existing projects and identify common security baselines. You can perform certain customizations to fit the project's needs. Take a look at this table:

OWASP projects	Project objective and reference
OWASP Top 10	OWASP Top 10 lists the 10 most critical web security issues. It also provides information on how to identify whether the application is vulnerable, how to prevent attacks, examples of attack scenarios, and related references to each critical security issue.
OWASP ASVS	The OWASP Application Security Verification Standard provides a list of application security requirements and can also be used as a security-testing checklist.
OWASP Testing Guide	The OWASP Testing Guide provides how-to test cases and suggested tools.
OWASP Security Knowledge Framework (SKF)	The OWASP SKF can help to build your security knowledge portal, which includes the OWASP ASVS checklist, security knowledge base, and code examples.
OWASP Security Mobile Testing Guide Project (MSTG)	This is a good reference for the mobile (Apple iOS and Android) application-testing guide, which provides the mobile-testing methodologies and also suggested testing tools.

Privacy

There are two kinds of privacy information that need to be protected. One is the sensitive information related to the application security, such as the password, API key, encryption key, CA certificate, and the other one is the **Personally Identifiable Information (PII)**, which is also regulated by GDPR. For the sensitive information review, the functions that relate to IAM, encryption, session management, logging, CA manager, and administration are those modules that directly handle the sensitive information. Here are the general testing guidelines for the privacy data-handling life cycle:

Data life cycle	Testing key points	Suggested testing tools
Transmission of data	• Ensure the sensitive information is not transmitted by GET • The secure communication protocol such as TLS v1.2, SSH V2, SFTP, SNMP V3.	SSLyze, NMAP, Wireshark
Storage of data	• Check whether sensitive information is encrypted • Check whether the permissions of the files are properly configured	TruffleHog
Encryption of data	No uses of weak encryption algorithms, such as MD5, RC4, Jackfish, and Tripple DES	Code-scanning tools
Data access and auditing	• Log any sensitive data query • ACL permissions	AuthMatrix
Removal of data	• No sensitive information in temp, exception files, and cookies • Check any plain-text sensitive information in memory and cache	GCORE WinHex LaZagne

In addition, there are some file types that are highly related to sensitive information. Here are some of the common files that may expose sensitive information and need either encryption or proper access permission controls in an application:

Files may include sensitive information	Files types
SSH key	`*rsa, *dsa, edcsa`
Cryptographic key	`Pckcs12, pfx, p12,   asc,`
Shell history files	`Bash_history, zsh_history`
Shell configuration file	`bashrc, zshrc, bash_profile, zsh_profile`
PHP configuration file	`.INC`
Docker configuration file	`Dockercfg`
MySQL command history	`Mysql_history`
Application or web logs	`.log`

For the PII handling review, please also refer to the following industry best practices:

- The GDPR checklist (`https://gdprchecklist.io/`) provides references for the data controller and the data processor
- The NIST SP 800-122 *Guide to Protecting the Confidentiality of PII* (`https://csrc.nist.gov/publications/detail/sp/800-122/final`) is also useful
- Information regarding Privacy Patterns can be found here: `https://privacypatterns.org/patterns/`

Security-testing domains

We have discussed web security testing and also privacy. The security testing must tie in closely to the business and the target of the application, which will be related to not only the testing scenario but also to the testing tools. Understanding the application domain knowledge is always the first step to plan the security testing. Here is a summary of industry references for each security testing domain. An organization may further develop its own domain-specific testing plan based on these references. Take a look at this table:

Security domain	Industry Security Best Practices and Testing Guide
Web security testing	• OWASP Testing Guide
Virtualization security testing	• NIST 800-125 Guide to Security for Full Virtualization Technologies • PCI DSS Virtualization Guidelines • Red Hat Virtualization Security Guide • SANS Top Virtualization Security Mistakes • ISCACA Virtualization Security checklist
Firmware security testing	• GitHub Awesome firmware security • GitHub Security of BIOS/UEFI System Firmware from Attacker and Defender Perspectives

Big-Data security testing	• NIST 1500-4 Big Data Interoperability Framework • CSA Big Data Security and Privacy Handbook
Privacy	• GDPR Checklist • NIST SP 800-122 Guide to Protecting the Confidentiality of PII
IoT security	• ENISA Baseline Security Recommendations for IoT • GSMA IOT Security Assessment
Container security	• NIST 800-190 Application Container Security Guide
Mobile security	• OWASP MSTG (Mobile Security Testing Guide)

Thinking like a hacker

Security testing requires a systematic approach to review an application with a comprehensive set of security-testing cases. We refer to some industry best practices and tools to plan security testing. On the other hand, we should also learn from white-hat or real hackers. The purpose of studying real threats and exploits is to review and improve the existing security testing methodologies and tools. The following sections contain some of the recommended references for real-world exploits.

Exploits and CVE

These resources provide the proof-of-concept (PoC) testing scripts and tools of CVEs. They're valuable because we may apply or customize those testing scripts to be parts of our security testing toolsets. The Security Focus, Packet Storm Security, and Exploit Database provide not only the CVEs information but also security testing tools and PoC scripts. Check out the following:

- Security Focus: The Security Focus lists the technical details of every CVE vulnerability.
- Packet Storm Security: In addition to the exploits, it provides lots of updated security tools and security whitepapers.
- Exploit Database: It provides the exploits, shellcode, security whitepapers, and also google hacking database.

For example, for the Java deserialization security issue, you may search the keyword *deserialization* for the specific vulnerable product, the testing scripts (mostly in Python), and the paper that describes the deserialization concept and testing techniques. It can be found at the Exploit Database `https://www.exploit-db.com/`

In addition, **Exploit kits** are also worth studying. These exploit kits can generate malicious payload and attack tools to target specific software vulnerabilities or create backdoor connections. ExploitPack and Metasploit are the most common testing framework in this category.

Hacker techniques

The **Adversarial Tactics, Techniques & Common Knowledge (ATT&CK)** gives a comprehensive list of malicious threats tactics and techniques for most platforms, including Windows, Linux, macOS, and mobile. For example, the **AppInit DLLs** in one of Windows Technique Matrix, the ATT&CK explains AppInit DLLs, examples, mitigation, detection and references (https://attack.mitre.org/wiki/Technique/T1103).

Here are the testing scripts that can be used to simulate the APT attacks or the ATT&CK. These can be used to test whether existing security solutions are able to detect those suspicious behaviors. Refer to the following:

- APT Simulator: It includes the toolset and PowerShell scripts to generate the attacks on Windows. https://github.com/NextronSystems/APTSimulator
- Atomic Red Team: It can generate the attack scenarios based on MITRE's ATT&CKhttps://github.com/redcanaryco/atomic-red-team

Malware Information

Understanding real-world malware attacks is another way to review our security defenses. The US-CERT is a valuable reference since it provides detailed technical analysis of major malware attacks, the detection suggestions, an indicator of compromise, the signatures of the malware, the impact of the applications, and the defensive technique solutions. For the "Alerts and Tips" section, check out the following:

- **US-CERT Alerts:** https://www.us-cert.gov/ncas/alerts

Security-Training environment

It's against the law to do security or penetration testing without permission. Developing the skills of security testing requires a proper testing environment or a training platform. These security-testing environments are purpose-built vulnerable web or mobile applications. Some security-testing environments even provide online tutorials to guide you through the security-testing tips. Refer to the OWASP projects listed below for a comprehensive list of online or offline virtualization images for the security-testing environment. If it's possible, set up an in-house security-testing environment instead of using the external online testing site. Here are some vulnerable application projects that can help to build a security-testing environment. Be aware that these are vulnerable applications, so set up these applications in a security-controlled environment. The following open source projects are examples of vulnerable web applications for security testing purposes:

- **OWASP Broken Web Application Project**
- **OWASP Vulnerable Web Application Directory Project**
- **OWASP Security Shepherd**
- **MITRE Vulnerable Mobile Apps**

To encourage the involvement of security testing, an in-house security testing competition may be held. The rewards can be based on the severity of the reported security issue. For external WhiteHat security researchers, consider setting up a security bug bounty program to reward the submitted vulnerabilities. For example, the Google Bug Hunter University defines defined rules of the non-qualifying findings and the reward program such as 'Google application Security Reward program' and the 'Google Bug Hunter University'.

Summary

In this chapter, we have suggested the setting up of a security-testing knowledge kit to include the testing guides and related security tools. The **OWASP Security Knowledge Framework (SKF)** provides an in-house security-testing knowledge portal with an OWASP ASVS checklist, security knowledge, and a code example by default. The security team can use the OWASP SKF to further customize the security-testing knowledge portal.

To develop a security-testing plan, we suggested referring to the industry references, such as an OWASP testing guide, a PCI penetration testing guide, a NIST 800-115, and a **Mobile Security Testing Guide (MSTG)**. One typical security-testing plan should include the testing objective, baseline, testing environment, testing strategy, identified high-risk modules, and also the recommended security-testing tools.

We also discussed some OWASP projects that can help the web and mobile applications security testing. In addition to this, we discussed the fact that how the applications handle the privacy information and sensitive data is also critical to security testing. We discussed the security-testing focus and tools for the data lifecycle and listed common system files that may include highly sensitive information.

In addition to web and mobile security, we also listed other security-testing domains and related industry references, including virtualization, firmware, big data, privacy, IoT security, and containers. Finally, to increase your security-testing knowledge, we shared some references that can help to understand the techniques that hackers use, such as exploits and CVE, hacker techniques, exploit kits, and a malware case study. The security-training environment can provide an in-house security-testing bed for the internal team to do hands-on security-testing practices.

In the next chapter, we will discuss whitebox security-testing tips.

Questions

1. The suggested *security testing kit* should include which of the following?
   1. Privacy checklist
   2. Testing toolkits
   3. Security testing plan templates
   4. All of the above

2. Which industry reference refers to the mobile security?
   1. OWASP testing guide
   2. NIST 800-115 pentest
   3. Moible Security Testing Guide (MSTG)
   4. PCI Pentest Guide

3. What is the testing strategy?
   1. It's a security checklist
   2. It defines the testing approaches for the high-risk functions
   3. It's a white-box testing
   4. It's a black-box testing

4. Which of the following is not a typical high-risk module?
    1. Administration management
    2. Authentication
    3. Installation
    4. Password reset

5. Which one of the following security tools is not used for web security?
    1. Nmap
    2. OWASP ZAP
    3. Arachni
    4. Burp

6. Which of the following communication protocols is not secure?
    1. TLS v1.2
    2. SSH v1
    3. SFTP
    4. SNMP v3

7. What can the ATT&CK resource not provide?
    1. Security testing tools
    2. Adversarial Tactics
    3. Adversarial Techniques
    4. Adversarial Knowledge

8. What is the OWASP Broken Web Application project used for?
    1. It's a web security scanning tool
    2. It's a security checklist
    3. It's a purpose-built vulnerable web application for security testing practices
    4. It's an automation-testing framework

Further reading

Visit the following URLs for more information:

- **GitHub Awesome PenTest**: https://github.com/enaqx/awesome-pentest/
- **PCI penetration guide**: https://www.pcisecuritystandards.org/documents/Penetration_Testing_Guidance_March_2015.pdf
- **NIST 800-115 Technical Guide to Information Security Testing and Assessment**: https://csrc.nist.gov/publications/detail/sp/800-115/final

- **GSMA IOT Security Assessment**: https://www.gsma.com/iot/future-iot-networks/iot-security-guidelines/
- **NIST 800-125 Guide to Security for Full Virtualization Technologies:** https://csrc.nist.gov/publications/detail/sp/800-125/final
- **ISCACA Virtualization Security checklist:** http://www.isaca.org/Knowledge-Center/Research/Documents/Virtualization-Security-Checklist_res_Eng_1010.pdf
- **GitHub Awesome firmware security**: https://github.com/PreOS-Security/awesome-firmware-security
- **GitHub Security of BIOS/UEFI System Firmware from Attacker and Defender Perspectives:** https://github.com/rmusser01/Infosec_Reference/blob/master/Draft/BIOS%20UEFI%20Attacks%20Defenses.md
- **NIST 1500-4 Big Data Security and Privacy:** https://www.nist.gov/publications/nist-big-data-interoperability-framework-volume-4-security-and-privacy
- **CSA Big Data Security and Privacy Handbook:** https://downloads.cloudsecurityalliance.org/assets/research/big-data/BigData_Security_and_Privacy_Handbook.pdf
- **NIST SP 800-122 Guide to Protecting the Confidentiality of PII:** https://csrc.nist.gov/publications/detail/sp/800-122/final
- **ENISA Baseline Security Recommendations for IoT:** https://www.enisa.europa.eu/publications/baseline-security-recommendations-for-iot/at_download/fullReport
- **GSMA IOT Security Assessment:** https://www.gsma.com/iot/future-iot-networks/iot-security-guidelines/
- **NIST 800-190 Application Container Security Guide:** https://nvlpubs.nist.gov/nistpubs/specialpublications/nist.sp.800-190.pdf

Whitebox Testing Tips 11

The testing plan gave an overview of the testing approach, risk assessment, and suggested testing tools. In this chapter, we will focus on whitebox testing tips.

Whitebox code review can be most effective to identify certain specific security issues, such as XXE, deserialization, and SQL injection. However, a whitebox review can be time-consuming if there are no proper tools or strategies. To have an effective whitebox test, we need to focus on specific coding patterns and high-risk modules. This chapter will give tips, tools, and key coding patterns to identify high-risk security issues.

We will cover the following topics in this chapter:

- Whitebox review preparation
- A bird's-eye view of the whole project
- High-risk modules
- Whitebox review checklist
- Top common issues
- Secure coding patterns and keywords
- Case study—Java Struts security review

Whitebox review preparation

Whitebox testing or source code review can be most effective to identify hidden security issues in the source code. Before we begin our whitebox source code review, there are some preparation and input will help us to judge how (approaches, tools) and what (which modules) to do the security source code review.

The following is a list we may check before performing the source code review; take a look at this table:

Whitebox testing input	Considerations
Source code	• Do we need a full buildable source code? • Does the source code include related import modules or headers? • These dependency source codes will help when we would like to trace the definition of certain APIs. However, if the whole source code is not available, it may require reverse engineering.
Threat-modeling documents	The threat-modeling provides a good reference to identify the high-risk modules and interfaces that we should focus on.
Architecture and design documents	The architecture and the design documents give us a good view of the design flow and the relationships of modules.
Automated static code analysis results	Before we do a whitebox review, it's a good idea to perform an automated security code scan first. The scanning result will not only make things easier, but it also gives us a hint regarding which parts we should focus on.
Application-related configuration	Some security frameworks may define the security policies in configurations that should also be reviewed. For example, the `web.xml` file in Spring MVC or the Spring Security framework is very critical to the access control.
Communication interface or ports	The purpose of listing external API interfaces and communication ports is to understand how they interact with external input from an untrusted source, insecure communication protocols, or mistakenly exposed APIs.

For some external dependencies or third-party components, there will be cases that we would like to do the certain analysis of the components to identify if there is no backdoor, weak encryption, hard or coded passwords without the availability of source code. This will require reverse engineering and dynamic run-time analysis. This table provides some of the tools for further reference:

Description	Tools
Cuckoo	Cuckoo Sandbox is an open source virtualized environment to do the static and dynamic analysis of any binary files. For more information refer to `https://cuckoosandbox.org`.
REMnux	REMnux includes lots of Linux toolkits for reverse engineering. For more information refer to `https://remnux.org/`.

Viewing the whole project

The top-down approach means we use the source code analysis tool to view programming flow diagrams, such as a class diagram, a call graph, or the dependency graph. The following table lists some recommended tools that will help you to analyze the source code more easily:

Tools	Description
Doxygen	It can generate documentation from the source code and also automatically visualize the relationships between modules, dependency graphs, and inheritance diagrams, by using the dot tool from Graphviz. Refer to the website at `www.doxygen.org`. To be able to generate documents from the source code, it requires proper comments and tags in the source code. Here are some tips that may be worth reading. Bear in mind that the generation of documents by doxygen can take a long time. Don't tie the doxygen to parts of the compiler jobs. Check out the following links for more information: • `https://www.rosettacommons.org/docs/latest/development_documentation/tutorials/doxygen-tips`. • `http://www.stack.nl/~dimitri/doxygen/manual/commands.html`.
Graphviz	It's not a code analysis tool, but it helps doxygen to generate diagrams. For more information, refer to `www.graphviz.org/Download.php`.
HTML Help Workshop	It's used to transform HTML files that are generated by doxygen to CHM documents. Check out `https://msdn.microsoft.com/en-us/library/windows/desktop/ms669985(v=vs.85).aspx`.
phpDocumentor	If the programming language of the project is PHP, the phpDocumentor will do a good job to generate the API documents and also the class inheritance diagram directly from the PHP source code. Check out `https://www.phpdoc.org/`.

Natural docs	It supports over 20 programming languages and allows developers to document the source code in a very straightforward way. Just bear in mind that the source document still requires the development team to comment the source code properly. Check out `http://www.naturaldocs.org/`. Here is an example of the comments in the source code:
	`// Function: Sum`
	`// Sum up two integers and returns the result.`
	`int Sum (int a, int b)`
	`{ return a + b; }`

Pandoc	It's a universal document format converter. Check out the following link for for more information: • `http://pandoc.org/try/`
Sphinx	It's mainly for Python documentation. Check out `http://www.sphinx-doc.org/`.

In summary, to generate the documents from the source code directly, we will use the following—natural docs and doxygen for general programming languages, phpDocumentor for PHP, and Sphinx for Python. These document generators are not magic. If the development team doesn't follow certain coding comment practices, the generated information will also be limited. For the whitebox review, we use the source code document generator to identify the security issues more efficiently. However, if the generated documents don't help a lot in that way, move on to the following review approaches. Consider the following sections carefully.

High-risk module

Once we have a good view of the whole project, we will need to identify those modules or functions that need further manual code review. We don't just do a manual code review with high-risk modules; we do automated code scanning for all the modules, and we do a further manual code review for those high-risk modules with potentially hidden security issues that may not be easily identified by automation scanning tools.

When we are identifying high-risk modules to prioritize the whitebox source code review modules, try to think like a hacker. *Which modules will interest a hacker? What information can be most valuable to a hacker? What is the weakest link out of all the applications?* The following table lists typical high-risk modules that should be considered for further whitebox review:

High-risk modules	Business functions
Authentication	• Accounts registration. • Login and CAPTCHA. • Password recovery or reset. • Password changes. • Identity and password storage and access control. • Account lockout control after multiple failures.
Authorization	• Sensitive resource access. • Administration management.

Administrative configuration	There are two kinds of review in configuration. One is the configuration values, and the other is how the application installs or updates the configuration. Generally, there are web, database, and service configuration needs to pay attention to.
Finance	• Payment functions. • Order and shopping carts.
File handling	• File upload. • File download. • File handling.
Database	• Database query operations. • Database create, add, update, and delete options.
API interface	• Restful API interfaces or other communication interfaces. • Third-party integration interfaces.
Legacy	• Modules that don't support secure communication. • Modules that may still use a weak encryption algorithm. • Uses of banned or dangerous APIs.
Encryption	• Uses of banned encryption algorithms. • Hard-coded sensitive information or comments in the source code during development, such as IP, email, password, or hidden hotkey.

Whitebox review checklist

It's suggested to have a checklist to do the whitebox review. A security checklist during a whitebox source code review can help the team decide what it should focus on. A typical security checklist for a code review may include critical security controls, such as authentication, data validation, authorization, session management, error handling, cryptography, logging, security configuration, administration functions, payment, money-related functions, and the handling of private data.

The reference sources of the security checklist can be from industry best practices or historical projects experiences. The contents of the checklist can be different based on the objective of the review.

Take a look at the following table:

Category of security checklist	Objectives and references
General security code review checklist	The objective is to provide the project team with a security code review checklist template. The project team may further add or customize the list based on the project profile. The following are the industry references links: • *OWASP Secure Coding Practices* at `https://www.owasp.org/index.php/OWASP_Secure_Coding_Practices_-_Quick_Reference_Guide`. • *OWASP Code Review Guide* at `https://www.owasp.org/index.php/Category:OWASP_Code_Review_Project`.
Top common issues	An ideal top-common-issues checklist is summarized based on historical project records, programming languages, or types of projects. If there is not enough project data to make the list, refer to the CWE or OWASP. The following are the industry references links: • *CWE Top 25 Most Dangerous Software Errors* at `http://cwe.mitre.org/top25/`. • `OWASP Top Ten Project` at `https://www.owasp.org/index.php/Category:OWASP_Top_Ten_Project`.
Specific security issues (struts, deserialization)	The objective is to focus on the security review of a specific security issue. There are some circumstances that we may find these kinds of security reviews helpful. The attacks again Java Struts framework are happening, and the team may want to check whether the struts-related implementation is vulnerable. One major security issue has been identified in project A, and the organization would like to know whether other projects also have a similar security issue. The driver to check for the specific security issue may be caused by the recently released CVE or the major security events news or one security issue reported by customers, and we would like to check whether all other projects have the same issue. Here is a list of examples in this category: • Struts security issue. • Java deserialization security issue. • REST API security.

Top common issues

A top-common-issues checklist can be very effective for a project team to decide what to focus on during secure code review. To build a top-common-security checklist, it's suggested to refer to the CWE Top 25. The security team and the project team may take the CWE Top 25 basis and in-house top security issues, based on historical project data, to reach a consensus of the top five security issues.

To summarize in-house top security issues is critical; it's because the CWE Top 25 may not be exactly the same for in-house projects, due to the business background, technology stacks, and the implementation. Once an in-house top-security-issue list is identified, it should also be listed with suggested mitigation approaches. Refer to the following table for what it may look like. The purpose of the table is to give a sample that you may also define the one fits your organization not just copy the whole list from CWE Top 25. Be aware that the following is just an example, not a comprehensive list. Let's take a look at the table:

Example of top issues	Mitigation approaches for the top security issues
CWE-89 SQL injection	A SQL injection can be detected effectively by tools for specific source code patterns. Focus on those SQL statements without using the prepared statement or the uses of $ as SQL parameters in iBATIS framework.
CWE-78 OS command injection	Due to the fact that the code-scanning tool can detect the OS command injection issue, the team decides to list those high-risk APIs that may result in command injection, and also develop a tool to do the source code search.
CWE-120 buffer overflow	Based on historical records, buffer overflow problems were one of the common issues. The team further identifies the common APIs that may cause the buffer overflow. Take C/C++ as an example listed: • `strcpy, strncpy_s, strncpy` • `strncat, strcat` • `sprint, snprintf` • `memcpy` • `memmove_s, memset, memset_s` • `scanf_s, gets, vscanf`

CWE-79 XSS	The team also identified that XSS was one of the top issues. To review the XSS issue, the team decided to list all potential APIs that may lead to XSS. Here are some of the examples—in JS/JSP/HTML, look for the following related functions: • `document.location` • `document.URL` • `document.write` • `document.open` • `eval` In Java, review the parameters for the following API: • `Request.getParameter` • `innerHTML.innerText` • `getAttribute` • `getHeader` • `getServerName`
CWE-306 missing authentication for critical function	A missing authentication for a specific URL or resource can be a common security issue that is difficult to detect with any tool. Which URLs can be visited by visitors without authentication, and which URLs need authentication are highly related to business logic. This kind of security issue is also difficult to be identified by a whitebox source code review. Based on historical project records, here are some tips for Java source patterns of the issue: • The uses of partial URL match API to determine the need for authentication, such as `StartsWith` and `EndsWith` • No path canonicalization before validation • No data normalization before validation

Secure coding patterns and keywords

The objective of a source code keyword or a specific patterns-based search technique is not to replace any other automated code-scanning tools. It's to support both the whitebox review and automated code-scanning tools by searching potentially high-risk strings. The security team may prepare or define a set of keywords or regular expression strings that can lead to security issues. Once the project team has a set of search strings, it may use any search tool, such as **GREP**, to do the search, and analyze the search results. This kind of search can be done with partial source code, and is programming-language independent. It's simple to search for a specific issue, as long as we have well-defined search strings.

The following diagram shows a general process of this kind of whitebox review technique:

Here is an example of how to search code for potential security risks, based on specific patterns or keywords. You may also refer to the *OWASP Code Review Guide 2.0, Appendix—Crawling Code* for further information and other programming languages.

Take a lok at the following table:

Category of security issues	Java code patterns/keyword examples
Command injection	Runtime.exec, ProcessBuilder
Buffer overflow risks	strcpy, strcat, sprint, sscanf, vscanf, gets
XML injection	SAXParser, DocumentBuilderFactory, BeanReader, XmlReader, DOMParser, SAXReader, XMLInputFactory
Sensitive information	• Backdoor, password, admin, root • Cipher, getInstance • MessageDigest.getInstance • Encode, ciphers, shareKey, token • URL, Email, IP address
HTTPS **man-in-the - middle (MITM)**	• ALLOW_ALL_HOSTNAME_VERIFIER • X509Certificate, X509TrustManager • getAcceptedIssuers
Insecure cryptography	• RC4, SSL, AES, DEC, ECB, MD5, SHA1 • Java.util.Random • Cipher.newInstance("DES • Cipher.getInstance("ECB
XSS	• document.location, document.URL • document.referrer, document.write, document.print • document.body.innerHTML • window.location, window.execScript • window.setTimeout, window.open • request.getParameter
De-serialization issue	• XMLDecoder • XStream • readObject, readResolve, readExternal

User data input	• getParameter, getQueryString, getRequest • getCookies, getInputStream, getReader • getInputSteam, getMethod, getReader • getRemoteUser, getServerName

Here are the security code-scanning tools in this category that can do source code, based on regular expression patterns. Normally, these tools will also have pre-defined vulnerable source code patterns and security signatures. It's suggested to review those security signatures and customize those regular expressions or strings to fit your project environment. Take a look at this table:

Tools	References
drek	• **Tool**: https://github.com/chrisallenlane/drek • **Signature**: https://github.com/chrisallenlane/drek-signatures/tree/master/signatures (refer to the *.yml)
Graudit	• **Tool**: https://github.com/wireghoul/graudit • **Signature**: https://github.com/wireghoul/graudit/tree/master/signatures (refer to the *.db)
VisualCodeGrepper (VCG)	• **Tool**: https://github.com/nccgroup/VCG • **Signature**: https://github.com/nccgroup/VCG/tree/master/VisualCodeGrepper/bin/Release (refer to the *.conf)
CRASS Grep IT	This tool is recommended because it requires no dependencies. It just needs one shell script to execute. • **Tool**: https://github.com/floyd-fuh/crass/blob/master/grep-it.sh • **Signature**: https://github.com/floyd-fuh/crass/blob/master/grep-it.sh (refer to the search "......")

These are all static code analysis tools that use a GREP-like search to identify vulnerable source code. This kind of source code review approach best works for banned APIs, dangerous APIs, weak encryption algorithm, or hard-coded secrets. It's flexible, so you can scan parts of source code without the need for the while buildable project, and it can be used to scan multiple programming languages, as long as the security code patterns signatures are properly defined.

Case study – Java struts security review

Susan, who is the CTO of a software company, seeks security team advice on struts. Susan understands that the security review of struts requires not only the domain knowledge of struts but also threats knowledge specific to struts. To identify the struts security requires automated code scanning, whitebox review, secure configuration review, and also blackbox with the malicious payload, the security team proposed the following security review approaches with industry practices resources. The purpose of the case study is not to give a comprehensive struts security review guide but to demonstrate how to proceed security whitebox review which is framework specific to Struts security.

Susan and the security team discuss possible review approaches and also deliver a struts security checklist for the project team as a code review baseline.

Struts security review approaches

The following table gives an example of the key review approaches for the Java struts frameworks:

Struts security review approaches	Objective and references
Struts security check	The security checklist is used for developers to do struts secure implementation and review. The struts official site provides a good reference. Check out for the link at `https://struts.apache.org/security/`.
Struts potential risks strings	In addition to code scanning, we may also search for specific strings that can lead to struts security. For struts security, we focus more on the secure configuration, `struts.xml`, instead of source code.
Struts exploit scripts	To test each vulnerability of struts, it's suggested to refer to the published exploit scripts. Refer to `https://www.exploit-db.com/search/?action=searchq=struts`.
OWASP dependency	Most of the known struts vulnerabilities were fixed in the latest releases. The OWASP dependency scanning tool can help to detect the uses of old versions of struts. Take a look at `https://www.owasp.org/index.php/OWASP_Dependency_Check`.

Struts security checklist

The security checklist will remind the team what it should focus on during the code review. Specifically, for the struts framework security, the struts security implementation checklist is summarized in the following points. The struts security reference source is at link `https://struts.apache.org/security/`:

- The **Config Browser Plugin** should be used only in the development environment
- Group actions in one namespace by security level
- Put all the JSP files under `WEB-INF` to avoid direct access of JSP files
- Disable the development mode `devMode`
- Reduce the logging level in the production environment
- UTF-8 encoding
- Validate the data input parameters for `getText()`
- Don't use a raw `${}` `EL` expression directly for the input parameters
- Disable the static method access
- Disable the dynamic method invocation

Struts security strings search in struts.xml and API

This list of keywords directly related to the struts security issues will help us to use a search tool (such as drek or Graudit) to locate and to identify the issue; take a look at the following table:

Struts security	Keyword search in bold
Development mode	`struts.devMode.` **Review tips**: The suggested value should be false in `struts.xml`.
Dynamic method invocation	`struts.enable.DynamicMethodInvocation.` **Review tips**: The suggested value should be false in `struts.xml`.
OGNL static method access	`struts.ognl.allowStaticMethodAccess.` **Review tips**: The suggested value should be false in `struts.xml`.

File upload	`Allowedtypes.`
	`maximumSize.`
	`allowedExtensions.`
	Review tips: These parameters should be defined to limit the file upload types, size, and extensions in `struts.xml`. Check out the link at `https://struts.apache.org/core-developers/file-upload.html.`

Data input injection	`findValue, getValue, setValue.` **Review tips**: Review the external input parameters of these APIs to avoid OGNL injection attacks in `struts.xml`.
Validation	`validate.` **Review tips**: The secure value of validating should be true in `struts.xml`.
Data input injection	`request.getParameter.` **Review tips**: Review the external input parameters of these APIs to avoid potential injection attacks.
Class loader manipulation	`getClass.` **Review tips**: Review the external input parameters of these APIs to avoid potential injection attacks.

Summary

We discussed the practices of the whitebox review. To have an effective whitebox review, there is some preparation and input needed, such as the source code, threat-modeling analysis, architecture and design documents, automated static code analysis report, configurations, and the list of communication interfaces.

There are several approaches to proceed the whitebox source code review. We can use doxygen and naturaldocs to generate documents and flow diagrams from the source code. It will help us to gain an overall understanding of the source code. Then, we identify the high-risk modules to do a manual code inspection. The high-risk modules are those that handle sensitive information, security controls, or administrative functions.

During the whitebox review, it's necessary to build a checklist. This comprises some of the recommended industry practices, such as OWASP Secure Coding Practices, OWASP Code Review Guide, CWE Top 25, and OWASP Top 10. Based on these practices, it's suggested an organization may build its own top common security issues with mitigation approaches.

Then, last but not least, we discussed the secure coding patterns and keywords. We listed some common Java code patterns for the security issues and introduced some tools, such as drek, Graudit, VCG, and CRASS Grep IT.

The case study gave a security code review example specific to the struts framework. In this case, the team applied some of the review approaches and also defined a struts-related security checklist.

In the next chapter, we will explore more security-testing toolkits in each security-testing domain.

Questions

1. Which of the following is not the input of whitebox review?
    1. Source code
    2. Threat-modeling documents
    3. Automated static code analysis results
    4. Antivirus scanning results

2. What are the tools doxygen and naturaldocs used for?
    1. Generating documents directly from source code
    2. Static code scanning
    3. Dynamic code scanning
    4. Reverse engineering

3. Which of the following are high-risk modules?
    1. Authentication
    2. Authorization
    3. API interfaces
    4. All of the above

4. Which one of the following APIs is not related to buffer overflow?
    1. strcpy
    2. strncat
    3. memcpy
    4. fwrite

5. What can cause missing authentication?
    1. The uses of partial URL match API to determine the need for authentication such as StartsWith and EndsWith
    2. No path canonicalization before validation
    3. No data normalization before validation
    4. All of the above

Further reading

Consider reading the following links for more information:

- **US CERT WhiteBox Testing**: `https://www.us-cert.gov/bsi/articles/best-practices/white-box-testing/white-box-testing`.
- **Security Code Scan – static code analyzer for .NET**: `https://security-code-scan.github.io/`
- **SEI CERT Coding Standards**: `https://wiki.sei.cmu.edu/confluence/display/seccode/SEI+CERT+Coding+Standards`.
- **Find Security Bugs**: `http://find-sec-bugs.github.io/`.
- **DevBug is an on-line PHP secure code analysis (SCA)**: `http://www.devbug.co.uk/`.
- **MITRE Secure Code Review**: `https://www.mitre.org/publications/systems-engineering-guide/enterprise-engineering/systems-engineering-for-mission-assurance/secure-code-review`.
- **MITRE Cyber Threat Susceptibility Assessment**: `https://www.mitre.org/publications/systems-engineering-guide/enterprise-engineering/systems-engineering-for-mission-assurance/cyber-threat-susceptibility-assessment`.
- **PCI Prioritized Approach Tool**: `https://www.pcisecuritystandards.org/documents/Prioritized-Approach-v3_2.xlsx`.
- **MSND How to Perform a Security Code Review for Managed Code**: `https://cwiki.apache.org/confluence/display/WW/Security+Bulletins`.
- **Apache Struts CVE lists**: `https://www.cvedetails.com/vulnerability-list/vendor_id-45/product_id-6117/Apache-Struts.html`.
- **Apache Struts File Upload**: `https://struts.apache.org/core-developers/file-upload.html`.

12
Security Testing Toolkits

In the previous chapter, we looked at white box testing tips. In this chapter, we will learn about a common (but not a comprehensive) set of security testing tools. The major elements of a network that involve security testing include web and mobile connections, configuration, communication, third-party components, and sensitive information. We will look at the testing tips and tools for each element. Furthermore, we will also learn how these tools can be executed both automatically and as tools that are built into continuous integration.

We will cover the following topics in this chapter:

- General security testing toolkits
- Automation testing criteria
- Behavior-driven security testing frameworks
- Android security testing
- Secure infrastructure configuration
- Docker security scanning
- Integrated security tools

General security testing toolkits

The objective of providing security testing toolkits is for project teams to understand what tools are available and apply the tools that they judge to be appropriate based on the business application scenario. There are many kinds of security testing tools. An organization may define one general testing toolkit for all projects, and also suggest other security testing tools based on those specific domains, such as automation, infrastructure, Docker, and BDD:

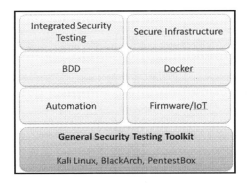

There are many kinds of Linux security distributions that have been installed and preconfigured with security tools. Kali, BlackArch, and PentestBox are the common Linux security distributions. PenetestBox is recommended because it doesn't need a Linux virtual machine environment to execute Linux utilities, and it can be executed natively on Windows. PenetestBox also includes many security tools, as does Kali Linux. For more information on each tool, go to the following links:

- Kali Linux: `https://www.kali.org/`
- BlackArch: `https://blackarch.org/`
- PentestBox: `https://pentestbox.org/`

As there can be hundreds of security tools in Kali or BlackArch Linux, it may not be feasible to require the security testing team to execute the security testing with all of the tools. It's suggested that you familiarize yourself with some of the key and common security tools.

The following table shows the recommended minimum security testing toolset (only open source or free tools are listed here):

Area that is being security checked	Common open source security tools
WhiteBox review	GraudIT or GREP-IT These tools are recommended because they don't require a whole buildable source code to identify the security issue for different programming languages: • GraudIT: `https://github.com/wireghoul/graudit` • GREP-IT: `https://github.com/floyd-fuh/crass/blob/master/grep-it.sh`
Web	BurpSuite, OWASP ZAP, Vega, SQLmap, Arachni
Vulnerability	Nessus, OpenVAS, OpenSCAP, NMAP
Networking	NMAP, WireShark, TCPDump, Hping, SSLScan, SSLyze, masscan

Automation testing criteria

We would like most basic and obvious web security testing cases to be done automatically while human testing is focused on deeper security issue reviews. The objective of automated web security testing is to integrate the security testing tools with a continuous integration framework, such as Jenkins. The web security testing can be automatically triggered every time the build is submitted. To be able to integrate web security testing tools with Jenkins, there are several key criteria that we need to consider:

- **Command console**: Most security testing tools provide a command console or GUI interface to operate the security testing procedures. It would be ideal for the tool to provide both interfaces. The command console can be used for Jenkins to trigger the execution of the security testing, and the GUI can help the human testing. From the automated testing point of view, the **command-line interface (CLI)** is a minimum requirement to integrate with Jenkins. The CLI interface also helps us to integrate with the unit test framework or BDD framework.
- **API interface**: The web security testing can be executed in a standalone attacker mode or a proxy mode. The API interface will allow us to interact with the testing tool programmatically during runtime. For example, the OWASP ZAP provides a REST API to automate all the operations using Python and also the ZAP CLI to interact with ZAP from the command line.

- **Output formats**: Most web security testing tools provide different kinds of reporting formats, such as HTML, PDF, XML, CSV, JSON, or console output. CSV, JSON, and XML are considered the basics if we would like to import the testing results together. Because of the various security tools and large quantities of results in the daily report, it's suggested that you apply integrated security testing tools, such as OWASP DefectDojo, to consolidate all the testing results in one dashboard (this option will be discussed later). In addition, some tools may provide the Jenkins plugin, which can help you to output the results in the Jenkins management console.

Based on these criteria, the suggested web security testing tools for automation are summarized in the following table. OWASP ZAP, Arachni, and W3af are three open source web security testing tools that provide CLI, API, and web GUI interfaces. Nikto and Wapiti are also good choices if you are looking for lightweight command-line tools. For web security testing, we also suggest using one additional tool to do the scanning because of the false positive rate of each tool.

Just be aware that the web security automated test can't complete all web security tasks. Some testing scenarios still require a human security tester to guide the tool and perform further verification, such as authentication, web page authorization, business logic-related tests, and multiple order submissions. The following table displays the tools and their features:

	Web GUI	CLI	REST API
OWASP ZAP	Yes	ZAP CLI	ZAP API
Arachni	Yes	Yes	Yes (It also provides Ruby libraries.)
W3af	Yes	Yes	Yes
Nikto	n/a	Yes	n/a
Wapiti	n/a	Yes	n/a

Behavior-driven security testing framework

BDD security testing is very suitable when your security testing reports will be shared with external vendors, or even internal, cross-team communication to understand what security testing cases are being executed. In addition, BDD security tests can help you to integrate all of the various kinds of security testing tools and consolidate testing reports based on the framework.

Let's look at a simple example to understand what behavior-driven security testing is. Under the behavior-driven security testing framework, the security testing scripts are the testing cases that are written in a human-readable language. It makes the security testing cases, and testing results, easily understood by non-security professionals. Here is an example of this human-readable script:

> **Scenario: The attack may execute a system command to gain valuable information.**
> **Precondition: Given the "ping" command line binary is available on the OS.**
> **When I launch a "ping" attack with:**
>   "Ping 127.0.0.1"
> **Then it should pass with regexp:**
>   "<1ms TTL=128"

The preceding example is a re-edited version based on GauntIT testing scripts. You may also refer to `https://github.com/gauntIT/gauntIt/tree/master/examples/` for more examples of defining security testing cases.

There are three open source tools in the BDD security testing framework. If you are familiar with Java BDD cucumber, then BDD security will be your best choice. If you would like to use Python with a BDD framework, refer to MITTN. GauntIT is programming-language independent, and can be easily extended to execute any tools and verify the results by defining a regular expression. GauntIT allows security testers to focus on the definition of the testing script, and is suitable for testers who have little knowledge of Java or Python. The BDD security frameworks and their featured tools are listed in the following table:

BDD security frameworks	Default security tools included
BDD security	OWASP ZAP, SSLyze, Nessus BDD Security is based on Java and Cucumber. • BDD Security: `https://www.continuumsecurity.net/bdd-security/`
MITTN	BurpSuite, SSlyze, and Radamsa API fuzzing MITTN is based on Python and Behave. • MITTN: `https://github.com/F-Secure/mittn`
GauntIT	CURL, NMAP, SSLyze, SQLmap, Garmr, heartbleed, dirb, Arachni • GauntIT: `http://gauntlt.org/`

Android security testing

Android security testing requires the reverse engineering analysis using APK files, permission analysis using Manifest, and internal components analysis using intents, services, broadcast, and content providers. Generally, the following are considered common testing tools when it comes to Android security testing:

Tools	Description
ApkTool	ApkTool is used to perform reverse engineering for Android APK files.
ByteCode View	ByteCode View is a Java Bytecode viewer and GUI Java decompiler.
Dex2JAR	Dex2JAR converts the DEX to a CLASS file.
JADX	JADX converts the DEX to a Java decompiler.
JD-GUI	JD-GUI is a GUI viewer that is used to read the source code of CLASS files.
Drozer	Drozer is an interactive security and attacks framework for the Android app.
Baksmali	Baksmali is an assembler/disassembler for the DEX format.
AndroBugs	AndroBugs takes an APK file as input and performs an APK security vulnerabilities scan.
AndroGuard	AndroGuard is a Python framework that can perform reverse engineering and malware analysis of the APK.
QARK	**Quick Android Review Kit (QARK)** works similarly to AndroBugs. It detects security vulnerabilities for APK files.
AppMon	AppMon can monitor API calls for both iOS and Android apps.

To install and configure the tools separately can be very time-consuming, so it is suggested that you use the following toolkits, which have most of the Android security testing tools preinstalled:

Toolkit	Description
AndroL4b	AndroL4b is an Unbuntu-based virtual machine that includes not only security testing tools, but also vulnerable APK labs for practice. • AndroL4b: `https://github.com/sh4hin/Androl4b/`
Appie	Appie is a portal for Android testing toolkits that can be executed in Windows without any installation and virtual machines. • Appie: `https://manifestsecurity.com/appie/`
PentestBox	PentestBox is similar to Appie, but also includes lots of other non Android-related security testing tools. • PentestBox: `https://tools.pentestbox.org/`

Last but not least, if you would like a fully automated APK and iOS security analysis that you can use by dragging and dropping an APK file to the Android security analysis platform, the MobSF (Mobile Security Framework) is what you will need, as shown in the following screenshots: Source: `http://github.com/MobSF/Mobile-Security-Framework-MobSF/`

MobSF/Mobile-Security-Framework-MobSF is licensed under the GNU General Public License v3.0.

The following screenshot shows the basic uses of MobSF.

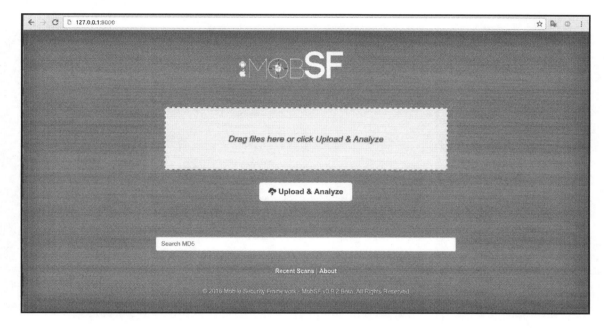

The following screenshot shows the MobSF security assessment results for the Manifest Analysis and the Code Analysis.

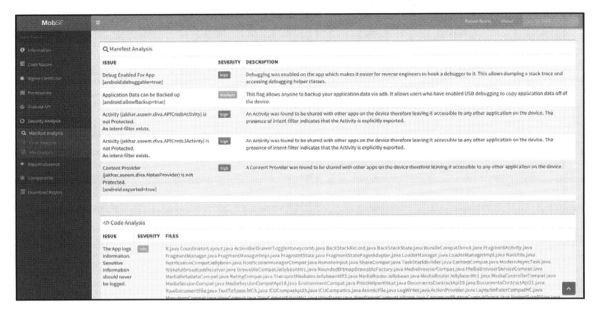

Securing infrastructure configuration

Securing the infrastructure configuration is vital in ensuring that the infrastructure configurations and system hardening are compliant with industry security best practices, such as CIS benchmarks, PCI-DSS, and the **National Checklist Program** (**NCP**). If the DevOps team have applied infrastructure tools, such as Chef or Puppet, it's highly recommended that you define the security configuration on top of these tools to achieve the goal of **infrastructure security as code**. This helps to move the infrastructure security from the operation stage to the development stage. The Inspec, Hardening Framework, and ServerSpec tools are tools that are used for checking infrastructure security configurations. You can learn more about them at the following links:

- Inspec: `https://www.inspec.io/`
- Hardening Framework: `https://Dev-Sec.io`
- Serverspec: `https://serverSpec.org/`

For an infrastructure environment that is not deployed with configuration management tools (Puppet, Chef, Ansible, or SaltStack), the following scanning tools are suggested:

- Lynis Security Auditing: `https://github.com/CISOfy/lynis`
- OpenSCAP: `https://www.open-scap.org/`
- CIS Benchmarks: `https://www.cisecurity.org/cis-benchmarks/`

These infrastructure security configuration review tools will reduce the operation team's and security team's efforts. The operation team may apply these tools before services deployment, and they may also do a regular check on the production environment. The development and testing team may use these tools to know whether any secure configurations are missing or incorrectly configured.

For a sample of the scanning result of OpenSCAP, go to `https://www.open-scap.org/wp-content/uploads/2015/09/ssg-rhel7-ds-xccdf.report.html`.

Docker security scanning

Docker technology is widely used for software deployment and cloud infrastructure. For Docker-specific security testing, the Docker Bench defines several security best practices and configurations for Docker containers deployment. The "CIS Docker Community Edition Benchmark" defines a security recommendation on the Docker host, daemon, container images, and container runtime. Generally speaking, there are three kinds of Docker security tools that do one of three different things:

- Scan for Docker security best practices based on CIS (Docker Bench, Actuary)
- Scan for known common vulnerabilities and exposures (CVEs) (Claire, Anchor Engine)
- Runtime threat analysis (Falco, Dagda)

Here are the open source security testing tools for Docker security:

Docker security tools	Purpose and reference
Docker Bench	Docker Bench is an automated script that checks the Docker security best practices compliance. The scanning rules are based on the CIS Docker Security Benchmark. • Docker Bench Security: `https://github.com/docker/docker-bench-security/` • Docker Benchmark: `https://benchmarks.cisecurity.org/`
Actuary	Actuary works similarly to Docker Bench. Additionally, Actuary can scan based on user-defined security profiles from the Docker security community. • Actuary: `https://github.com/diogomonica/actuary/`
Clair	Clair is a container image security static analyzer for CVEs. Clair: `https://github.com/coreos/clair`
Anchor Engine Anchor Cloud	Anchor Cloud and Anchor Engine scan the Docker images for CVEs. Anchor Engine is a hosted tool and Anchor Cloud is a cloud-based tool. • Anchor Engine: `https://github.com/anchore/anchore-engine` • Anchor Cloud: `https://Anchore.com/cloud/`
Falco	Falco is a Docker container runtime security tool that can detect anomalous activities. • Falco: `https://sysdig.com/opensource/falco/`
Dagda	Dagda is an integrated Docker security tool that provides runtime anomalous activities detection (Sysdig Falco), vulnerabilities (CVEs) analysis (OWASP dependency check, Retire.JS), and malware scanning (CalmAV). • Dagda: `https://github.com/eliasgranderubio/dagda/`

Integrated security tools

As there are many security testing tools, we may like the testing results to be integrated into one dashboard, or to execute the tool through a unified interface. If you are looking for such an integrated security testing management tool, here are some of the open source and free tools to consider:

Tools	Tools included by default
JackHammer	JackHammer, provided by Ola, is an integrated security testing tool. It provides you with a dashboard to consolidate all the testing results. The key difference is that JackHammer includes mobile app security scanning and source code static analysis tools. The supported open source security scanners include Brakeman, Bundler-Audit, Dawnscanner, FindSecurityBugs, PMD, RetireJS, Arachni, Trufflehog, Androbugs, Androguard, and NMAP. The following screenshots show a typical example of its integrated interface. • JackHammer: `https://github.com/olacabs/jackhammer` • Additional information: `https://jch.olacabs.com/userguide/`
Faraday	Faraday is an integrated penetration testing environment, and provides a dashboard for all the testing results. It integrates with over 50 security tools. • Faraday: `https://www.faradaysec.com/#why-faraday` • Additional information: `https://github.com/infobyte/faraday/wiki/Plugin-List`
Mozilla Minion	Mozilla Minion is also an integrated security testing tool that includes the following plugins by default: • ZAP • Nmap • Skipfish • SSLScan You can find Mozilla Minion at `https://github.com/mozilla/minion/`.

Penetration testing toolkit	Penetration testing toolkit provides a unified web interface for many Linux scanning tools, such as nmap, nikto, WhatWeb, SSLyze, fping, URLCrazy, lynx, mtr, nbtscan, automater, and shellinabox. • Penetration testing toolkit: `https://github.com/veerupandey/Penetration-Testing-Toolkit`
Seccubus	The key advantage of using Seccubus is that it integrates with various kinds of vulnerability scanner testing results, and also compares the differences between each scan. It includes the following scanners: • Nessus • OpenVAS • NMAP • Nikto • Medusa • SSLyze • SSL Labs • TestSSL.sh • SkipFish • ZAP You can find Seccubus at `https://github.com/schubergphilis/Seccubus`.
OWTF	**Offensive Web Testing Framework (OWTF)** is an integrated security testing standards OWASP testing guide and includes PTES and NIST tools. • OWTF: `https://owtf.github.io/` • Additional information: `https://owtf.github.io/online-passive-scanner/`
RapidScan	RapidScan is a mult-itool that includes a web-vulnerability scanner. The security scanning tools that it contains include nmap, dnsrecon, uniscan, sslyze, fierce, theharvester, and golismero.
DefectDojo	The OWASP DefectDojo is a security tool that can import and consolidate various security testing tool outputs into one management dashboard. DefectDojo: `https://github.com/DefectDojo/django-DefectDojo`

Summary

In this chapter, we learned about security testing toolkits. Based on the elements that are to be tested, there are Kali Linux, BlackArch, and PentestBox, which are the Linux security distributions that provide general security testing toolkits. As there are many tools, we suggested a minimum set of security tools to cover the white box review, web connection, vulnerability, and network security.

We also showed the key factors of security automation tools and compared the capabilities of some web security tools for supporting the CLI and REST API interfaces. The BDD Security framework was also introduced for the support of an automated framework. We looked at BDD Security, MITTN, and GauntIT.

Some other security testing tools were also discussed. For Android security testing, MobSF (Mobile Security Framework) was recommended for a quick-win, fully automated analysis platform. For infrastructure security, we looked at the Lynis Security Auditing, OpenSCAP, or CIS Benchmarks security scanning tools to detect insecure configurations. For Docker security, there are three kinds of security tools—namely, the CIS security configuration best practices, the scan for known vulnerabilities, and the runtime threat analysis. Finally, we introduced the integrated security tools, which can help you to integrate and consolidate all the testing results.

In the next chapter, we will discuss security automation with continuous integration.

Questions

1. Which one of the following is not a Linux distribution for security testing? Ans: d
    1. Kali Linux
    2. BlackArch
    3. PentestBox
    4. OSSEC

2. The OWASP ZAP, Vega, and Arachni tools are used for which of the following security tests?
    1. Web security
    2. Network security
    3. Intrusion detection
    4. Integrity monitoring

3. Which one of the following tools is used for vulnerability scanning?
    1. WireShark
    2. OpenVAS
    3. TCPDump
    4. Hping

4. Which one of the following is not a minimum criterion for automated testing?
    1. GUI interface
    2. CLI interface
    3. API interface
    4. Output formats

5. What're the benefits of using BDD security?
   1. Integration with all tools
   2. Consolidated testing results
   3. Easy to communicate across the team
   4. All of the above

6. Which one of the following is not used for Docker security?
   1. Scanning for Docker security best practices based on CIS (Docker Bench, Actuary)
   2. Appie
   3. Scanning for known CVEs. (Claire, Anchor Engine)
   4. Runtime threats analysis. (Falco, Dagda)

7. Which of the following is not mainly focused on infrastructure security?
   1. Inspec
   2. Hardening Framework
   3. Serverspec
   4. PentestBox

Further reading

For more information visit the following URLs:

- **GauntIT examples**: `https://github.com/gauntIT/gauntIt/tree/master/examples/`
- **United States Government Configuration Baseline (USGCB)**: `https://csrc.nist.gov/projects/united-states-government-configuration-baseline/`
- **National Checklist Program Repository**: `https://nvd.nist.gov/ncp/repository`
- **Docker Secure Deployment Guidelines**: `https://github.com/GDSSecurity/Docker-Secure-Deployment-Guidelines`
- **Vulscan**: `https://github.com/scipag/vulscan`
- **AttifyOS distribution for IoT security testing**: `https://github.com/adi0x90/attifyos`

- **Attify Firmware Analysis Toolkit**: `https://github.com/attify/firmware-analysis-toolkit`
- **CHIPSEC Platform Security Assessment Framework**: `https://github.com/chipsec/chipsec`
- **List of penetration testing resources**: `https://github.com/enaqx/awesome-pentest`
- **List of penetration testing resources**: `https://github.com/wtsxDev/Penetration-Testing`

Security Automation with the CI Pipeline

13

We have reviewed white box testing tips and security testing toolsets. This chapter will focus on security practices in the development phases, as well as how to integrate tools such as Jenkins into continuous integration. In the development phases, we explored the techniques of using IDE plugins to secure code scanning, and suggested some static code analysis tools. For the build and package delivery, secure compiler configurations and dependency vulnerability checks will also be introduced. Finally, web security automation testing approaches and tips will also be discussed in this chapter.

We will cover the following topics in this chapter:

- Security in continuous integration
- Security practices in development
- Web testing in proactive/proxy mode
- Web automation testing tips
- Security automation in Jenkins

Security in continuous integration

Most of the development team's daily activities include coding, compiling/building, testing, and deployment. Our goal is to build security automation practices into these activities. In the coding stage, the development team can use IDE plugins to do security source code analysis. In the build stage, we scan for the secure hardened compiling options and the known vulnerabilities of the dependency components, as well as the secure source code for the whole project.

Once the build is ready and installed on the staging environment, more comprehensive security scanning will be performed, such as dynamic web security testing by OWASP ZAP, infrastructure configuration security, and secure communication protocols. In the production deployment, security scanning will also be performed regularly, and will be more focused on security monitoring instead of the source code or dynamic web security testing.

The following diagram shows the security practices in each phase, namely, coding, build, testing, and production deployment:

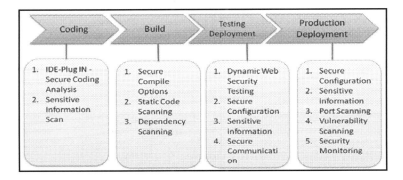

Security practices in development

The security practices of the development team consist of secure coding and secure build delivery. For the secure coding, we can have an IDE plugin do the code scanning, or we can also require security unit testing and run a static code scan of the whole project. For the secure build delivery, we need to ensure that the compiler options are configured properly and review all the dependency components for known vulnerabilities. The following diagram shows the overall security practices we can plan into the development stage. We will introduce some of the open source security tools and practices for these security activities in the upcoming sections:

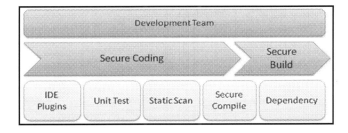

IDE plugins to automate the code review

The key advantages of using the IDE plugins to perform the automated security code review is that the tools can provide informative suggestions for fixes during the coding stage. It works in a similar way to a spellchecker. This will reduce lots of code review efforts and security defects that can't be detected by blackbox testing. The disadvantage is that this kind of static code scanning may introduce some annoying false positives, and the developer team may ignore or forget to use the IDE plugins to do static secure code analysis.

The following table shows some of the open source IDE plugins that can help developers to detect security and coding errors. Only open source tools are listed here, although there are also many good commercial tools that are available.

DevSkim is recommended not only because it can support multiple languages, but also because it supports a wide range of IDEs, such as VS, VS Code, Sublime Text, and so on. In addition, writing scanning rules for DevSkim is also simple in JSON format. Refer to `https://github.com/Microsoft/DevSkim/wiki/Sample-Rule` for more information:

Tools	Supported programming language	Reference
FindSecBugs	Java	• `https://find-sec-bugs.github.io/`
PMD	Java	• `https://pmd.github.io/`
DevSkim	All	• `https://github.com/Microsoft/DevSkim`

Although we would like the code review to be done automatically by the tools, there may be an occasion where we want to execute a team peer code review and require a team collaboration portal to comment on or discuss the code quality. For a team code review platform, the following open source tools are recommended:

- **Gerrit:** It provided a web-based UI code review for the GIT source code. `www.gerritcodereview.com`
- **Phabricator:** Phabricator is an open source tool which integrates not only code review tools but also bug tracking. `www.phacility.com`

For the peer code review practices, consider creating a code review checklist or refer to the OWASP cheat sheet or OWASP SCP (secure coding practices):

Static code analysis

Static code scanning analysis is an effective source-level security inspection in CI frameworks, such as Jenkins or Travis. The development team may not fully apply IDE code-scanning plugins to do the secure code analysis. In that case, the static code analysis adoption into the CI framework will help to enforce the secure code scanning for all projects. In other words, the integration with the static security code analysis tools and Jenkins is a must in the development stage.

The following table lists some of the static code analysis tools. You can also refer to Chapter 8, *Secure Coding Best Practices*, for other suggested tools:

Tools	Supported Programming language	Characteristics
Grep Rough Audit	All	It's a simple script to detect security flaws in the source code by using GREP and regular expression for common security patterns.
Flawfinder	C/C+	It's a simple tool to scan for the security issue in C/C++ security issue in C/C++ source code.
Brakeman	Ruby on Rails	Brakeman is mainly focused on the security issue in Ruby code.
SonarQube	All	The SonarQube is a source code quality analysis tool.
GREP IT	All	It's one Linux shell script which can do the code scanning. No other dependencies required.
NodeJsScan	NodeJS	It's mainly used to scan NodeJS security issue.
ScanJS	JavaScript	The ScanJS can identify the uses of high-risk JavaScript API such as eval, execScript, document.write and so on.
Bandit	Python	It scans the security issue for Python source code.

Secure compiler configuration

The secure compiler configuration means that you can enable the compile-time defenses against memory corruption issues to execute unexpected exploit code. These mitigations may include RELRO, **address space layout randomization (ASLR)**, **NoExecute (NX)**, stack canaries, and **position-independent executables (PIE)**. These secure compiler configurations should be done during the development stage.

The following table shows some of the available mitigation:

Mitigation	Visual Studio compiler options
Stack randomization	/DyNAMICBASE
Buffer overrun defenses	/GS
NoExecute (NX)	/NXCOMPAT
Exception handler protection	/SAFESEH

The following table shows the common build flags for GCC and G++ compiler drivers:

Mitigation	Compiler and linker flags for GCC
Address	-fPIC
NoExecute stack	-Wl, -z, noexecstack
GOT protection	-Wl, -z, relro
Stack protector	-fstack-protector
ASLR	Echo 1 > /proc/sys/kernel/randomize_va_space

The following tools can be used to verify the correct secure compiler configuration:

- **CheckSEC for Linux**: www.trapkit.de/tools/checksec.html
- **Microsoft BinScope**: https://www.microsoft.com/en-us/download/details.aspx?id=44995

The secure compiler configurations are low-hanging fruits for the buffer overflow security mitigations. This security practice is often neglected by the development team. Make sure that the security configurations are done at compile time, and also verify the binary packages in the testing stage.

Dependency check

Known vulnerabilities in third-party components or dependencies are considered to be parts of the OWASP Top 10 List of Using Components with Known Vulnerabilities. These known vulnerable components should be identified at an early development stage. It is also suggested that you perform the vulnerability scanning of the dependency components not only in the development stage but also in the production stage on a regular basis.

The following tools will help you scan for vulnerable components:

Tool	Supported languages
OWASP Dependency Check	The OWASP Dependency Check scans for dependency vulnerabilities in Java, Ruby, PHP, JavaScript, Python, and .NET.
Retire.JS	Retire.JS scans for vulnerable JavaScript libraries.
Snyk	Snyk scans for the JS, Ruby, Python, Java vulnerabilities.

Web testing in proactive/proxy mode

Dynamic web testing tools, such as OWASP ZAP, Arachni, Wapiti and W3af, normally provide two modes of security testing: proactive mode and proxy mode. The proactive mode means that you launch the testing tools and perform security testing directly on the web services. The tester may decide on the types of security testing (such as XSS or SQLi) of the target web service. However, the key disadvantage of this kind of testing is that you could miss certain permission-required web pages, or web pages that may require the right order of page visits. The following diagram shows the approach of proactive mode:

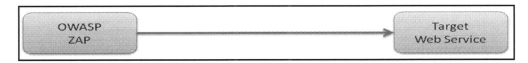

The proactive mode

The proxy mode, which can also be understood as MITM, means that the security testing tool is running as a proxy and intercepting traffic between the browser client and the target web services. In the proxy mode, the security testing tool OWASP ZAP will detect potential security vulnerability issues based on the intercepted traffic.

Take OWASP ZAP as an example. Say that we want OWASP ZAP to be executed in proxy mode. This will require the following configurations:

1. Launch the OWASP ZAP as proxy mode.
2. Configure the client-side proxy to the OWASP ZAP proxy.
3. Install the CA certificate in the OWASP ZAP proxy.

Proxy mode works best for the project team if they have set up functional automation, such as Selenium or Robot Framework. Selenium or Robot Framework will help to guide the OWASP ZAP to walk through the web pages, especially those required permission pages:

The proxy mode

In practice, it's recommended that you execute the web security testing in both modes with more than one tool. This is because every security tool may have its own strength and weakness of security attacks and detection engines. For example, OWASP ZAP and Arachni may be running in proactive scanning and spider mode. Furthermore, you can also use the Selenium automation client to guide the Vega or OWASP ZAP to visit authenticated pages, and to do deeper fuzz testing on the specified web service. Refer to the following diagram for the testing scenarios:

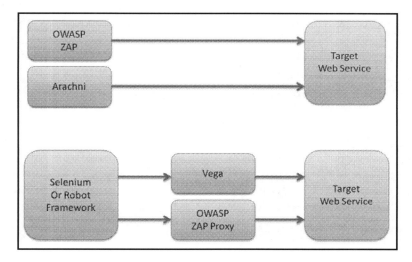

Web automation testing tips

Simply install and launch OWASP ZAP. Active and passive scanning can only give us a preliminary testing result for public web services. The following table contains some suggested tips to improve the testing efficiency and effectiveness for uses of web automation testing tools, such as ZAP or Arachni:

Testing tips	Description
Integration	To do automated integration, try to understand that the web security tools provide the following: • Headless execution mode • Command-line interface • REST API • Jenkins plugin (this may be optional as long as one of te preceding tools is provided) For example, the OWASP ZAP (`https://github.com/Grunny/zap-cli/`) provides the ZAP CLI interface, which also helps make the integration easier.
Authorization testing	To test the guest, user, and admin permissions for every web service's URL or resources will require proper predefined navigation workflows. The testing scenario may include the following: • Session fixation, reuses, expiration • User, role, guest, administration permissions • Login, logout, and reauthentication behaviors There are two main approaches for the security testing: • Use Selenium or Robot Framework to do the authentication and use OWASP ZAP to detect the security issue • Preconfigure the pages or URLs that require authentication in OWASP ZAP or Arachni
Scanning scope	Dynamic web testing may take a very long period of time. Properly configure the scanning scope to include or exclude the URLs that are being tested. Only apply a complete full scan when the application passes the smoke testing. A complete scan can be scheduled to be done on a nightly basis.

API fuzz	The web service may provide several REST JSON or SOAP XML APIs. It's suggested that you get a complete API list and specifications. Do the fuzz testing on the parameters of each API. Once this has been done, run the OWASP ZAP or the Arachni in proxy mode to intercept all the API calls. Then, investigate these API calls for further fuzz testing with the parameters in the payload. For the fuzz security payload test, consider replacing the value of the parameters with the following data in the fuzzDB: • `https://github.com/fuzzdb-project/fuzzdb/` • `https://github.com/minimaxir/big-list-of-naughty-strings/` Radamsa can be used to automatically generate fuzzing data: • `https://github.com/aoh/radamsa`
Business logic	Some web UI workflows need to be operated in order, such as shopping for items, ordering the items, and payment. Here are some approaches to help you handle this kind of security testing: • Use existing functional Selenium automation UI testing and run the OWASP ZAP or Arachni in proxy attack mode. • Use the script provided by OWASP ZAP to integrate with Selenium. Refer to the Zap webdriver (`https:/github.com/continuumsecurity/zap-webdriver`) as an example. • Apply the BDD Security framework (`https://github.com/continuumsecurity/bdd-security/`). • Manually operate the web pages to navigate the flow and save the ZAP sessions for further security scanning.

Security automation in Jenkins

In this section, we will discuss how to configure Jenkins to trigger the automated testing, and also introduce some of the security plugins.

The following table shows an example of how to configure the command-line ZAP, which can be triggered periodically and remotely by a predefined URL:

Steps	Configuration steps
New item	New Item | Enter an Item Name | *"Security Testing"* | Freestyle Project | OK
General	Project Name: *"Security Testing"*

Build Trigger	The automation testing can be triggered by the schedule in the following ways. The Build Trigger defines how the tasks can be triggered. There are two modes supported: one is the scheduled mode and the other is the remote trigger by the REST API:
	
	    Build Periodically: *45 9-17/2 * * 1-5*
	The automation testing can also be triggered remotely by sending the HTTP request:
	
	    Trigger builds remotely: *ZAP*
	Once it's defined, this will be the URL that can be triggered remotely to kick off the automation execution:
	`https://<JenkinsHost:8080>/job/Security Testing/build?token=ZAP`

Build	Build | Add Build Step
	Execute the Windows batch command:
	`echo ---- the execution of OWASP ZAP for Active Scan----`
	`    zap cli  active-scan  http://targetWeb/`
	`echo ---- The end of OWASP ZAP active Scan ----`

There are some open source security scanning tools that also provide Jenkins plugins. In practice, these Jenkins plugins are optional. If you have few projects and would like to manage the security scanning status in the Jenkins dashboard, these Jenkins plugins will be good choices. However, if you have a lot of projects with various kinds of security testing scans, it's still suggested that you build your integrated security testing framework. Please also refer to the `Chapter 12`, *Security Testing Toolkits*, for details. The following table lists the common Jenkins plugins that are related to software security assessment:

Jenkins Security plugins	Description
ZAP	ZAP is a dynamic web scanning tool.
Arachni Scanner	Arachni Scanner is a dynamic web scanning tool.
Dependency Check plugin	The Dependency Check plugin detects vulnerable dependency components.
FindBugs	FindBugs is a static code analysis tool for Java.
SonarQube	SonarQube is a code quality analysis tool.
360 FireLine	360 FireLine is a static code scanner for Java.

HTML Publisher Plugin	The HTML Publisher plugin generates the testing results in HTML.
Log Parser Plugin	The Log Parser plugin parses the testing results of the security testing tools, such as the number of XSS detected or the number of errors.
Static Analysis Collector	The Static Analysis Collector plugin can consolidate the results from all other static code analysis plugins, such as Checkstyle, Dry, FindBugs, PMD, and Android Lin.

Summary

In this chapter, we learned about the security practices that take place during the continuous integration cycle in the coding, building, testing, and production deployment phases. For the development stage, we perform secure code scanning, secure compiling checks, and also vulnerable third-party component review. For the static code analysis, we also introduced some of the open source scanning tools for different programming languages. We have also learned how to enable compile-time defenses against buffer overflows, such as ASLR and NX.

For web security testing, we introduced testing approaches in proactive and proxy modes and discussed web automation testing tips to improve the testing effectiveness in terms of business logic, API fuzz, scanning scope, authorization, and integration. We also looked at Jenkins configurations and security automation plugins in Jenkins, such as ZAP, Arachni, Dependency Check, FindBugs, and SonarQube. In the next chapter, we will learn about incident response.

Questions

1. What security practices are related to secure coding?
    1. Security scanning using IDE plugins
    2. Security unit testing
    3. Static code scanning
    4. All of the above

2. What does the tool DevSkim do?
    1. Reverse engineering
    2. It is an IDE plugin for static code scanning
    3. Web security scanning
    4. Network security

3. What techniques are used to defend against memory overflow attacks?
    1. Stack randomization
    2. Nonexecution
    3. Exception handler protection
    4. All of the above

4. What's the main purpose of using dependency check tools?
    1. Software integrity
    2. Implements access control
    3. Scans for known vulnerabilities
    4. Data encryption

5. What security testing can Radamsa be used for?
    1. API fuzz testing
    2. Integrity monitoring
    3. Dynamic analysis
    4. Mobile application

Further reading

- **GitHub automated testing resources**: `https://github.com/atinfo/awesome-test-automation`
- **Hardening compiler and linker flags**: `https://developers.redhat.com/blog/2018/03/21/compiler-and-linker-flags-gcc/`
- **Automated security testing for REST APIs**: `https://github.com/flipkart-incubator/Astra`

14
Incident Response

Security testing plans, whitebox testing tips, security toolsets, and automation were illustrated in previous chapters. Starting with this chapter, we will now discuss incident responses for a security operation team. We will mainly discuss the key activities in the key phases of the incident response process: preparation, containment, detection, and post-incident analysis. The field of incident response includes how to handle public CVE vulnerability, how to respond to whitehat or security attacks, how we evaluate each security issue, the feedback loop to the development team, and the tools or practices we may apply in incident response. The topics that will be covered in this chapter are as follows:

- Security incident response process
- Security operation team structure
- Incident forensics techniques

Security incident response process

Establishing a security incident response process is a must for not only very large enterprises but also small businesses. Cybersecurity laws or GDPR require not only a security incident process, but they also require a security incident notification to be sent to the supervisory authority and key stakeholders. A complete security incident process involves the security incident handling team, human resources, the legal department, and also external supervisory groups. Although there are many security technologies and tools that can help to identify, protect, detect, respond, and recover from threats, PR and public communication play critical roles in non-technical parts. We will mainly focus on the security activities during the preparation, detection, containment, and post-incident handling stages based on NIST SP 800-62.

Here are some of the recommended industry references related to security incident response:

- NIST SP 800-62 Computer Security Incident Handling Guide (`https://csrc.nist.gov/publications/detail/sp/800-61/rev-2/final`)
- SANS Incident Handler Handbook (`https://www.sans.org/reading-room/whitepapers/incident/incident-handlers-handbook-33901`)
- ENISA Cloud Computing Benefits, risks, and recommendations for information security (`https://resilience.enisa.europa.eu/cloud-security-and-resilience/publications/cloud-computing-benefits-risks-and-recommendations-for-information-security`)
- MITRE Ten Strategies of a World-Class Cyber Security Operations Center (`https://www.mitre.org/sites/default/files/publications/pr-13-1028-mitre-10-strategies-cyber-ops-center.pdf`)
- FIRST (`https://www.first.org/education/FIRST_PSIRT_Service_Framework_v1.0`)

NIST SP 800-62 defines the incident response life cycle as consisting of four phases: preparation, detection and analysis, containment eradication and recovery, and post-incident activity. We will introduce some practical tools for each phase in the upcoming sections:

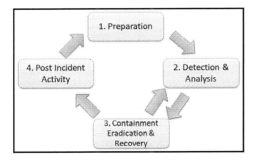

Preparation

The preparation is the most critical part of the incident process. We cannot completely predict or avoid any security incident, but we can plan to have full preparation for a security incident. The preparation covers all the required processes, analysis tools, security technologies, and team resources to prevent and handle a security incident. Preparation not only helps in preventing security incidents but also minimizing the damage caused during a security incident.

Here are some suggested security practices to be performed in the incident response preparation phase:

- Incident handler communication plan
- Incident analysis hardware and software tools (refer to the section on incident forensics)
- Existing networking diagram and baselines
- Prevention controls, such as risk assessments, host security, network security, malware protection, user awareness, and training (refer to the CIS security controls)
- The blue and red team security exercise (refer to the following table)
- Bounty program for whitehat hackers or security researchers to submit security issues

It's suggested that you perform internal attack simulations regularly to test the effectiveness and weakness of existing endpoint and network detection security solutions, such as antivirus software, IPS, IDS, and firewalls. The security team can also analyze the existing logging and alerting capabilities and the response time. These kinds of simulated attacks give the security team a chance to review and optimize the existing security framework.

The following open source tools can help to generate an internal attack simulation without compromising business operations. These tools don't generate real attack samples, but simulate the behaviors of hacking or **advanced persistent threat (APT)** behaviors:

Tools	Simulation of APT
DumpsterFire	The DumpsterFire tool includes various kinds of simulated attack scenarios, such as an account attack, file download, drop files, command execution, and web access in Python. It provides a user-friendly menu to customize the security incidents, even for those who don't understand Python.
METTA	The METTA tool allows the security team to customize the simulation of APT attacks based on MITRE ATT&CK. The simulated APT behaviors defined by YAML include credential access, evasion, discovery, execution, exfiltration, lateral movement, persistence, and privilege escalation.
Red Team Automation (RTA)	The Red Team Automation tool is a collection of Python and PowerShell scripts that can simulate over 50 malicious behaviors based on ATT&CK.
Atomic Red Team (ART)	The Atomic Red Team tool provides Windows, macOS, and Linux shell scripts to simulate the MITRE ATT&CK.

| APT Simulator | The APT Simulator tool is a collection of Windows BAT scripts that simulate APT behaviors. |
| Network Flight Simulator | The Network Flight Simulator tool can be used to generate malicious network traffic, such as DNS tunneling, C2 communication, DGA traffic, and port scans. |

During the security incident handling, the team may be occupied by the case, but forget to record the information. An incident case-tracking tool will help to keep records of the relevant information. The open source tool FIR (Fast Incident Response) is a security incident case-management tool that can help to record, track, and archive all the findings for each security incident case. This information will help to build an in-house security incident handling knowledge base and generate an incident report for post-mortem analysis (you can find the tool at `https://github.com/certsocietegenerale/FIR/`).

Detection and analysis

Identifying the signs of a security incident requires the deployment of various security solutions and log sensors. The sources of infections include IDS/IPS, SIEM, antivirus, file-integrity monitoring, OS/network logs, and public and known vulnerabilities. The deployment of the whole enterprise's security controls may refer to the CIS Critical Security Controls for Effective Cyber Defense (you can find the information at `https://www.cisecurity.org/controls/`).

These consist of 20 security controls, as summarized in the following table. There are many commercial solutions in each security control, but only open source solutions are listed in the table:

Cybersecurity controls	Examples of security techniques and open source tools
CSC1: Inventory of Authorized and Unauthorized Devices	Endpoint security, Asset Management
CSC2: Inventory of Authorized and Unauthorized Software	Endpoint security, Asset Management
CS3: Secure Configurations for Hardware and Software on Mobile Devices, Laptops, Workstations, and Servers	CIS Security Benchmark, OpenSCAP.

CSC4: Continuous Vulnerability Assessment and Remediation	OpenVAS Nmap OWASP Dependency Check OWASP Dependency-Track vulscan
CSC 5: Controlled Use of Administrative Privileges	Strong password complexity Auditing logs for root and administrator activities
CSC 6: Maintenance, Monitoring, and Analysis of Audit Logs	Syslog, Event Logs, SIEM ELK GrayLog Security Onion Malicious Traffic Detection
CSC 7: Email and Web Browser Protections	Email Protection, Anti-Spam, Web Application Firewall ModSecurity Email Encryption Scramble Linux Malware Detection
CSC 8: Malware Defenses	Endpoint Protection, Antivirus, HIDS/HIPS OSSEC ClamAV
CSC 9: Limitation and Control of Network Ports, Protocols, and Services	Nmap OpenSCAP
CSC 10: Data Recovery Capability	Bacula
CSC 11: Secure Configurations for Network Devices, such as Firewalls, Routers, and Switches	CIS Security Benchmark
CSC 12: Boundary Defense	Firewall, IPS, HoneyPot Security Onion
CSC 13: Data Protection	OSQuery Data Vault
CSC 14: Controlled Access Based on the Need to Know	Data Classification, Firewall, VLAN, Logging
CSC 15: Wireless Access Control	VPN, SSL Certificate, WAP2
CSC 16: Account Monitoring and Control	Log Analysis Tools Fail2ban

CSC 17: Security Skills Assessment and Appropriate Training to Fill Gaps	Security Training and Labs Resource CybraryIT
CSC 18: Application Software Security	OWASP
CSC 19: Incident Response and Management	NIST SP800-61 Computer Security Incident Handling Guide FIR (Fast Incident Response)
CSC 20: Penetration Tests and Red Team Exercises	Refer to some of the open source tools we suggested in the *Preparation* section

When a security incident case is received, the security team should perform a prioritization of the security incident based on the impact that it has. The NIST SP800-61 Computer Security Incident Handling Guide suggests quantifying the impact level by the functional impact, the PII information impact, and the recoverability effort:

- The functional impact means the impact on business functions
- The PII information impact is the **confidentiality, integrity, and availability (CIA)** of the sensitive information
- The recoverability effort refers to the amount of time and resources needed to recover from the incident

The following table shows some sample definitions of each security incident alert level:

Priority	Impact	Response
High	The functional impact, information leakage, or recoverability effort is classed as high.	Requires immediate human response.
Medium	The functional impact, information leakage, or recoverability effort is classed as medium.	Requires response within 24 hours.
Low	The functional impact, information leakage, and recoverability effort are all defined as low.	Requires response during routine tasks.
Notification	No major signs are directly related to the functional impact or information leakage, but it can be a potential security issue.	Just a notice. This can be part of a quarterly threat-trending analysis.

Containment and recovery

The short-term objective of containment is to isolate the infected hosts before a complete solution is ready. On the other hand, the long-term objective of recovery is to look for a security control that can avoid a similar security incident in the future, or that can perform automatic recovery when the security incident is detected.

For the containment, there are typical network- or host-containment criteria established by network policy enforcement. Whenever one of the criteria is met, the containment actions can include blocking that specific host, redirecting the traffic to apply the latest security patches, and rejecting specific communication traffic or ports.

The following are common security policy enforcement criteria that will trigger the network or host containment:

- The host hasn't installed any antivirus products.
- The antivirus pattern/engine versions are not updated.
- There are known vulnerable components on the host.
- There is suspicious communication traffic on the specified ports.
- A known virus is detected on the hosts.
- There is outgoing communication to an external known malicious IP or domain. Refer to the following resources:
    - http://iplists.firehol.org/
    - https://www.spamhaus.org/drop/
    - https://rules.emergingthreats.net/fwrules/emerging-Block-IPs.txt
    - https://check.torproject.org/exit-addresses

In terms of recovery, the objective is to restore the infected applications or hosts back to normal operation. The activities of recovery not only include restoring the system but also removing compromised files, applying the latest patches, securing communication ports, increasing the complexity of passwords, and improving security controls, such as permission configurations, HIDS, SELinux, and firewalls.

Post-incident activity

Hosting a *lessons learned* meeting or post-mortem analysis report can help the team to learn from the incident. The primary objective of the lessons learned meeting is to look for the improvement of each phase during the security incident response process. This kind of meeting is often neglected once the security issue is solved. It's suggested that you at least document the process of the security incident and incorporate it into the knowledge base.

For a lessons learned meeting, the meeting should focus on how the team can improve together and prevent a similar issue in the future instead of blaming someone for the error. The inputs of the post-mortem meeting typically include the proposed security control changes, the case-handling information, and the root cause analysis report. It's expected that the team will think on what specific actions can be done to prevent similar issues. For example, specific email phishing awareness training can be increased. The security scanning rules in IDS can be optimized to reduce false positives. Security incident forensics can be done by automation. The period of the known vulnerabilities installation cycle can be shortened. These are the potential outputs of the meeting with the consensus among the stakeholders, such as the security, IT, development, business, and legal teams.

The expected post-mortem output report typically includes certain key sections answering key questions, such as what happened, the impact, root cause analysis, short-term and long-term mitigations, the activities that occurred during the incident timeline, what should be improved, and what should be kept. Here is an example of a post-mortem meeting output report:

Overview of the issue

One of the services was identified as having abnormal unavailability. The WebLogic process had a CPU usage of 100%, and the log showed an abnormal and suspicious outbound IP connection.

What happened and the impact

Business Functional Impact: Some of the services slowed down, and were unable to respond to the requests. The running process occupied 100% of the CPU resources. No data-leakage risks were identified.

Root Cause Analysis

- IT identified that it was the WebLogic process that frequently had a CPU usage of over 80%.

- After the security team checked the Linux connection logs, it was confirmed that the WebLogic process had an outbound connection to external hosts that were related to cryptojacking (cryptojacking refers to the use of compromised hosts to mine cryptocurrency).
- After searching the CVE database by the security team, the issue was likely related to CVE 2017-3248.

Mitigation and Solutions

- Short-term before the security patch is ready: Apply firewall rules to block outbound communication traffic to the cryptojacking servers, and inbound connections to the victim host.
- Long-term:
  - Apply WebLogic security patch.
  - Update the antivirus security patterns.
  - Optimize the host-based intrusion detection rules for high-CPU usage processes and abnormal outbound connections behaviors.

Activities during the timeline

Day 1 1000: IT service monitoring identified service unavailability.

Day 1 1020: IT identified that a WebLogic process occupied 100% CPU usage, and collected related logs for further analysis. As the issue happened frequently and impacted the service's availability, the case was also escalated to the security team to identify whether it was a security incident.

Day 1 1040: Security team completed the log analysis and identified abnormal connections.

Day 1 1145: The IT team was informed, and decided to disconnect the outbound connection to the malicious IP.

What should be improved or kept

- Keep: Good collaboration between IT and security team.
- Improvement: Automated log collection and analysis tools.
- Improvement: Virtual patch by firewall before a security patch is ready.
- Improvement: Networking log correlation with threat knowledge from `http://iplists.firehol.org/`.

Security incident response platforms (SIRP)

When handling a security incident, there will be lots of information that needs to be processed and analyzed. An ideal security incident response platform should be able to do the following:

- Receive alerts and security events from different sources (SIEM, IDS, email)
- The security incident case management should allow a security analyst to add related logs, IOCs, or findings during the incident case handling life cycle
- Compare its analysis with external threat information, such as VirusTotal, to identify the malicious behaviors of a file, hash, domain, or IP address

The open source tool TheHive can help you to provide a security incident response management platform. TheHive can also work with MISP, which is a threat intelligence platform for sharing and correlating indicators of compromise (which indicate that a targeted attack has taken place) and vulnerability information. Refer to the following documentation for more information:

- `https://thehive-project.org/`
- `http://www.misp-project.org/index.html`

For more information on how TheHive, CorTex, and MISP can integrate together for a threat incident response, go to `https://blog.thehive-project.org/2017/06/19/thehive-cortex-and-misp-how-they-all-fit-together/`.

SOC team

The **security operations center** (**SOC**), also known as the **computer incident response team** (**CIRT**), is the security team that handles and monitors daily security events. The organizational structure of SOC can include parts of the existing IT team, an outsourced team, or a dedicated security team. No matter what kind of structure it has, there are several key functions that the team will have:

Key functions	Description
Security incident analysis and forensics (call center)	This function team may include the Tier 1 case handling in the 24/7 security monitoring center. The Tier 1 team typically handles the case by following the predefined checklist or SOP to perform initial root-cause analysis or mitigation based on the incidents.

Security operations and administration	This functional team involves the following routine security activities. These are regular security checking activities for the production environments: • Network scanning (weekly) • Vulnerability scanning (weekly) • Penetration testing (monthly) • Security awareness training (bi-monthly) • Security log trending analysis (monthly) • Security administration and monitoring (daily) • Patch or security signature update (daily/weekly)
Security tools engineering	The security engineering team implement security tools for the security call center or security operations team. The security tools can be security automation, suspicious behaviors detectors, forensic analysis tools, security configurations checker, threat intelligence integration, threat signatures creation, and so on.

The SOC team can consist of parts of an IT call center or a dedicated security team depending on the size of the whole organization. A typical dedicated SOC team structure is shown in the following diagram:

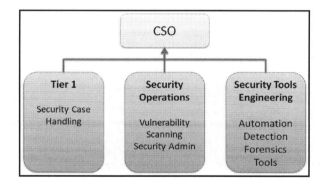

Incident forensics techniques

The primary objective of incident forensics for an organization is to answer the following questions:

- Is the host infected with a malicious program?
- How did the host get infected?
- What can be improved to avoid the infection?

The NIST SP 800-86 Guide to Integrating Forensic Techniques into Incident Response defines four major phases to perform digital forensics on a compromised computer:

- **Collection**: Collect all the relevant logs of the compromised computer or networking activities logs
- **Examination**: Extract and correlate the information that may highly relate to suspicious behaviors
- **Analysis**: Analyze all the information for root causes of the malicious infection
- **Reporting**: Conclude the summary results

The forensics techniques require the capability of the incident response team to perform the analysis. In the following table, we have listed some quick-win solutions that can perform semi-automated forensics, including collection, examination, and analysis:

Category	Tools	Purpose and usage scenario
Log Collection	OSX Collector	Mac OS X Log Collector is an automated forensic evidence collection for macOS. The Python script, osxcollector.py, is the script that performs all the collection jobs. The tool will generate a JSON file as a summary of the collected information.
Log Collection	IR Rescue	IR Rescue is a Windows and Linux script for collecting host forensic data. For the Windows version, it integrates several utilities from the from Sysinternals and NirSoft.
Log Collection	FastIR Collector	FastIR Collector (for Linux) only requires one Python script to collect all related logs in Linux. For Windows systems, it will require additional modules and tools. Refer to `https://github.com/SekoiaLab/Fastir_Collector` for more information.
Malware Detector	Linux Malware Scanner	Free malware scanners for Linux are available from the following links: CalmAV: It's an open source antivirus software for Windows. Linux Malware Detect (LMD): It's an open source antivirus software for Linux.
Suspicious Files Analysis	Cuckoo	Cuckoo is an automated malware analysis system. It can analyze the dynamic runtime and static behaviors of the unknown and suspicious files under Windows, Linux, macOS, and Android.

Client/Server log collector and analysis	GRR Rapid Response	You can use Google Remote Live forensics for incident response. It will require the installation of a Python agent on the target hosts to collect the logs and on the Python server to do the analysis.

Client/Server log collector and analysis	OSQuery	The OSQuery tool works in a similar way to GRR. The key difference is that OSQuery provides an SQL query to perform endpoint analysis.
		 For more information, you can read the documentation at the following links:
		 `https://osquery.io/`
		 `https://osquery.readthedocs.io/en/stable/`
		 `deployment/anomaly-detection/`

Summary

In this chapter, we discussed the security incident response process and shared some of the industry practices, such as the NIST SP800-62, SANS Incident Handler Handbook, and MITRE's Ten Strategies of a World-Class Cyber Security Operations Center. We explored the incident response activities based on the phases defined by the NIST SP800-62, which are the preparation, detection and analysis, containment eradication, and post-incident activity phases.

In the preparation phase, we introduced some of the simulated attack tools for the red/blue team exercise. In the detection phase, we suggested applying CIS Critical Security Controls for Effective Cyber Defense to assess the detection and analysis capabilities. We introduced some containment security policies when looking at the containment phase. In the post-incident phase, we learned how to do a post-mortem review and looked at one incident post-mortem sample report. To link all the information from the different phases and teams, it's suggested that you have a **security incident response platform** (SIRP).

Last but not least, we discussed the SOC organization and the key functions that it should have. We also looked at some incident forensics techniques and tools.

In the next chapter, we will discuss security monitoring. Security incident response may be a one-time event for security case handling, but security monitoring will be a constant security-monitoring activity.

Questions

1. What's the right order of the security incident response phases?
    1. Detection -> Preparation -> Containment -> Post-Incident Analysis
    2. Containment -> Detection -> Preparation -> Post-Incident Analysis
    3. Preparation -> Detection -> Containment -> Post-Incident Analysis
    4. Preparation -> Containment -> Detection -> Post-Incident Analysis

2. What best describes a bounty program?
    1. It's an incentive program for security researchers to submit security issues
    2. It's a security awareness training program
    3. It's an in-house security penetration exercise
    4. It's a security design camp

3. What's the purpose of attack simulations?
    1. To test the weakness of endpoint detection
    2. To test the detection capability of network security
    3. To test the logging and alerting capability of the security system
    4. All of the above

4. What does the CIS Critical Security Controls for Effective Cyber Defense define?
    1. It defines the 20 security controls for the whole enterprise security
    2. It defines incident response processes
    3. It defines the secure coding practices
    4. It defines security automation practices

5. The ELK, Graylog, and Syslogs are mainly used in which of the following security controls?
    1. Monitoring and Analysis of Audit Logs
    2. Email and Web Browser Protections
    3. Malware Defenses
    4. Data Recovery Capability

6. Which should not be used to quantify the impact level?
   1. The functional impact
   2. The malware detection capability
   3. The PII information impact
   4. The recoverability efforts

7. Which one of the following is the incorrect role/responsibility for the SOC team?
   1. The primary objective of the Tier 1 call center is to perform malware analysis
   2. The security operations team should perform network scanning on a regular basis
   3. The security tools engineering team is in charge of security tools implementation
   4. The security log analysis should be regularly summarized and analyzed

8. What is the correct description of "cryptojacking "?
   1. Unauthorized use of a compromised host to mine cryptocurrency
   2. Encryption of the compromised host without permission
   3. Unauthorized access to the encrypted information
   4. Unauthorized encryption of the compromised host

Further reading

- **NIST SP 800-62 Computer Security Incident Handling Guide**: `https://nvlpubs.nist.gov/nistpubs/specialpublications/nist.sp.800-61r2.pdf`
- **ENISA Cloud Computing Benefits, risks, and recommendations for information security**: `https://www.enisa.europa.eu/publications/cloud-computing-risk-assessment`
- **Handbook for Computer Security Incident Response Teams (CSIRTs)**: `https://resources.sei.cmu.edu/library/asset-view.cfm?assetid=6305`
- **SANS Security Checklists & Step by Step Guides**: `https://www.sans.org/score/checklists`
- **Awesome Incident Response**: `https://github.com/meirwah/awesome-incident-response/`
- **InfoSec Tools**: `https://secure.dshield.org/tools/`
- **Forming an Incident Response Team**: `https://www.auscert.org.au/publications/forming-incident-response-team`

- **Awesome Forensics**: https://github.com/cugu/awesome-forensics/
- **Awesome Incident Response**: https://github.com/meirwah/awesome-incident-response/
- **Awesome List of Digital Forensic Tools**: https://github.com/ivbeg/awesome-forensicstools/
- **Awesome Malware Analysis Tools**: https://github.com/rshipp/awesome-malware-analysis/
- **Incident Response Playbooks**: www.incidentresponse.com/playbooks/
- **SANS Incident Handler's Handbook**: https://www.sans.org/reading-room/whitepapers/incident/incident-handlers-handbook-33901
- **Incident Response Process**: https://response.pagerduty.com
- **NIST Framework for Improving Critical Infrastructure Cybersecurity**: https://www.nist.gov/publications/framework-improving-critical-infrastructure-cybersecurity-version-11
- **Microsoft TechNet Responding to IT Security Incidents**: https://technet.microsoft.com/en-us/library/cc700825.aspx
- **MITRE's Ten Strategies of a World-Class Cybersecurity Operations Center**: https://www.mitre.org/sites/default/files/publications/pr-13-1028-mitre-10-strategies-cyber-ops-center.pdf
- **Security 101 for SaaS Startup**: https://github.com/forter/security-101-for-saas-startups/blob/english/security.md
- **InfoSec Security Training and Labs Resource**: https://github.com/onlurking/awesome-infosec
- **vFeed - The Correlated Vulnerability and Threat Intelligence Database Wrapper**: https://github.com/toolswatch/vFeedhttps://vfeed.io/
- **MITRE ATT&CK**: https://attack.mitre.org/wiki/Main_Page
- **Red Team Automation**: https://github.com/endgameinc/RAT
- **Atomic Red Team**: https://github.com/redcanaryco/atomic-red-team
- **APT Simulator**: https://github.com/NextronSystems/APTSimulator
- **Network Flight Simulator**: https://github.com/alphasoc/flightsim
- **Awesome Information Security:** https://github.com/onlurking/awesome-infosec

- **NIST SP800-61 Computer Security Incident Handling Guide:** https://csrc.nist.gov/publications/detail/sp/800-61/rev-2/final

15
Security Monitoring

The topic of incident response was discussed in the previous chapter. In this chapter, we will introduce some security monitoring techniques. The objective of this chapter is to prepare our security monitoring mechanism to protect and prevent our cloud services from being attacked. To be prepared for this, our security monitoring procedures should include logging, monitoring the framework, threat intelligence, and security scanning for malicious programs. The topics that will be covered in this chapter are as follows:

- Logging policy
- Security monitoring framework
- Source of information
- Threat intelligence toolset
- Security scanning toolset
- Malware behavior matching—YARA

Logging policy

The general objective of security monitoring is to understand the existing security posture of the data, the network, endpoint hosts, gateway, cloud services, web services, databases, applications, and security configurations. This monitoring can be done by various kinds of security tools, such as host IDS, network IDS/IPS, antivirus software, firewalls, and also **security information and event management (SIEM)**. The security monitoring scenario will decide which logs should be collected, what should be monitored, and the focus of the threat visualization.

If the logs are collected too often, the information can be overwhelming and occupy too many resources, such as storage and network traffic. On the other hand, if the logs that are collected are not detailed enough, it's likely that the security professionals may not be able to identify potential risks or perform the post-mortem of a security event.

The NIST SP 800-92 Guide to Computer Security Log Management suggests that the log collection configuration should be based on the security impact to the systems. It is suggested that the logging collection and retention policies should be based on the value of the data and the business impact. An organization may define such security policies to manage the whole log infrastructure. The following table is an example of some logging policies:

Examples of logging configuration settings by NIST SP 800-92:

Category	Low impact	Moderate impact	High impact
How long to retain log data (Keep in mind that the cybersecurity law may also have explicitly requested the log retention period. The number here is just an example.)	One to two weeks	One to three months	Three to 12 months
How often to rotate logs	Optional (if performed, at least every week, or for every 25 MB)	Every six to 24 hours, or every 2 to 5 MB	Every 15 to 60 minutes or every 0.5 to 1.0 MB
How frequently the organization requires the system to transfer log data to the log management infrastructure, if it has this policy	Every 3 to 24 hours	Every 15 to 60 minutes	At least every five minutes
How often log data needs to be analyzed locally (through automated or manual means)	Every 1 to 7 days	Every 12 to 24 hours	At least six times a day
Whether log file integrity checking needs to be performed for rotated logs	Optional	Yes	Yes
Whether rotated logs need to be encrypted	Optional	Optional	Yes
Whether log data transfers to the log management infrastructure need to be encrypted or performed on a separate logging network	Optional	Yes, if feasible	Yes

Security monitoring framework

Once the security detection solutions are in place, security monitoring management can be planned to perform security events correlation analysis. The purpose of the security monitoring framework is not to replace existing endpoint or network security solutions, it's to provide the security posture, the security trending, and the security events correlation of the whole environment. Some advanced security monitoring frameworks may even apply machine learning for the security events correlation to identify the abnormalities. Don't just assume that setting up a security monitoring management framework will do everything related to security monitoring. Building a complete security monitoring framework involves incorporating the following key components:

- **Log collector**: This is responsible for collecting and forwarding all the logs to the security monitoring team for further analysis. In the production environment, the concern of the log collection is the performance impact of the host and the number of logs needed to be forwarded. Syslog is the most common way to send the logs to security monitoring management.

- **Security monitoring (SIEM)**: This gives the security administrator a visualized security overview of the whole environment. An ideal SIEM can even do automated security correlation analysis based on predefined rules to identify abnormalities and potential risks.

- **Threat intelligence**: Threat intelligence is used to correlate the collected in-house security logs with external threat information, such as blacklisted IPs, Tor exit nodes, known malicious domains, user agents, file hashes, and the **indicators of compromise (IOC)**.

- **Threat intelligence feeds**: These form the threat database that includes known current threat information provided by cybersecurity communities, security vendors, or customer submissions. An organization may use the external threat intelligence feeds to correct internal security events in order to identify whether there are any suspicious activities, such as internal hosts connected to a known cybercrime IP.

In practice, it's suggested that you build the threat intelligence and security monitoring after the security scanning solutions, such as host IDS/IPS and network security, are deployed and optimized. Security monitoring and threat intelligence may help you to visualize and correlate the security events across hosts and network segments, but those security monitoring technologies still rely on the host and network IDS/IPS detection and actions.

The following diagram shows the typical scope of security monitoring:

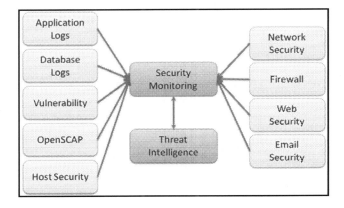

Source of information

The various log sources will help you to provide security events in different respects. Here are some of the general recommendations of the security monitoring focuses:

Source of information	Security monitoring focuses
Application logs	These are the operational and error logs generated by the application. If the application is a web service, the logs may be included in Apache or nginx logs: • Monitor the user activities, especially those activities that involve access to sensitive data • Monitor the major changes of user profiles, such as login IPs, abnormal endpoint devices, non-browser connection clients, and concurrent connections from different IP sources • Monitor the activities of administration and service accounts • Monitor login failures and web errors, such as 401, 404, and 501
Host security, database logs	These mainly rely on the host-based IDS/IPS detection logs, OS, and database logs: • Successful and failed authentication of users • Administrative access and changes • Unauthorized login failure • Major configuration file changes, such as mysql.cnf • Database accounts added • Massive data transmission to specific hosts

Vulnerability	The OpenVAS or NMAP scanning results of CVE vulnerabilities Insecure communication ports or protocols, such as Telnet, SSH v1, SSL, and FTP
OpenSCAP	The adoption of OpenSCAP scanning tools can help you to identify the insecure configuration of the applications, OS, database, and web services
Network security, firewalls	Rely on the network IDS/IPS detection logs, and also the logs from the load balancer, switches, and routers. For the updated firewall rules for IPtables, Snort, and Suricata, refer to the EmergingThreats website.
Web security	Rely on the web application firewall detection logs: • Client IP is from a blacklisted IP • User-agent associated with suspicious clients • Too many errors in the weblogs, such as 401, 404, and 500 • Refer to the OWASP ModSecurity CRS which includes the web application firewall ruleset.
Email security	Reply to the email security scanning and detection logs: • Unusual mail receivers or senders • Malicious attachment files • Malicious URL in the message body

Threat intelligence toolset

The purpose of threat intelligence is to help an organization to prepare for known and unknown threats. To address the unknown threats, the external threat feeds can be used to identify whether the existing environment may have similar threats, and also be used to optimize the security detection rules. For example, a known cybercrime IP or the Tor exit IP can be used to block the outbound connection IP lists in the firewall.

Integrate the internal threat log information, and the external threat feeds will help to combine the known and unknown threats and take proactive steps. The whole threat intelligence process normally includes the following key components:

- **The log collector**: This is used to collect the internal system, applications, and security logs
- **SIEM/visualization**: This is used to visualize the security posture in one dashboard

- **Threat intelligence platform**: This is used to correlate the internal and external threat information
- **Threat intelligence feeds**: This is the external threat database, such as the blacklist IP, malicious hash, suspicious domain, and so on

Here are some of the open source tools that will help you to build the whole threat intelligence solution:

Category	Open source security tools
Log collector/sensor	**Syslog-NG**: Syslog-ng is an enhanced log daemon which can handle not only standard syslog message but also unstructured data. **Rsyslog**: Rsyslog stands for a rocket-fast **system** for **log** processing. **FileBeat**: Filebeat provides a backpressure-sensitive protocol that controls the flow of sending data to Logstash or Elasticsearch **LogStash**: Logstash is a data processing pipeline that collects the data, transforms it, and then sends it to Elasticsearch.
SIEM/visualization	**Kibana**: Kibana provides the visualization of the Elasticsearch data. **ElasticSearch**: Search, index and analyze the data in real time. **AlienValut OSSIM**: It's an open source SIEM (Security Information and Event Management) solution provided by AlienValut. **Grafana**: It provides a quick solution for log query and visualization regardless of the data store. **GrayLog**: It's an open soure solution for enterprise log management.
Threat intelligence platforms	**MISP - open source threat intelligence platform**: The MISP is the threat sharing platform which can search and correlate IoC (Indicators of Compromise), threat intelligence feeds and vulnerability information.
Threat intelligence feeds	**External threat feeds for blacklisted IP list and firewall rules suggestions**: • `https://rules.emergingthreats.net/fwrules/` • `https://www.spamhaus.org/drop/` • `https://rules.emergingthreats.net/fwrules/emerging-Block-IPs.txt` • `https://check.torproject.org/exit-addresses` • `http://iplists.firehol.org/`

Security scanning toolset

Here are some open source tools that can perform security monitoring, scanning, and detection. Although your organization may have some commercial security solutions in place, these open source security detection rules can be a good reference when optimizing the existing security detection, such as the IDS/IPS, firewall, and web security.

You may find the following rules helpful to update or improve your existing firewall rules:

- **Wazuh host IDS rules**: Host-based intrusion defense rules.
- **OSSEC host IDS rules**: Host-based intrusion defense rules.
- **ModSecurity WAF rules**: Web Application Firewall rules.
- **Suricata network IDS/IPS rules**: Network-based intrusion prevention firewall rules.
- **Snort network IDS/IPS rules**: Network-based intrusion prevention firewall rules.

The table lists the security monitoring tools in each category.

Category	Open source security monitoring tools
All-in-one security scanning (host, network, visualization)	**Security Onion**: `https://github.com/Security-Onion-Solutions` This includes several open source security tools, such as Elasticsearch, Logstash, Kibana, Snort, Suricata, Bro, OSSEC, Sguil, Squert, and NetworkMiner.
All-in-one host-based IDS, secure configuration, and visualization	The Wazuh integrates the OSSEC (a host-based IDS), OpenSCAP (secure configuration scanner), and Elastic Stack (threat visualization).
Secure configuration	The OpenSCAP defines the secure configuration for OS, Web, database, and application.
Vulnerability	The OpenVAS and OWASP dependency are two of popular open source vulnerability scanners.
Antivirus	The CalmAV is the open source antivirus for Windows. The LMD (Linux Malware Detect) is the Linux version open source antivirus.
Host IDS/IPS	The OSSEC and Samhain are two of open source host IDS/IPS solutions to be considered.
Web application firewall (WAF)	The ModSecurity which is one of OWASP open source project is a light-weight web application firewall.

Network IDS/IPS	Snort and Suricata are two of the popular open source network IDS/IPS solutions. These two solutions also provide frequently updated rules.

Malware behavior matching – YARA

YARA (`https://virustotal.github.io/yara/`) is a pattern-matching Swiss army knife for malware detection. YARA rules consist of the descriptions of malware characteristics based on textual or binary patterns. YARA can be used to perform malware detection, and the detection signatures can also be easily defined. The YARA scanner/rules can be seen as an antivirus scanner and signatures.

For example, say that one host identifies suspicious webshell activities, but the antivirus software does not detect any suspicious activities. The security administrator can use the YARA detector with predefined YARA rules to scan all the files on the host or to scan the collected logs. Here is one example of a YARA rule to detect the web shell:

```
rule  php_webshell : webshell
{
    meta:
        description = "This is a sample of a PHP webshell detection rule."
    strings:
        $x1 = "eval(\\\x65\\x76\\x6C"
        $x2 = "Dim wshell, intReturn, strPresult"  fullword   ascii
    condition:
        filesize < 15KB and all of them
}
```

The YARA rules define two characteristics of a web shell. When the YARA rules are scanned with any binary files, and if the files match the conditions where the file size is less than 15 KB and the criteria stipulated under x1 and x2 are also met, then the YARA scanner will identify a match.

The YARA scanner can be executed as a standalone command-line tool or as a Python plugin. Refer to the YARA introductory guide *Compiling and Installing YARA* to get your YARA scanner on Windows, Linux, and macOS. You can find the guide at `https://yara.readthedocs.io/`.

The latest YARA rules—as well as the signatures and detection of malware, malicious emails, webshells, packers, documents, exploit kits, CVEs, and cryptography—can be found at the following links:

- `https://github.com/Yara-Rules/rules`
- `https://github.com/Neo23x0/signature-base`
- `https://github.com/InQuest/awesome-yara`

Summary

In this chapter, we discussed using the NIST 800-92 Guide to Computer Security Log Management to define the logging policy. We also explored the key components of a security monitoring framework, such as the log collector, SIEM, and threat intelligence. The security monitoring framework requires a source of information logs. We also discussed the source of information and stated what we are looking for in the logs. The application logs, host security logs, database logs, vulnerability scanning results, network security logs, and web and email security logs are typically the source logs for security monitoring.

We also introduced the toolset that you need to build your own in-house threat intelligence framework. We apply the threat intelligence framework to identify known and unknown threats. Some of the open source tools that are used to build a threat intelligence framework are also shared, such as the MISP—an open source threat intelligence platform. There are three key categories of tools—, the log collector, the SIEM/visualization, and the threat intelligence feeds. On the other hand, open source security scanning toolsets are also available, such as Security Onion, host IDS, vulnerability scanner, antivirus, WAF, network security, and the adoption of YARA.

In summary, security monitoring relies on the security scanning tools, the correlation of logs from various sources by SIEM, and also the threat intelligence feeds that are used to identify known and unknown threats.

Questions

1. Which of the following is not a part of the security monitoring framework?
    1. Log collector
    2. Security monitoring
    3. Threat intelligence
    4. Encryption

2. What kinds of logs will help security monitoring?
    1. Application logs
    2. Host security logs
    3. Vulnerability scanning results
    4. All of the above

3. Which of the following facts is not directly related to web security?
    1. Client IP is from blacklisted IP
    2. User-agent is associated with suspicious clients
    3. Unusual mail receivers or senders
    4. Too many errors in the weblogs, such as 401, 404, 500

4. Which one of the following tools is not a log collector/sensor?
    1. Syslog
    2. Kibana
    3. FileBeat
    4. LogStash

5. What is Security Onion used for?
    1. It's an all-in-one security scanning and monitoring tool (host, network, visualization)
    2. It's a vulnerability scanner
    3. It's an antivirus scanner
    4. It's a WAF (web application firewall)

6. What is YARA?
    1. It's an encryption module
    2. YARA is a pattern-matching Swiss army knife for malware detection
    3. It's a vulnerability scanner
    4. It's an automation framework

Further reading

- **SANS Continuous Monitoring—What It Is, Why It Is Needed, and How to Use It**: https://www.sans.org/reading-room/whitepapers/analyst/continuous-monitoring-is-needed-35030
- **PCI DSS Part 11 - Regularly test security systems and processes**: https://www.pcisecuritystandards.org/document_library?category=pcidssdocument=pci_dss
- **Guide to Computer Security Log Management (SP 800-92)**: https://ws680.nist.gov/publication/get_pdf.cfm?pub_id=50881
- **NIST 800-137 Information Security Continuous Monitoring**: https://nvlpubs.nist.gov/nistpubs/legacy/sp/nistspecialpublication800-137.pdf
- **Loki - Simple IOC and Incident Response Scanner**: https://github.com/Neo23x0/Loki
- **Malware Indicators**: https://github.com/citizenlab/malware-indicators
- **OSINT Threat Feeds**: https://www.circl.lu/doc/misp/feed-osint/
- **SANS How to Use Threat Intelligence effectively**: https://www.sans.org/reading-room/whitepapers/analyst/threat-intelligence-is-effectively-37282
- **NIST 800-150 Guide to Cyber Threat Information Sharing**: https://nvlpubs.nist.gov/nistpubs/specialpublications/nist.sp.800-150.pdf

16
Security Assessment for New Releases

Now that we have finished looking at security monitoring, we are going to learn about security assessment for new releases in this chapter. Cloud services may have frequent releases and updates. It's a challenge for the development, operations, and security teams to release their work within a short time frame and to finish the minimum required security testing before releases. In this chapter, we will look at the security review policies and the suggested checklist and testing tools for every release. For testing integration, the BDD security framework and other integrated security testing framework will also be introduced in this chapter.

These are the main topics that will be covered in this chapter:

- Security review policies
- Security checklist and tools
- BDD security framework
- Consolidated testing results

Security review policies for releases

An organization should define its own security assessment policies for every release. For a major or new application release, there is no doubt that a full security assessment is needed. However, should we do the same for a patch release, especially when it's a time-sensitive and business-critical release? Having a clear understanding of the application release scope and objective will help the security team to plan the necessary security assessment scope.

The following table shows an example of the relationship between the application releases and the security assessment scope:

Application release objective	Security assessment scope
New or major application release	Full assessment
Third-party component update	Assessment based on the third party and the integration interfaces
Patch releases	Targeted assessment based on patch scope
Emergency releases	The security testing scope is limited to ensure that there are no major security issues

When a team receives more projects with more frequent releases, it may be unrealistic for one security team to handle all of the security assessment of all of the projects. Therefore, it's recommended that you define what security assessment should be done by the product development team and what will be done by the security team. Typically, the security team will help to prepare the security checklist, toolkits, and guidelines that will be used by the product team to do the self-assessment. Please also refer to the next section for a more complete list of security checklists and tools. The following table shows an example of the security assessment activities' execution by the development, security, and DevOps teams:

Security review stage	Example key security practices	Executed by
Self-assessment	• Review the OWASP ASVS checklist • Review the OWASP Top 10 checklist • Execute the defined automated security tools, such as ZAP, NMAP, and SQLmap • Fix major security issues	Product development team
Pre-release	• Submit the self-assessment testing results and the prerelease package to the security team • The security team focuses on the assessment with the highest risk modules • The security team performs the acceptance security testing, which includes not only the packages, but also the secure configurations of the whole system, such as Linux, MySQL, and NginX • Manual and automated application and network security testing will be performed by the security review team, and you will receive your review results (see the following results section for more details)	Security team

| Production | Perform regular security scans for the following:
• Known CVEs of software components
• Secure configurations
• Network communications, such as ports and insecure protocols
• OWASP Top 10 security issues | Operation and security team |

Security checklist and tools

The scope of the security checklist we will discuss here is mainly for pre-production deployment releases. The DevOps and the security team do the final testing before the deployment to production. In the best-case scenarios, those defined security checklists can be done automatically. This will help the DevOps team perform regular security checks, even after the deployment to production. Refer to the *Further reading* section for the reference sources of every tool. The following table shows the feature being checked, the security testing approaches, and the suggested security testing tools:

Security category	Security testing approaches	Suggested security testing tools
Hidden communication ports or channels	• Ensure that there are no hidden communication ports or backdoors • Ensure that there are no hidden hardcoded secrets, passwords, or hard keys • Check for unnecessary system maintenance tools • Perform a source code review for networking communication, such as Java-related API `connect()`, `getPort()`, `getLocalPort()`, `Socket()`, `bind()`, `accept()`, `ServerSocket()` • Listening to `0.0.0.0` is forbidden	NMAP Graudit TruffleHog Snallygaster Hping masscan
Privacy information	• Search for the plaintext password and key in the source code • Search for the personal information for the GDPR compliance • The personal information can be modified and removed by the end user • The personal information can be removed within a defined period	TruffleHog Blueflower YARA PrivacyScore Snallygaster
Secure communication	• SSH v2 instead of Telnet • SFTP instead of FTP • TLS 1.2 instead of SSL TLS 1.1	NMAP WireShark SSLyze SSL/TLS tester

Third-party components	• CVE check • Known vulnerabilities check • Hidden malicious code or secrets	OWASP Dependency check LMD (Linux Malware Detection) OpenVAS NMAP CVEChecker
Cryptography	• Ensure that there is no weak encryption algorithm • Ensure that there are no secret files on the public web interfaces	Graudit SSLyze Snallygaster
Audit logging	**Ensure that the operation and security teams can log the following scenarios:** • Non-query operations, including success and failure actions • Non-query scheduled tasks • API access or tool connections that execute administration tasks	GREP
DoS attacks	**The testing of the DoS is to ensure if the application failure is as expected. The DoS scenario may cover the following:** • TCP Sync flooding • HTTP Slow • HTTP Post Flooding • NTP DoS • SSL DoS	Pwnloris Slowloris Synflood Thc-sll-DoS Wreckuests ntpDoS
Web security	**To develop a policy concerning web security, you can refer to the OWASP Testing Guide and OWASP Top 10:** • Injection • Authentication • Data exposure • XXE • Broken access control • Security misconfiguration • XSS • Insecure deserialization • Known vulnerabilities • Insufficient logging and monitoring	Refer to OWASP Testing Guide v4 OWASP ZAP BurpSuite Arachni Scanner SQLMap
Secure configuration	**Ensure that the configurations of applications, web services, databases, and the OS are secure. The secure configurations are based on the CIS security benchmark and OpenSCAP.**	OpenSCAP Docker Bench Security Clair

Fuzz testing	The purpose of fuzz testing is to generate dynamic testing data as input to check whether the application will fail unexpectedly.	API Fuzzer Radamsa American Fuzzy lop FuzzDB Wfuzz
Mobile app security	Refer to the OWASP Mobile App Security Testing Guide for a good set of guidelines to apply to your security policy.	Mobile Security Framework
Top common issue	Draw up a list of the most common security issues based on projected historical data.	CWE/SANS Top 25 Most Dangerous Software Errors
Security compliance	Security compliance that is based on business needs may also be included, such as GDPR or PCI DSS.	Refer to the specific security compliance requirements

BDD security framework

As there are various kinds of security testing tools, it may be time-consuming to analyze the testing results generated by every testing tool. When simply reading the security testing results, it may be hard to tell what security testing cases are executed. For example, the security testing reports generated by NMAP can be understood by the security testing team, but may not be easily understood by the DevOps team. Those are the issues that the BDD security framework can solve. The purpose of the adoption of the BDD security framework is to integrate all security testing tools and to define all the security testing cases by using human-readable user-story statements.

To build the whole automation framework, it's suggested that you have the security testing tools in place first, such as NMAP, SSLyze, SQLmap, ZAP, and Arachni. Don't try to build the BDD security automation framework when those security tools and practices are not ready.

After all, the BDD security framework is used to consolidate all the security tools and results in defined user stories, and requires each security testing tool to perform the execution:

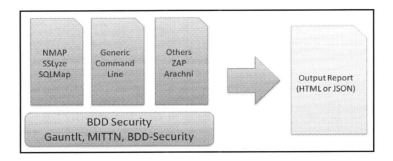

The following table is a comparison of the open source BDD security tool with other options. These frameworks are flexible enough to perform security tool integration and to provide consolidated testing results. If you are looking for a BDD framework that can be executed on both Windows and Linux, and that can be integrated with other tools, then GAUNTLT can be considered. GAUNTLT provides the *generic command-line* adapters, which allow you to execute any command-line tool:

	MITTN	**GAUNTLT**	**BDD Security**
Programming language	Python	Ruby	Java
BDD framework	Behave	Cucumber	Cucumber Selenium
Windows/Unix	Unix	Both	Both
Default plugins	BurpSuite SSLyze Radamsa	NMap SSLyze SQLMap Garmr Generic command line	ZAP SSLyze Nessus

Consolidated testing results

If your security team has performed the security testing using various kinds of security tools, one of the challenges is the consolidation of all the output. The BDD framework that we looked at previously is one of the solutions. However, if you don't build another BDD framework and would just like to consolidate all the testing outputs, then OWASP DefectDojo may be the solution for you (see `https://github.com/DefectDojo/django-DefectDojo` for more information).

The key advantage of using DefectDojo to consolidate all the security testing tool outputs is the ability to present the results in one dashboard alongside the metrics, as shown in the following screenshot:

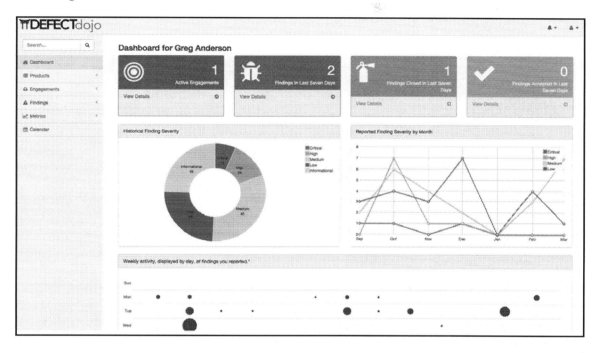

Source: `https://github.com/DefectDojo/django-DefectDojo`

The following table shows the open source security tool output formats that DefectDojo can import:

Open source security tools	Output format
Arachni Scanner: `http://www.arachni-scanner.com/`	JSON
Bandit: `https://github.com/PyCQA/bandit`	JSON
Burp: `https://portswigger.net/burp`	XML
Dependency Check: `https://www.owasp.org/index.php/OWASP_Dependency_Check`	XML
Nikto: `https://github.com/sullo/nikto`	XML
NMAP: `https://nmap.org/`	XML
OpenVAS: `http://www.openvas.org/`	CSV
Retire.JS: `https://retirejs.github.io/retire.js/`	JSON

ssllabs-scan: `https://github.com/ssllabs/ssllabs-scan`	JSON
Trufflehog: `https://github.com/dxa4481/truffleHog`	JSON
Visual Code Grepper (VCG): `https://github.com/nccgroup/VCG`	CSV or XML
ZAP: `https://www.owasp.org/index.php/OWASP_Zed_Attack_Proxy_Project`	XML
Generic Findings Import	CSV

Summary

In this chapter, we looked at how to establish a security review policy for every release. We learned that it was recommended that the security assessment scope is based on the application release objective. For example, a new and major application release should have a full security assessment. A third-party component update release may focus on the integration interfaces instead of a full-scope assessment. In addition, the security review can be done in different stages, such as the self-assessment by the product development team, the prerelease assessment by the security team, and the product security assessment by the operations team.

The security checklist and the related testing tools for the pre-production deployment release were also discussed. The key area of the security checklist includes hidden communication interfaces, privacy information, secure communication, third-party components, cryptography, audit logging, DoS attacks, web security, configuration, fuzz testing, and lists of recent top issues.

To integrate all the testing cases with different tools, the use of a BDD security framework was recommended. There are three open source BDD security frameworks—MITTN, GAUNTLT, and BDD-Security. If a BDD security framework is not used, we suggested using OWASP DefectDojo, which can help to consolidate all the various kinds of security testing tool outputs to present the results in one dashboard.

In summary, the process (security release policies, checklists, and testing strategies), the technologies (security testing tools and frameworks), and the teams' (development, operation, and security team) involvement are the keys to ensuring the security of every release.

Questions

1. What security assessment may apply to a new or major application release?
   1. Full assessment
   2. Assessment based on the patch scope
   3. Assessment based on the third party and the integration interfaces
   4. The security testing scope is limited to ensure no major security issues

2. Which of the following is not one of the self-assessment activities that should be done by the product development team?
   1. Review the OWASP ASVS checklist
   2. Security awareness training program
   3. Execute defined automated security tools, such as ZAP, NMAP, and SQLmap
   4. Fix major security issues

3. Which of the following is not the security testing approach for checking hidden communication interfaces?
   1. Listening to 0.0.0.0 is forbidden
   2. Searching for hidden hard-coded secrets, password, or hard key
   3. Searching for personal information
   4. Unnecessary system maintenance tools

4. Which of the following communication protocols is insecure?
   1. SSH v2
   2. SFTP
   3. TLS 1.2
   4. Telnet

5. Which one of the following tests is not for DoS?
   1. TCP sync flooding
   2. HTTP slow
   3. HTTP post flooding
   4. CVE checking

Further reading

- **SAS Cloud Security Framework Audit Methods**: `https://www.sans.org/reading-room/whitepapers/cloud/cloud-security-framework-audit-methods-36922`
- **Securing Web Application Technologies Checklist**: `https://software-security.sans.org/resources/swat`
- **Application Server Security Requirements Guide**: `https://www.stigviewer.com/stig/application_server_security_requirements_guide/2018-01-08/`
- **Mozilla Checklist for Releases**: `https://wiki.mozilla.org/Releases/Checklist`
- **SANS Security Policies**: `https://www.sans.org/security-resources/policies/#template`
- **CWE/SANS Top 25 Most Dangerous Software Errors**: `http://cwe.mitre.org/top25/`

17
Threat Inspection and Intelligence

In the previous chapter, we discussed the security assessment for every release. In this chapter, we will cover threat inspection and intelligence. This chapter focuses on how to identify and prevent known and unknown security threats, such as backdoors and injection attacks, using various kinds of log correlation. We will introduce the logs that are needed, how those logs are connected, and the potential symptoms of attacks. Some open source threat detection will be introduced. Finally, we will introduce how to build your own in-house threat intelligence system.

We will cover the following topics in this chapter:

- Unknown threat detection
- Indicators of compromises
- Security analysis using big data frameworks

Unknown threat detection

The threat landscape is in a constant state of flux, with newly emerging, sophisticated technologies. The investment associated with security protection to handle the dynamic threat landscape is also becoming huge. Security protection is shifting from known threat detection to the early prevention of unknown threats. Big data frameworks, machine learning, and threat intelligence are the technologies that help to achieve the detection of unknown threats. Correlation analysis of abnormal events is key to detecting potential unknown threats.

The following diagram shows the concept of correlation or machine learning with different data sources:

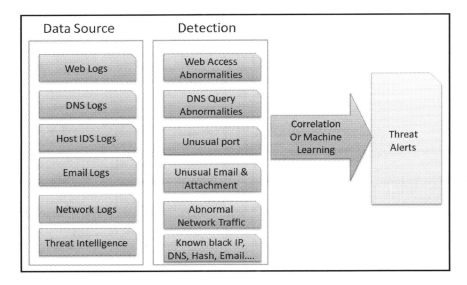

The objective of network traffic analysis is to identify abnormal internal host traffic communications. The challenge posed by network traffic analysis is that the amount of data can be overwhelming. In addition, in order to be able to identify abnormalities, network administrators will need to perform network traffic profiling, such as defining a network communication whitelist or network traffic baseline. Although big data and machine learning may help in terms of analysis, it still requires IT network administrators to define the normal and abnormal network traffic categorization rules.

The following are some typical abnormal network traffic examples:

Abnormal network traffic	Potential threats
Port/host scan	The port or host scan behaviors mean one of the hosts may have been infected by a malware program, and the malware program is looking for vulnerabilities, other services, or hosts on the network.
A high number of outbound DNS requests from the same host	This is a symptom of **Command and Control (C&C)** malware, establishing communication between the infected host and the C&C server using the DNS protocol.
A high number of outbound HTTP requests from the same host	This is a symptom of C&C, establishing communication between the infected host and the C&C server using the HTTP protocol.

Periodical outbound traffic with same-sized requests or during the same period of time every day	This is a symptom of C&C malware, establishing communication between the infected host and the C&C server.
Outbound traffic to an external web or DNS listed as a known threat by threat intelligence feeds	The user may be tricked through social engineering to connect to an external known threat web or the C&C connection is successfully established.

To visualize the network threat status, there are two recommended open source tools: Malcom and Maltrail (Malicious Traffic detection system). Malcom can present a host communication relationship diagram. It helps us to understand whether there are any internal hosts connected to an external suspicious C&C server or known bad sites.

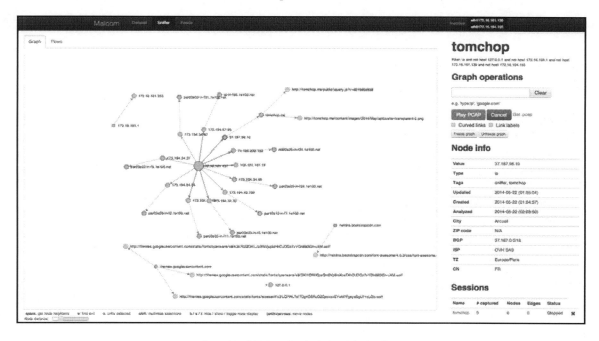

Source: https://github.com/tomchop/malcom#what-is-malcom

The other one is the Malicious traffic detection system (Maltrail), which correlates external threat intelligence feeds to identify a known malicious domain name, a suspicious URL, IP or the user-agent header:

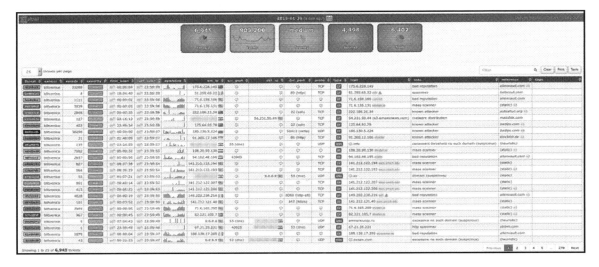

Source: https://github.com/stamparm/maltrail

Indicators of compromises

An analysis of hosts for suspicious behaviors also poses a significant challenge due to the availability of logs. For example, dynamic runtime information may not be logged in files and the original process used to drop a suspicious file may not be recorded. Therefore, it is always recommended to install a host IDS/IPS such as OSSEC (Open Source HIDS SEcurity) or host antivirus software as the first line of defense against malware. Once the host IDS/IPS or antivirus software is in place, threat intelligence and big data analysis are supplementary, helping us to understand the overall host's security posture and any known **Indicators of Compromises (IoCs)** in existing host environments.

Based on the level of severity, the following are key behaviors that may indicate a compromised host:

Abnormal host behaviors	Potential threats
Multiple compromised hosts' data communication to external hosts	The compromised hosts are sending data to external C&C servers.
The host connects to an external known APT IP address or URL and/or downloads a known malicious file	The host shows an indication of compromise from APT or a malware attack.
Several unsuccessful login attempts	One of the internal compromised hosts is trying to log in in order to access critical information.
An email message that includes a dangerous URL or malicious file	Attackers may use social engineering to send emails for target attacks. Include the email senders in the watch list.
Rare and unusual filenames in process/service/program start	The malware installs itself to start up so as to continue to act even after rebooting. One of the common ways in which malware can achieve persistence is as follows: In the case of Windows, using **AutoRuns** to check whether the host is compromised with suspicious malware is recommended. `https://docs.microsoft.com/en-us/sysinternals/downloads/autoruns`
Unusual event and audit logs alert	The following system event or audit logs may need further analysis: • Account lockouts • Users added to the privileged group • A failed user account login • Application error(s) • Windows error reporting • BSOD • The event log was cleared • The audit log was cleared • A firewall rule change

An analysis of web access is also very critical, since the majority of internet connections are based on the HTTP protocol. There are two major scenarios regarding web access. One is the internal hosts that connect to external websites, and the other is the hosted web services connected by internal or external hosts. The following table lists some of the common techniques and tools for web access analysis:

Web access analysis	Detection techniques
External source client IP	The source of IP address analysis can help to identify the following: • A known bad IP or TOR exit node • Abnormal geolocation changes • Concurrent connections from different geolocations The MaxMind GeoIP2 database can be used to translate the IP address to a geolocation: `https://dev.maxmind.com/geoip/geoip2/geolite2/#Downloads`
Client fingerprint (OS, browser, user agent, devices, and so on)	The client fingerprint can be used to identify whether there are any unusual client or non-browser connections. The open source ClientJS is a pure JavaScript that can be used to collect client fingerprint information. The JA3 provided by Salesforce uses SSL/TLS connection profiling to identify malicious clients. **ClientJS**: `https://clientjs.org/` **JA3**: `https://github.com/salesforce/ja3`
Web site reputation	When there is an outbound connection to an external website, we may check the threat reputation of that target website. This can be done by means of the web application firewall, or web gateway security solutions. `https://www.virustotal.com/`
Random Domain Name by **Domain Generation Algorithms (DGAs)**	The domain name of the C&C server can be generated by DGAs. The key characteristics of the DGA domain are high entropy, high consonant count, and long length of a domain name. Based on these indicators, we may analyze whether the domain name is generated by DGAs and could be a potential C&C server. **DGA Detector**: `https://github.com/exp0se/dga_detector/` In addition, in order to reduce false positives, we may also use Alexa's top one million sites as a website whitelist. Refer to `https://s3.amazonaws.com/alexa-static/top-1m.csv.zip`.
Suspicious file downloads	Cuckoo sandbox suspicious file analysis: `https://cuckoosandbox.org/`

	In the case of DNS query analysis, the following are the key indicators of compromises:
DNS query	• DNS query to unauthorized DNS servers. • Unmatched DNS replies can be an indicator of DNS spoofing. • Clients connect to multiple DNS servers. • A long DNS query, such as one in excess of 150 characters, which is an indicator of DNS tunneling. • A domain name with high entropy. This is an indicator of DNS tunneling or a C&C server.

Security analysis using big data frameworks

After discussing some of the common techniques for detecting unknown potential threats, we are going to introduce some open source frameworks to do security analysis with threat intelligence and big data technologies. You may consider applying these open source solutions as a basis if you are planning to build a security log analysis framework that can do the following:

- Machine learning and correlation with the IoCs
- Analysis involving external threat intelligence feeds
- Data enrichment such as GeoIP information
- Visualization and querying of the relationships of IoCs

Project	Key features
TheHive project	TheHive provides threat incident response case management that allows security analysts to flag IOCs. The Cortex can perform analysis with threat intelligence services such as VirtusTotal, MaxMind, and DomainTools. There are over 80 threat intelligence services supported. The Hippocampe provides a query interface through a REST API or a Web UI: `https://thehive-project.org/`
MISP	This is mainly a threat intelligence platform to share IoCs and indicators of malware. The correlation engine helps to identify the relationships between attributes and indicators of malware: `https://www.misp-project.org/` The MISP provides over 40 threat intelligence feeds. Refer to `https://www.misp-project.org/feeds/`.

Apache Metron	Apache Metron is a SIEM (threat intelligence, security data parsers, alerts, and a dashboard) and also a security analysis (anomaly detection and machine learning) framework based on Hadoop's big data framework: `https://metron.apache.org/`. Typical technology components used to build a big data framework include the following: • Apache Flume • Apache Kafka • Apache Storm or Spark • Apache Hadoop • Apache Hive • Apache Hbase • Elasticsearch • MySQL

These open source solutions can work together with one another. For example, TheHive can be used as a security operation center to manage security incident cases with IoC information, and integrate TheHive with MISP to query external threat intelligence feeds. Moreover, Metron can perform log data enrichment and analysis with machine learning to identify abnormalities.

In addition, there are also some open source analysis frameworks based on the **Elasticsearch, Logstash, Kibana (ELK)**. Refer to the following list:

- **Response Operation Collection Kit (ROCK) NSM**: `http://rocknsm.io/`
- **A Hunting Elasticsearch, Logstash, Kibana (ELK) with advanced analytical capabilities**: `https://github.com/Cyb3rWard0g/HELK`
- **Cyber Analytics Platform and Examination System (CAPES)**: `http://capesstack.io/`

TheHive

TheHive is a security incident response platform that integrates **Malware Information Sharing Platform (MISP)**. The Cortex can help to analyze observables using external threat analysis services such as VirusTotal, DomainTools, and MaxMind. The Hippocampe provides the REST API or Web UI to enable users to carry out analysis reports and perform queries.

The following diagram shows the collaboration between TheHive, Cortex, SIEM, and also MISP:

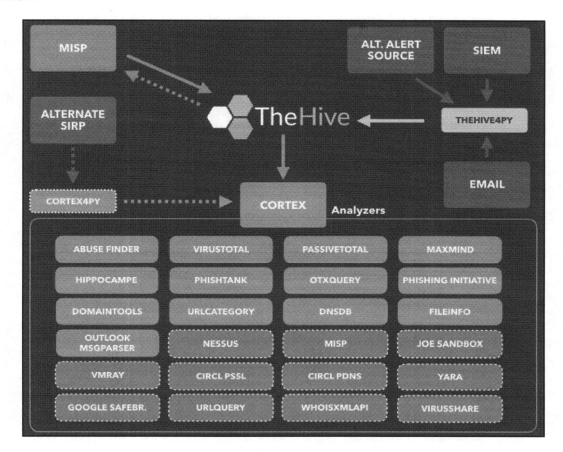

MISP – an Open Source Threat Intelligence Platform

MISP is a Threat Intelligence Platform that can carry out correlations with threat attributes, IOCs, and indicators. MISP can also generate Snort/Suricata IDS rules, STIX, and OpenIOC detection rules based on the IOCs observed.

The following diagram refers to MISP (Malware Information Sharing Platform):

The following diagram shows one of the identified threat and threat relationship diagram in the MISP.

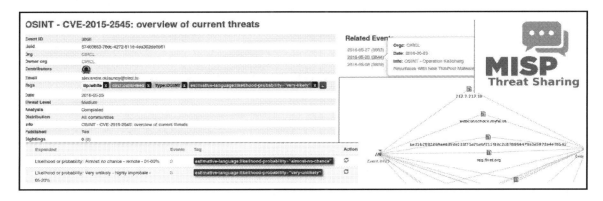

Source: http://www.misp-project.org/features.html

In addition to MISP, you may also refer to the open source **Your Everyday Threat Intelligence (YETI)** platform solution, which also provides a similar threat intelligence platform. Refer to `https://yeti-platform.github.io/`.

Apache Metron

Apache Metron is a cybersecurity application framework that can perform big data analysis to identify anomalies. The framework provides the following key characteristics:

- The processing, enrichment, and labeling of the data source for security analysis, search, and query.
- Anomaly detection using machine learning algorithms
- SIEM-like capabilities (alerting, threat intelligence framework, agents to ingest data sources)
- A pluggable framework for various kinds of data sources and that can add parsers for new data sources

Please refer to the following diagram of Apache Metron:

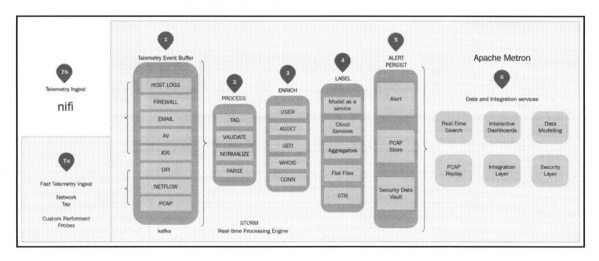

Summary

In this chapter, we discussed unknown threat detection techniques involving identifying abnormalities in network traffic and host behaviors. To identify and visualize potential threats in network traffic, we introduced two open source tools—Malcom and Maltrail. Malcom helps connection relationship diagram and also potential C&C server connections.

As regards the host behaviors, we explained IOCs and discussed some abnormal host behaviors for potential threats. Different aspects of web access log analysis were also discussed, including an external source of client IP, client fingerprints, website reputation, DGAs, and DNS query.

We also suggested some open source frameworks for an organization that would like to build an in-house security analysis big data framework. TheHive and MISP can collaborate in connection with threat analysis. Apache Metron provides security analysis based on a Hadoop big data framework.

In the next chapter, we will discuss business fraud and service abuses.

Questions

1. What is the purpose of detecting a high number of outbound DNS requests from the same host?
   1. It's an indicator of ransomware
   2. It is a port scan behavior
   3. It's an indicator of a C&C connection
   4. It's a normal behavior
2. What does IOC stand for?
   1. Indicator of Compromise
   2. Information of Compromise
   3. Inspection of Computer
   4. Injection of Computer
3. Which of the following can be an indicator of potential attacks in event logs?
   1. BSOD
   2. An event log was cleared
   3. A failed user account login
   4. All of the above

4. For the purpose of web log analysis, why do we analyze the external source client IP?
   1. To identify whether it's a known bad IP or TOR exit node
   2. To identify whether there are any abnormal geolocation changes within a short space of time
   3. To identify any concurrent connection from different geolocations
   4. All of the above

5. What does DGA stand for ?
   1. Domain Generation Algorithms
   2. Data Generation Algorithms
   3. Denormalization Generation Algorithms
   4. Duplication Generation Algorithms

6. Why are we able to detect the domain name generated by DGAs?
   1. It's a downloader malware
   2. It's an indicator of a C&C server
   3. It's an indicator of ransomware
   4. It's an indicator of a brute force attack

Further reading

- **Windows security log events**: https://www.ultimatewindowssecurity.com/securitylog/encyclopedia/default.aspx
- **SANS detecting DNS tunneling**: https://www.sans.org/readning-room/whitepapers/dns/detecting-dns-tunneling-34152
- **SANS – A practical big data kill chain framework**: https://www.sans.org/reading-room/whitepapers/warfare/practical-big-data-kill-chain-framework-35487
- **Your everyday threat intelligence**: https://yeti-platform.github.io/
- **Malware Information Sharing Platform (MISP)**: https://www.circl.lu/doc/misp/
- **MISP GDPR compliance**: http://www.misp-project.org/compliance/gdpr/information_sharing_and_cooperation_gdpr.html
- **Apache Metron architecture**: https://cwiki.apache.org/confluence/display/METRON/Metron+Architecture

- **Cyber threat intelligence and information sharing**: `https://www.nist.gov/publications/cyber-threat-intelligence-and-information-sharing`
- **Guide to cyber threat information sharing**: `https://nvlpubs.nist.gov/nistpubs/specialpublications/nist.sp.800-150.pdf`
- **Threat intelligence: What it is, and how to use it effectively**: `https://www.sans.org/reading-room/whitepapers/analyst/threat-intelligence-is-effectively-37282`
- **NIST SP 800-92 A guide to computer security log management**: `https://csrc.nist.gov/publications/detail/sp/800-92/final`
- **SANS 2018 cyber threat intelligence survey**: `https://www.sans.org/reading-room/whitepapers/threats/cti-security-operations-2018-cyber-threat-intelligence-survey-38285`
- **ROCK (Response Operation Collection Kit) NSM**: `http://rocknsm.io/`
- **A Hunting Elasticsearch, Logstash, Kibana (ELK) with advanced analytical capabilities**: `https://github.com/Cyb3rWard0g/HELK`
- **Cyber Analytics Platform and Examination System (CAPES)**: `http://capesstack.io/`

18
Business Fraud and Service Abuses

The previous chapter discussed threat inspection and intelligence. In this chapter, we will look into business fraud and service abuses. Cloud services introduce new types of security risks, such as transaction fraud, account abuses, and promotion code abuses. This online fraud and abuse may result in financial losses or gains, depending on which side of the fence you sit.

Therefore, the objective of this chapter is to provide guidelines and rules on how to detect these kinds of behaviors. We will also discuss typical technical frameworks and technical approaches needed to build a service abuse prevention or online fraud detection system.

In this chapter, we will cover the following topics:

- Business fraud and abuse scenarios
- Business risk detection framework
- PCI DSS compliance

Business fraud and abuses

We have discussed lots of security technologies in terms of defense or the detection of malicious activity. On the other hand, the online black market is also looking for different opportunities in order to make money or benefit from unsuspecting users and e-commerce web services. These kinds of cyber criminal activities are exploiting business transaction loopholes in order to make financial gains.

Here are some of the common activities associated with the online black market:

Business scenario	Cyber criminal activities
For the promotion of new user registration, a e-commerce site may give a $10 coupon or certain discounts	**Account cheating**: • Cyber criminals may register massive accounts to obtain coupons and discounts. They then resell these coupons.
A shopping site may sell a limited number of special edition goods	**Scalper**: • Cyber criminals may register massive accounts to purchase the goods and resell them at higher prices
Shopping search query results are sorted by the ratings and sales volume of the online seller	**Non-genuine orders**: • Online sellers may make a deal with cyber criminals to manipulate massive non-genuine orders and ratings in order to be listed in the top rankings of the query results
A shopping site account is normally registered with an email, phone number, and ID	**Account takeover**: • A cyber criminal poses as a genuine user, and gains control of an account to make unauthorized transactions • In addition, cyber criminals may carry out brute-force attacks on the accounts and reregister using a different email address or phone number to gain financial benefits

The following diagram gives an overview of the business fraud risk in terms of accounts, content, payments, and promotion:

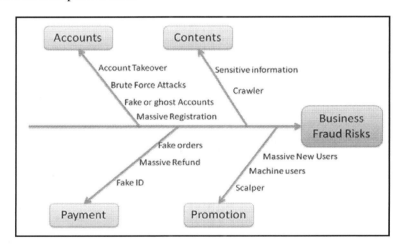

You may wonder whether the selling of limited edition goods within a limited timeframe can be a good thing. After all, it attracts the attention of the public and there is nothing illegal in it. However, **scalper** behavior also applies to online business transactions. Online **scalper** behavior may occupy a gray area in the eyes of the law, but it does break the original intention of the business. Eventually, all online business will be affected as it becomes prevalent on a larger scale.

Business risk detection framework

The key objective of building a business risk framework is to identify whether it's an authentic transaction, which means that normal users or sellers follow normal business rules in order to effect business transactions on the e-commerce platform. On the other hand, a business risk framework is able to detect whether the transactions, accounts, or sellers are suspicious and controlled by cyber criminals. The key relationship between cyber criminals and a shopping site are shown in the following diagram:

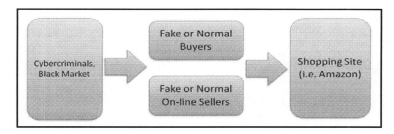

A business fraud and abuse detection framework requires tight integration with online businesses; in particular, security policies must understand the rules of business logistics. In addition, the framework must be able to retrieve the key business activity logs, including login, registration, user behavior, password reset, payment, and purchase operations.

Not every online business function requires real-time fraud detection. User account registration, promotions, orders, and payment and business transactions are the key functions that require risk management. When these online services receive requests from clients, business services will query the real-time fraud detection service to decide whether the transaction should proceed or not. The real-time fraud detection service decides the business risks based on predefined security rules, offline profiling analysis, and other sources of supporting information.

The key objective of the offline analysis is to build a user behavior profile that can help to identify whether it's the normal user or a user controlled by cyber criminals. Several pieces of information are required to be able to identify whether the client is a cyber criminal.

Let's consider a scenario. There is one user logging in via the **Jimmy** account. How can we identify whether this person is actually Jimmy, or whether it's someone else who has stolen Jimmy's account?

To answer this question, we will look into the IP, account, device, and usage profiling. The query results of the profiling are shown in the following table.

Case 1 represents normal user behavior, since it explains that Jimmy used one device to do 20 logins within the same city.

However, case 2 definitely requires further investigation as it is highly suspected that cyber criminals are behind it. This shows that Jimmy was doing 20 logins with 10 different devices in 10 different cities:

Cases	Account	Number of login operations	Device profiling	GeoIP
1	Jimmy	20	1	Same city
2	Jimmy	10	10	10 different cities

A typical business fraud detection framework is shown in the following diagram:

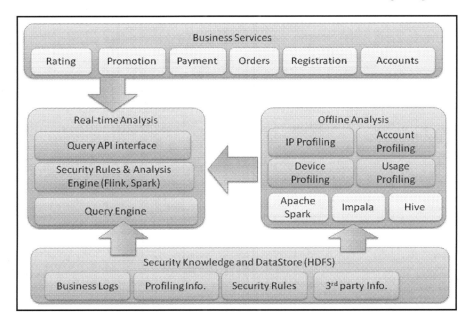

Profiling	Description
IP profiling	IP profiling is designed to identify the IP behaviors of the account and the device. IP profiling involves the following attributes: • Geolocation • VPN, Proxy, Gateway, or TOR (these IPs will require the user to undertake further verification) • A known black IP address
Device fingerprints	A device fingerprint is the information collected in relation to a remote client device or browser for the purpose of identification. We use device fingerprints to establish whether the remotely connected device is the one normally used by the user/account. For example, for the same account, logging into the e-commerce service with a different mobile phone every day is definitely a sign of abnormality. Here are some of the common device fingerprints: • Machine type, CPU, virtualization • OS version, software plugin, fonts • A concurrent connection for the same device fingerprints • Geolocation for the same devices on the same day • The same device fingerprints used by a number of different accounts • Multiple different device fingerprints used by the same user account
Machine versus human behaviors	The objective of the behavior analysis is to identify whether the source of the request is manipulated by a malicious program or a real human: • Keyboard usage • Mouse movements • User agent; HTTPS fingerprints
Account profiling	The following attributes are related to the account. If one of the attributes, such as an email address, is identified as suspicious, it is very likely that all other accounts related to this email will be be suspicious. Therefore, we will build a suspicious watch list of the following information: • Email address • Shipping address • Bank account number • Telephone number • Social networking friends • Payment
Usage profiling	Based on historical usage, we can also identify whether it's a normal user or just a one-time user attempting to abuse the services or business promotion code: • Page-visiting history • Historical communication with sellers • Purchase history and habits

The purpose of doing profiling is to build a basis of normal and common behavior according to historical usage or statistics. The offline analysis of profiling can be IP profiling, device fingerprints, machine behaviors, accounts, and usage. Using this user profiling data, we will be able to tell whether a user has been hacked or can potentially be manipulated by cyber criminals.

In addition, we can also analyze the page-visiting behaviors to identify whether it's a machine buyer or real human buyer. Just be aware that cyber criminals are also trying to make machine behaviors closer to human behaviors to avoid those detection rules. These behaviors may be an indicator reference but they can not be the only evidence to decide whether it's a machine buyer. Following are some key differences between normal users and machine users:

Normal human buyer	Machine buyer
Finds the products by keyword search	No search behavior Locates the specific product page directly Skips the landing page
Looks into similar products to do some sort of comparison	Just focuses on the specific product under promotion
There may be in excess of 20 seconds' browsing time per product	Less than three seconds
The real user may have a communication history with the seller	The machine buyer account has no communication history
The real user may have rating feedback history for products purchased previously	No rating feedback history

At the time of writing (2018), there is still no proper open source framework for fraud risk detection as a whole, although there are modules for performing device fingerprints and threat intelligence services to identify the blacklist IP. Establishing an entire fraud risk management framework may be a challenge for a small or medium-sized business.

Following are some of the mitigation and security approaches to consider:

Fraud mitigation	Description
PCI compliance	The minimum requirement for an online retailer is to be PCI-compliant. Ensure that the related third party vendor and payment gateway are PCI-compliant.
Define threshold	This is considered to be the easiest implementation in terms of mitigating the fraud risks. Some of the common thresholds to limit usage may include the following: • Account lockout for a certain period after a number of login failures • Limiting the number of coupe usage per device/account • Limiting the number of transactions per device/account/day A proper definition of the threshold will require certain statistics from the historical data.
Two factor re-authentication	Ask the user to perform re-authentication for key actions such as payment.
CAPTCHA	The adoption of CAPTCHA is used to differentiate humans from robotic software programs.
Phone authentication	Send an authentication code to the phone number for the purchase action. This is also the first step in two-factor authentication since it proves that the user has the phone.
GeoIP or IP reputation	Look for the geolocation of the client source IP address, since the IP address may be difficult to fake. Check the following: • Whether the IP address is in the blacklist • Whether the GeoIP appears in abnormal locations across the globe

PCI DSS compliance

The PCI **Data Security Standard (DSS)** is considered a must, and is a minimum security requirement for organizations that deal with credit card information or online payment practices. There are 12 security requirements, plus two additional requirements, for the shared hosting providers and TLS:

- **Requirement 1**: Install and maintain a firewall configuration to protect the cardholder data
- **Requirement 2**: Do not use vendor-supplied defaults for system passwords and other security parameters
- **Requirement 3**: Protect stored cardholder data

- **Requirement 4**: Encrypt transmission of cardholder data across open, public networks
- **Requirement 5**: Use and regularly update antivirus software or programs
- **Requirement 6**: Develop and maintain secure systems and applications
- **Requirement 7**: Restrict access to cardholder data by businesses according to a need-to-know basis
- **Requirement 8**: Assign a unique ID to each person with computer access
- **Requirement 9**: Restrict physical access to cardholder data
- **Requirement 10**: Track and monitor all access to network resources and cardholder data
- **Requirement 11**: Regularly test security systems and processes
- **Requirement 12**: Maintain a policy that addresses information security for all personnel
- **Appendix A1**: Additional PCI DSS requirements for shared hosting providers
- **Appendix A2**: Additional PCI DSS requirements for entities using SSL/early TLS

During the PCI DSS compliance implementation, the PCI DSS suggests a **prioritized approach**, with six milestones for the 12 security requirements and sub-requirements. The following are the key concepts for the six milestones:

1. Don't store sensitive information if there is no need
2. Protect systems and networks, and be prepared to respond to a system breach
3. Secure payment card applications
4. Monitor and control access to your systems
5. Protect stored cardholder data
6. Finalize remaining compliance efforts, and ensure all controls are in place

Following is the mapping to the key category; please also refer to the reference for the detailed sub-requirements in each milestone:

	PCI DSS security requirments
Don't store sensitive information if there is no need	• **Requirement 1**: Install and maintain a firewall configuration to protect cardholder data • **Requirement 3**: Protect stored cardholder data • **Requirement 9**: Restrict physical access to cardholder data • **Requirement 12**: Maintain a policy that addresses information security for all personnel

Protect systems and networks, and be prepared to respond to a system breach	• **Requirement 1**: Install and maintain a firewall configuration to protect cardholder data • **Requirement 2**: Do not use vendor-supplied defaults for system passwords and other security parameters • **Requirement 4**: Encrypt transmission of cardholder data across open, public networks • **Requirement 5**: Use and regularly update anti-virus software or programs • **Requirement 8**: Assign a unique ID to each person with computer access • **Requirement 9**: Restrict physical access to cardholder data • **Requirement 11**: Regularly test security systems and processes • **Requirement 12**: Maintain a policy that addresses information security for all personnel
Secure payment card applications	• **Requirement 2**: Do not use vendor-supplied defaults for system passwords and other security parameters • **Requirement 6**: Develop and maintain secure systems and applications
Monitor and control access to your systems	• **Requirement 7**: Restrict access to cardholder data by businesses according to a need-to-know basis • **Requirement 8**: Assign a unique ID to each person with computer access • **Requirement 10**: Track and monitor all access to network resources and cardholder data • **Requirement 11**: Regularly test security systems and processes
Protect stored cardholder data	• **Requirement 3**: Protect stored cardholder data • **Requirement 9**: Restrict physical access to cardholder data
Finalize remaining compliance efforts, and ensure all controls are in place	• **Requirement 1**: Install and maintain a firewall configuration to protect cardholder data • **Requirement 6**: Develop and maintain secure systems and applications • **Requirement 12**: Maintain a policy that addresses information security for all personnel

PCI DSS prioritized approach reference source:

- `https://www.pcisecuritystandards.org/documents/Prioritized_Approach_v3.xlsx`

- `https://www.pcisecuritystandards.org/documents/Prioritized-Approach-for-PCI_DSS-v3_2.pdf`

Summary

In this chapter, we discussed some typical business fraud and abuse cases, including account cheating, online scalpers, non-genuine orders, and account takeovers. The major categories of business fraud risks are accounts, content, payments, and promotion.

We suggested some detection rules and typical frameworks for building your own business risk detection services. To identify normal and abnormal user behavior, we need to build a user profile. Aspects of profiling include IP profiling, device fingerprints, machine behaviors, accounts, and usage.

In addition to detection, we also explored some mitigation approaches, such as PCI compliance, the threshold, 2FA, CAPTCHA, GeoIP, and IP reputation. Last, but by no means least, the prioritized approach for PCI DSS compliance was listed. PCI DSS compliance is regarded as a minimum security requirement for any credit card data-handling or e-commerce services.

In the next chapter, we will focus on the security requirements of privacy and GDPR compliance cases.

Questions

1. What is account takeover?
   1. Online sellers may make a deal with cyber criminals to manipulate massive non-genuine orders
   2. A computer criminal poses as a genuine user, and gains control of an account to make unauthorized transactions
   3. Cyber criminals may register massive accounts to purchase goods
   4. Cyber criminals may register massive accounts to obtain coupons and discounts
2. What business risks and fraud may be related to the accounts?
   1. Account takeover
   2. Brute force attacks
   3. Large-scale registration
   4. All of the above

3. Which one of the following is not directly related to promotion abuses?
    1. Massive new users
    2. Machine users
    3. Crawler
    4. Scalper

4. What are the key characteristics of profiling with a view to detecting potential business abuse risks?
    1. IP
    2. Account usage
    3. Device fingerprints
    4. All of the above

5. Which one of the following is not included in IP profiling?
    1. Geolocation
    2. CPU type
    3. A known black IP address
    4. TOR exit node

6. Which one of the following can be used for device fingerprints?
    1. CPU type
    2. OS version
    3. Software plugin
    4. All of the above

7. What are the key characteristics for identifying machine behavior?
    1. The landing page is skipped
    2. There is a very short browsing time for each product
    3. There is no communication history
    4. All of the above

Further reading

- **Reporting internet-related crime**: https://www.justice.gov/criminal-ccips/reporting-computer-internet-related-or-intellectual-property-crime
- **European Cybercrime Centre**: https://www.europol.europa.eu/about-europol/european-cybercrime-centre-ec3
- **Interpol**: https://www.interpol.int/Crime-areas/Cybercrime/Cybercrime
- **Cyber Crime Response Agency**: https://www.ccra.agency
- **TLS Fingerprint**: https://github.com/LeeBrotherston/tls-fingerprinting
- **Fingerprintjs2**: https://github.com/Valve/fingerprintjs2
- **JA3**: https://github.com/salesforce/ja3
- **All cybercrime IP feeds by FireHOL**: http://iplists.firehol.org/
- **PCI Security Document Library**: https://www.pcisecuritystandards.org/document_library

19
GDPR Compliance Case Study

In the previous chapter, we explored business fraud and service abuses. In this chapter, we will talk more about GDPR case studies. The **General Data Protection Regulation (GDPR)** has set an enforcement date; May 25, 2018. Any organization that has not complied with data protection rules by this date may face heavy fines. This chapter will take the GDPR compliance as a case study to apply to software development. It discusses the GDPR software security requirements it should include in coming releases. We will also explore some practical case studies, such as personal data discovery, data anonymization, cookie consent, data-masking implementation, and web privacy status.

We will cover the following topics in this chapter:

- GDPR security requirement
- Case studies

GDPR security requirement

There are 11 chapters in the GDPR. To take GDPR into product development consideration, chapters 1 to 4 are most relevant to the product requirement planning. All of the GDPR chapters are shown in the following diagram. The number in the brackets means the number of articles in that chapter.

Let's take a look at it:

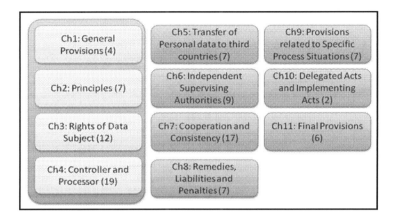

Privacy rights	Detailed description
Privacy notice (data controller)	The product should provide a privacy notice. The contents of the privacy notice should include the following: • How to collect and use the personal data • How cookies will be used • How to protect personal data. • How to manage your personal data • How to protect children's personal data • Third-party services • International transfer of personal data
Lawfulness of processing (All)	Any interface that collects personal data in the background without the user's consent is forbidden. For example, uploading troubleshooting logs without user consent or sending the phone IMEI in the background.
Data minimization (All)	• The product must ensure not to collect the data that isn't relevant to the product's functions. • The data-masking (anonymization or pseudonymization) must apply to personal data. The pseudonymization can allow re-identification, but the anonymization cannot be re-identified. The following personal data should be considered anonymization: • Names (surnames and first names) • Postal addresses, telephone numbers • IDs (credit card numbers, social security numbers)
Consent (data controller)	• Before the data collection, the product must provide the Agree or Disagree options to the data subject. • For the data collection consent options, it's forbidden to have a default value as agree. • The consent authorization actions must be logged. • Any further changes in personal data processing should have another user's consent.
Right to object to data processing (data controller)	• The product must provide options for users to stop data processing for any direct marketing purposes. • The product must provide an option for the user to remove their own personal data at any time. • Once the user decides to be removed from the data processing, the period of the personal data retention should be configurable if the related personal data is still required by law.
Rights of data subject (rectification, access, informed)	• The product should provide an interface for the user to add, update, and remove for their own personal data. • If the product needs to connect to the internet, it must inform and gain the user's consent. • The installation of any software update or application must also have the user's consent. • The feedback information for the improvement of user experiences must also have the user's consent. • It must have user consent before sending the troubleshooting logs. • Personal data should take appropriate security control, such as access control and encryption.
Right to data portability	• The product must provide the data export capability. The data export format can be a machine-readable format such as XML, CSV, and JSON.

Data transfer	• The data communication should be in a secure channel. • If personal data is to be transferred to a third party, the user must be asked for consent. • Without the user consent, the data is forbidden to transfer out of **European Economic Area** (**EEA**).
Right to be forgotten	• Once the objective of the data processing is done, the related data should be removed or anonymized, especially for temporary data. • Once the user has decided to revoke the user account, the related personal data should also be able to be removed automatically. • The product should provide a data-removal mechanism.

Based on these privacy rights, the GDPR security requirements for products and services can be summarized in the following table. Let's take a look at it.

In practice, here are some of the common issues in the product design. Take a look at this table:

Common product design issue	Expected behaviors for the GDPR compliance
The product doesn't remove related personal data once the user revokes the account.	Provide data-removal mechanism
The product doesn't provide an interface for the user to export their own personal data.	Provide the data export mechanism to CSV or XML formats
The default value of the user consent is always Agree.	There shouldn't be a default value of Agree on the user consent page
There is no option for the user to stop further data processing for marketing purposes.	Provide an option for the user to choose not to get involved with marketing profiling
The upload of troubleshooting logs that include personal information doesn't do anonymization and doesn't have the user's consent.	Have the user consent, and do anonymization for any troubleshooting logs
The product doesn't provide the interface for the user to update or edit their own personal information.	Provide an interface for the user to edit or update their own personal information

Furthermore, here are the recommended GDPR self-assessment checklists. The online assessment report also provides practical suggested actions to improve the data protection and GDPR compliance. Take a look at this table:

Category of self-assessment checklist	Description
Data protection self-assessment for controllers	It's an on-line self-assessment checklist. At the end of the assessment, it will give a report with the overall rating, guidance, and suggested actions. The assessment mainly covers the following four areas: • Lawfulness, fairness and transparency • Individuals' rights • Accountability and governance • Data security, international transfers and breaches According to GDPR article 4, the 'controller' means the natural or legal person, public authority, agency or other body which, alone or jointly with others, determines the purposes and means of the processing of personal data;
Data protection self-assessment for processors	According to GDPR article 4, the 'processor' means a natural or legal person, public authority, agency or other body which processes personal data on behalf of the controller. The assessment covers the following areas: • Documentation • Accountability and governance • Individual rights • Data security For the GDPR compliance, the data processors may have fewer security requirements as compared to the data controllers.
Information security	The information security assessment includes the followings: • Management and organizational information security • Your staff and information security awareness • Physical security • Computer and network security • Personal data breach management
Direct marketing	The assessment is to check the personal data handling for the direct marketing activities such as include phone, email, postal, fax.
Records management	The records management checklist includes the following four major areas: • Management and organizational records management • Records creation and maintenance • Tracking and offsite storage • Access to records
Data sharing and subject access	It evaluates the data sharing policies in the following areas: • Data sharing governance • Data sharing records • Privacy information • Security measures • Requests for personal data process
GDPR compliance checklist	The GDPR checklist evaluates general security requirements in the followings: • Your data • Accountability & management • New rights • Consent • Follow-up • Special cases

Case studies

In this section, we will discuss the practical GDPR cases for the GDPR implementation issue, with suggested approaches or open source tools. The cases will cover data discovery, database anonymization, cookie consent, data masking, and website privacy. These are typical practical scenarios that directly relate to GDPR compliance.

Case 1 – personal data discovery

Company A has been running several services and databases with lots of legacy-running applications for several years. The database and IT administrators would like to do **personally identifiable information (PII)** scanning to gain an overview of all the personal data distribution status. In this case, company A would need a **PII discovery tool**, which can define the PII data type, and be able to search for various kinds of files and databases. Take a look at this diagram:

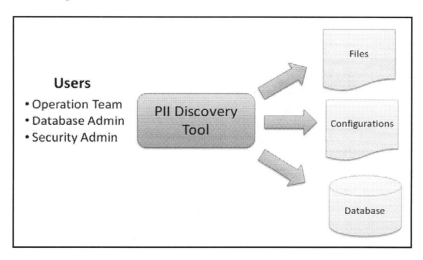

For an open source tool, the RedataSense data discovery tool is recommended, since it supports multiple databases and can identify personal data by a dictionary and regular expressions. Here is the reference source of the sensitive data discovery tool: `https://github.com/redglue/redsense`.

In addition, it's also suggested to search for highly sensitive and secret information, such as the API key, encryption password, hash value, and so on. The common pattern of these values is the high entropy, although some of the passwords may still be configured as plain text, or a default value without encryption. The following tools are recommended to use regularly to scan and identify the storage of the secret information. DumpsterDriver is a Python script that can search for secrets in local files, while truffleHog is mainly used to scan the secrets on the Git repository.

For more information on these tools, go to the following URLs:

- DumpsterDiver: It's a Python Script which can search for secrets in local files can be found here: `https://github.com/securing/DumpsterDiver`
- TruffleHog: It scans the secrets on GIT repository which can be found here.
  : `https://github.com/dxa4481/truffleHog`

Case 2 – database anonymization

During the development and testing process, it's forbidden to allow a development team to access the production databases for any testing or evaluation purposes, due to the risks of unintended disclosure and privacy laws. However, on the other hand, the production data may help the development team for the performance, security, and development evaluation. Therefore, the need for a database anonymization tool that can generate a database full of anonymized data is very important.

The data flow of the database anonymization tool is shown in the following diagram. Although the tool can technically transform the production database into an anonymization database, it's highly recommended to generate anonymization data based on database schema only (empty database). It's because transforming the data from the production database may possibly miss certain personal-data-related columns to be anonymized. The tool that helps to generate the data is supposed to keep the similar production data format. Look at this diagram:

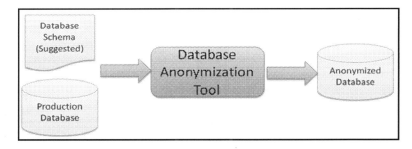

The table below summarizes the data anonymization tools and the scenario to apply to.

Data anonymization tools	Key Adoption Scenario
Data anonymization (`https://github.com/ dataanon/data-anon`)	It's a Java library that can help to generate anonymization data. There are lots of anonymization strategies that can be defined such as Random Email, Random FirstName, Random Int, Random String, and so on.
Data defender, data discovery, and anonymization toolkit (`https://github.com/armenak/ DataDefender`)	It supports several major databases, such as MS SQL Server, MySQL, and Oracle. The data anonymizer can generate the anonymization data, based on pre-defined rules.
ARX Data Anonymization Tool (`https://arx.deidentifier. org/`)	The ARX can flexibly define the transformation rules and export the data into an anonymization dataset.
Database anonymizer `https://github.com/ Divanteltd/anonymizer`	It can work with the existing database to anonymize, truncate, and empty the table. It can also work with JSON-encoded data for anonymization.
Data anonymization `https://sunitparehk.github. io/data-anonymization/`	It's a ruby data anonymization library used to build MySQL anonymized data dumps.

Case 3 – cookie consent

For the compliance of GDPR, the cookie that is used to uniquely identify the person or device should be treated as personal data. (according to the 'General Data Protection Regulation Recital 30'). Consider the following original quotation:

> *"Natural persons may be associated with online identifiers provided by their devices, applications, tools, and protocols, **such as internet protocol addresses, cookie identifiers** or other identifiers such as radio frequency identification tags. This may leave traces which, in particular when combined with unique identifiers and other information received by the servers, may be used to create profiles of the natural persons and identify them."*

Therefore, under the GDPR, the development of the website will need a common cookie consent policy and framework. Traditionally, the approach *By visiting this site, you must accept cookies* or the loading cookies immediately on the first landing page or the uses of the third-party cookie, such as Google Analytics, may not be compliant with GDPR without users' consent. For the compliance of GDPR, there are some cookie consent approaches to be considered. Just be sure to consult with legal advice for which approaches best fit your online services.

Generally, there are two main common approaches for the cookie consent notices. The soft opt-in cookie consent is shown with the **OK** button and the link to the privacy policy when a visitor first visits your website, by default. The notice will show again in 30 days. There will not be any cookie-loading behavior on the first landing page until the user clicks other links or accepts the cookie. Look at this screenshot:

The other approach is to show the cookie consent banner with the **OK** button and **Cookie Settings**, which include the privacy policy and also the cookie opt-out options to filter cookies based on specific services. The following snapshots show the concept of cookie consent behaviors. Take a look at this screenshot:

The cookie settings are shown in this screenshot:

Refer to the further section for some of the open source GDPR cookie consent implementations.

Case 4 – data-masking library for implementation

For the development team, for the implementation of services that relate to personal information handling, there will be a need for data-masking APIs, which are used to anonymize personal data. The typical use cases to do the data masking include data export, reporting or query results based on access roles, troubleshooting logs, the communication between third-party components, and the export of production databases. Take a look at this diagram:

Here are some of the common data-masking APIs, based on the programming languages:

- Data masking (JavaScript library): https://github.com/scokmen/data-mask
- Chlorine finder (Java library): https://github.com/dataApps/chlorine-finder
- CommonRegex (Python library): https://github.com/madisonmay/CommonRegex
- ARX Data Anonymization Tool (Python library): https://arx.deidentifier.org/

Case 5 – evaluating website privacy status

The website privacy scanner is used for the operation or security team that would like to know all of the third-party cookies' behaviors in the web services. It's likely that one of the embedded third-party services may have cookie behaviors that the website administrator may not be aware of. Therefore, having an online privacy scanner to do periodical cookie scanning for all the sources of cookies is also critical to comply with GDPR. Look at this diagram:

Here are the recommended privacy scanner tools that can not only scan the cookie-tacking behaviors but also the adoption of TLS and HTTP security headers behaviors:

- Privacy score: https://privacyscore.org/
- Privacy-friendly check: https://webbkoll.dataskydd.net/en/

Summary

In this chapter, we discussed the security requirements of products and services for GDPR compliance. Generally, the security requirements cover the privacy notice, lawfulness of processing data, data minimization, consent, the right to object to data processing, the rights of the data subject, the right to data portability, data transfer, and the right to be forgotten.

We also illustrated some of the common product design issues. For example, the product doesn't provide an interface for the user to edit or export their own personal data. The default value of the user consent is always **Agree**. Furthermore, we also shared the self-assessment checklists for the GDPR data protection.

Five practical GDPR case studies were also discussed with a description of the issue, the suggested actions, and the open source tools to use. The cases covered data discovery, database anonymization, cookie consent, data masking, and website privacy.

In the upcoming final chapters, we will sum up the challenges and FAQs of DevOps security by discussing roles such as security management, development, testing, and security monitoring teams.

Questions

1. Which one of the followings should be included in the privacy notice?
    1. How to protect personal data
    2. How to manage your personal data
    3. How to protect children's personal data
    4. All of the above
2. What is "Data Minimization"?
    1. Keeping the data size as small as possible
    2. The product must ensure not to collect data that is irrelevant to the product functions
    3. Compressing personal data
    4. Encrypting personal data

3. Which of the following is not correct when it comes to rules regarding data consent?
   1. The product must provide the Agree or Disagree options to the data subject after the data collection
   2. For the data collection consent options, it's forbidden to have a default value as Agree
   3. The consent authorization actions must be logged
   4. Any further changes in personal data processing should have another user's consent

4. Which one of the following is the expected behavior for the GDPR compliance?
   1. The product doesn't remove related personal data once the user revokes the account
   2. The default value of the user consent is always Agree
   3. Provide the data export mechanism to CSV or XML formats
   4. The product doesn't provide the interface for the user to update or edit their own personal information

5. Which one of the following may need data anonymization?
   1. Email
   2. First name
   3. Age
   4. All of the above

Further reading

Visit the following URLs for more information:

- **NIST SP 800-122 Guide to Protecting the Confidentiality of Personally Identifiable Information (PII)**: `https://csrc.nist.gov/publications/detail/sp/800-122/final`
- **GDPR EU**: `https://www.gdpreu.org/`
- **CSA Code of Conduct for GDPR Compliance**: `https://cloudsecurityalliance.org/media/press-releases/cloud-security-alliance-issues-code-of-conduct-self-assessment-and-certification-tools-for-gdpr-compliance/`
- **Cookie consent**: `https://github.com/insites/cookieconsent`

- **Data protection self-assessment for controllers:** https://ico.org.uk/for-organisations/resources-and-support/data-protection-self-assessment/controllers-checklist/
- **Data protection self-assessment for processors:** https://ico.org.uk/for-organisations/resources-and-support/data-protection-self-assessment/processors-checklist/

- **Information security data protection self-assessment:** https://ico.org.uk/for-organisations/resources-and-support/data-protection-self-assessment/information-security-checklist

- **Direct marketing data protection self-assessment:** https://ico.org.uk/for-organisations/resources-and-support/data-protection-self-assessment/direct-marketing-checklist

- **Records management data protection self-assessment:** https://ico.org.uk/for-organisations/resources-and-support/data-protection-self-assessment/records-managment-checklist

- **Data sharing and subject access data protection self-assessment:** https://ico.org.uk/for-organisations/resources-and-support/data-protection-self-assessment/data-sharing-and-subject-access-checklist/

DevSecOps - Challenges, Tips, and FAQs

20

The adoption of DevSecOps is a continuous learning process and takes a lot of stakeholder involvement, process optimization, business priority conflicts, and customization of security tools, as well as a security knowledge learning curve. The intention of this chapter is to give you some hands-on tips, challenges, and FAQs based on a functional roles perspective.

We will cover the following topics in this chapter:

- DevSecOps FAQs for security management
- DevSecOps FAQs for the development team
- DevSecOps FAQs for the testing team
- DevSecOps FAQs for the operations team

DevSecOps for security management

Q: Are there any suggested industry best practices for secure development and deployment in DevOps?

The OWASP SAMM (Software Assurance Maturity Model), Microsoft Security Development Lifecycle (SDL) and the SafeCode provide practical security practices for the DevOps or agile development.

- OWASP SAMM: `https://github.com/OWASP/samm`
- Microsoft SDL for Agile: `https://www.microsoft.com/en-us/SDL/Discover/sdlagile.aspx`
- SafeCode: `https://safecode.org/publications/`

Q: What are the security risks of a cloud service?

The CSA has defined the top threats to cloud computing on their website (`https://cloudsecurityalliance.org/group/top-threats/`), which are listed as follows:

- Data Breaches
- Insufficient identity, credential, and access management
- Insecure interfaces and APIs
- System vulnerabilities
- Account hijacking
- Malicious insiders
- Advanced persistent threats
- Data loss
- Insufficient due diligence
- Abuse and nefarious use of cloud services
- Denial of service
- Shared technology vulnerabilities

Q: What are the security requirements in terms of GDPR compliance?

The following table lists the GDPR security requirements for a software/service of the data processor and data controller:

GDPR requirements	Data processor	Data controller
Provide a data privacy declaration	Must	Must
Data collection requires a user's explicit consent to allow data collection and also to allow the user to disable the data collection	Must	Must
For the purposes of error troubleshooting, the user must be informed whether the collection of logs includes personal information	Must	Must
The collection of a user's cookies requires the user's consent. Refer to `https://www.cookielaw.org/the-cookie-law/` for more details.	Must	Must
If the data is collected for marketing analysis purposes, the application must allow users to disable the analysis	Recommended	Must
Provide the ability to remove data securely after the data expires	Must	Must

If the data will be provided to third-party partners, it must have the user's explicit consent	Recommended	Must
Provide the ability for the user to query and update the data	Recommended	Must
Delete any temporary data that is no longer in use	Recommended	Must
Provide the ability to export the data	Recommended	Must
Secure data transmission	Must	Must
Secure local data storage with encryption, access control, and logging security controls	Must	Must

DevSecOps for the development team

Q: What are the recommended security architecture patterns?

- Open Security Architecture Patterns: `http://www.opensecurityarchitecture.org/cms/library/patternlandscape`
- Security and privacy reference architecture: `http://security-and-privacy-reference-architecture.readthedocs.io/en/latest/index.html`
- Shiro: `http://shiro.apache.org/`
- OWASP Cheat Sheet Series: `https://www.owasp.org/index.php/OWASP_Cheat_Sheet_Series`

Q: What are the common security frameworks that are used to build secure software?

Security improvement area	Open source security and privacy framework
Authentication	• Gluu for multiple-factor authentication and social login • ReCAPTCHA • Git-Secret for the protection of sensitive information in the source code
Authorization	• Gluu for the user consent management • Apache Shiro Session Management • OWASP CSRF Guard
API manager	• Kong • API umbrella • WSO2 API manager
Data input/output	• OWASP HTML Sanitizer Project • Commons validator • ValidateJS • OWASP Java Encoder
Privacy	• ARX De-Identifier data anonymization tool • Apache Atlas for data governance • PrivacyScore for the web privacy assessment • CookieConsent

Q: There are lots of third-party components and dependencies that are released and deployed with a software package. Are there any recommended tools to assess the security risks?

- RetireJS: `https://retirejs.github.io/retire.js/`
- OWASP Dependency Check: `https://www.owasp.org/index.php/OWASP_Dependency_Check`
- Cuckoo Sandbox: `https://cuckoosandbox.org/`

Q: What are the recommended security deliverables in the design and coding stage?

Stage	Deliverables
Requirement	• Customer security requirement analysis • Security standards compliance analysis • Security industry best practices (that is, OWASP ASVS, CSA CCM)
Design	• Threat modeling analysis report • Secure design checklist self-assessment report
Coding	• Static secure coding scanning report • High-risk module security assessment report • Secure compiler and linker flags status • Forbidden or unsafe uses of APIs scanning report

Q: What are the recommended resources for the secure coding best practices?

- OWASP Secure Code Review: `https://www.owasp.org/index.php/Category:OWASP_Code_Review_Project`
- Common Weakness Enumeration (CWE): `https://cwe.mitre.org/data/index.html`
- CERT Secure Coding: `https://www.securecoding.cert.org/confluence/display/seccode/SEI+CERT+Coding+Standards`
- Android Secure Coding: `https://www.jssec.org/dl/android_securecoding_en.pdf`

Q: What are the secure compiler and link flags that are used to mitigate the buffer overflow exploit attack?

Refer to the secure compiling table in `Chapter 8`, *Secure Coding Best Practices.*

DevSecOps for the testing team

Q: What testing tools are suggested for data privacy assessment?

Data life cycle	Testing key points	Suggested testing tools
Transmission of data	• Ensure that the sensitive information is not transmitted by GET • The secure communication protocol, such as TLS v1.2, SSH V2, SFTP, SNMP V3	SSLyze, NMAP, Wireshark
Storage of data	• Check whether sensitive information is encrypted • Check that the permissions of the files are properly configured	TruffleHog: `https://github.com/dxa4481/truffleHog`
Encryption of data	No uses of weak encryption algorithms, such as MD5, RC4, Jackfish, and Tripple DES	Code-scanning tools: `https://github.com/floyd-fuh/crass/blob/master/grep-it.sh`
Data access and auditing	• Logging any sensitive data query • CL permissions	AuthMatrix: `https://github.com/SecurityInnovation/AuthMatrix`
Removal of data	• Check that there is no sensitive information in temp, exception files, and cookies • Check any plain-text sensitive information in the memory and cache	GCORE WinHex: `https://www.x-ways.net/winhex/` LaZagne: `https://github.com/AlessandroZ/LaZagne`

Refer to `Chapter 10`, *Security-Testing Plan and Practices*, for more details.

Q: What are the industry security testing guides of each security domain?

Security domain	Security testing guide
Web security testing	• OWASP Testing Guide: `https://www.owasp.org/index.php/OWASP_Testing_Project`
Virtualization security testing	• NIST 800-125 Guide to Security for Full Virtualization Technologies: `https://csrc.nist.gov/publications/detail/sp/800-125/final` • PCI DSS Virtualization Guidelines: `https://www.pcisecuritystandards.org/documents/Virtualization_InfoSupp_v2.pdf` • Red Hat Virtualization Security Guide: `https://access.redhat.com/documentation/en-us/red_hat_enterprise_linux/7/html-single/virtualization_security_guide/index` • SANS Top Virtualization Security Mistakes: `https://www.sans.org/reading-room/whitepapers/analyst/top-virtualization-security-mistakes-and-avoid-them-34800` • ISCACA Virtualization Security Checklist: `http://www.isaca.org/Knowledge-Center/Research/Documents/Virtualization-Security-Checklist_res_Eng_1010.pdf`
Firmware security testing	• GitHub Awesome Firmware Security: `https://github.com/PreOS-Security/awesome-firmware-security` • GitHub Security of BIOS/UEFI System Firmware from Attacker and Defender Perspectives: `https://github.com/rmusser01/Infosec_Reference/blob/master/Draft/BIOS%20UEFI%20Attacks%20Defenses.md`
Big data security testing	• NIST 1500-4 Big Data Interoperability Framework: `https://www.nist.gov/publications/nist-big-data-interoperability-framework-volume-4-security-and-privacy` • CSA Big Data Security and Privacy Handbook: `https://downloads.cloudsecurityalliance.org/assets/research/big-data/BigData_Security_and_Privacy_Handbook.pdf`
Privacy	• GDPR Checklist: `https://gdprchecklist.io/` • NIST SP 800-122 Guide to Protecting the Confidentiality of **Personally Identifiable Information (PII)**: `https://csrc.nist.gov/publications/detail/sp/800-122/final`
IoT security	• ENISA Baseline Security Recommendations for IoT: `https://www.enisa.europa.eu/publications/baseline-security-recommendations-for-iot/` • GSMA IOT Security Assessment: `https://www.gsma.com/iot/future-iot-networks/iot-security-guidelines/`
Container security	• NIST 800-190 Application Container Security Guide: `https://nvlpubs.nist.gov/nistpubs/specialpublications/nist.sp.800-190.pdf`
Mobile security	• OWASP **Mobile Security Testing Guide (MSTG)**: `https://github.com/OWASP/owasp-mstg`

Refer to `Chapter 10`, *Security-Testing Plan and Practices*, for more details.

Q: What are the suggested white box review tools that use regular expressions or string patterns to search for high-risk source code?

Tools	References
DREK	Tool: `https://github.com/chrisallenlane/drek` Signature: `https://github.com/chrisallenlane/drek-signatures/tree/master/signatures` (refer to the `*.yml` file)
GrAudit	Tool: `https://github.com/wireghoul/graudit` Signature: `https://github.com/wireghoul/graudit/tree/master/signatures` (refer to the `*.db` file)
Visual Code Grepper (VCG)	Tool: `https://github.com/nccgroup/VCG` Signature: `https://github.com/nccgroup/VCG/tree/master/VisualCodeGrepper/bin/Release` (refer to the `*.conf` file)
CRASS Grep It	The CRASS Grep IT tool is recommended because it requires no dependencies. All it needs is one shell script to execute. Tool: `https://github.com/floyd-fuh/crass/blob/master/grep-it.sh` Signature: `https://github.com/floyd-fuh/crass/blob/master/grep-it.sh`

Refer to the tips shown in `Chapter 11`, *Whitebox Testing Tips*, for more details.

Q: What are the recommended open source tools for BDD security frameworks?

BDD security frameworks	Default security tools included
BDD-Security	OWASP ZAP, SSLyze, Nessus BDD-Security is based on Java and Cucumber. BDD-Security: `https://www.continuumsecurity.net/bdd-security/`
MITTN	BurpSuite, SSlyze, and Radamsa API fuzzing MITTN is based on Python and Behave. MITTN: `https://github.com/F-Secure/mittn`
Gauntlt	CURL, NMAP, SSLyze, SQLmap, Garmr, Heartbleed, dirb, Arachni Gauntlt: `http://gauntlt.org/`

Refer to `Chapter 12`, *Security Testing Toolkits*, for more details.

Q: What are the suggested open source Docker security scanning tools?

Docker security tools	Purpose and reference
Docker Bench	Docker Bench is an automated script that checks whether the system is compliant with Docker security best practices. The scanning rules are based on the CIS Docker Security Benchmark. Docker Bench: `https://github.com/docker/docker-bench-security/` CIS Docker Security Benchmark: `https://benchmarks.cisecurity.org/`
Actuary	Actuary works in a similar way to Docker Bench. Additionally, Actuary can do the scanning based on user-defined security profiles provided by the Docker security community. Actuary: `https://github.com/diogomonica/actuary/`
Clair	Clair is a container image security static analyzer for CVEs. Clair: `https://github.com/coreos/clair`
Anchor Engine	The Anchor Engine scan the Docker images for known vulnerable CVEs. Anchor Engine: `Https://github.com/anchore/anchore-engine` In addition, the Anchor also provides cloud version, refer to the 'Anchor Cloud'
Falco	Falco is a Docker container runtime security tool that can detect anomalous activities. Falco: `https://sysdig.com/opensource/falco/`
Dagda	Dagda is an integrated Docker security tool that provides runtime anomalous activities detection (Sysdig Falco), vulnerability (CVE) analysis (OWASP dependency check, Retire.JS), and malware scanning (CalmAV). Dagda: `https://github.com/eliasgranderubio/dagda/`

Refer to `Chapter 12`, *Security Testing Toolkits*, for more details.

Q: What are the integrated security testing tools that can consolidate the various testing tool results?

Faraday

Faraday is an integrated penetration testing environment and provides a dashboard for all the testing results. It integrates with over 50 security tools.

Faraday: `https://www.faradaysec.com/#why-faraday` Refer to `https://github.com/infobyte/faraday/wiki/Plugin-List` for a list of the available plugins.

Tools	Tools included by default
JackHammer	JackHammer, provided by Ola, is an integrated security testing tool. It provides a dashboard to consolidate all the testing results. The key difference is that JackHammer includes mobile app security scanning and source code static analysis tools. The supported open source security scanners include Brakeman, Bundler-Audit, Dawnscanner, FindSecurityBugs, PMD, RetireJS, Arachni, Trufflehog, Androbugs, Androguard, and NMAP. JackHammer: `https://github.com/olacabs/jackhammer` Ola: `https://jch.olacabs.com/userguide/`
Mozilla Minion	Mozilla Minion is also an integrated security testing tool that includes the following plugins by default: • ZAP • Nmap • Skipfish • SSLScan Mozilla Minion: `https://github.com/mozilla/minion/`
Penetration Testing Toolkit	The Penetration Testing Toolkit provides a unified web interface for many Linux scanning tools, such as Nmap, nikto, WhatWeb, SSLyze, fping, URLCrazy, lynx, mtr, nbtscan, automater, and shellinabox. Penetration Testing Toolkit: `https://github.com/veerupandey/Penetration-Testing-Toolkit`
Seccubus	The key advantage of using Seccubus is that it integrates with various kinds of vulnerability scanner testing results and also compares the differences between each scan. It includes the following scanners: • Nessus • OpenVAS • NMAP • Nikto • Medusa • SSLyze • SSL Labs • TestSSL.sh • SkipFish • ZAP Seccubus: `https://github.com/schubergphilis/Seccubus`
OWTF	**Offensive Web Testing Framework (OWTF)** is an integrated security testing cases which include the OWASP testing guide, PTES and NIST testing standards. OWTF: `https://owtf.github.io/`OWTF guide: `https://owtf.github.io/online-passive-scanner/`
RapidScan	RapidScan is a multi-tool that contains a web-vulnerability scanner. The security scanning tools that it contains include Nmap, dnsrecon, uniscan, sslyze, fierce, theharvester, and golismero.

DefectDojo	The OWASP DefectDojo is a security tool that can import and consolidate various security testing tool outputs into one management dashboard. DefectDojo: `https://github.com/DefectDojo/django-DefectDojo`

Refer to `Chapter 12`, *Security Testing Toolkits*, for more details

Q: What are the common security Jenkins plugins?

Jenkins plugins	Description
ZAP	ZAP is a dynamic web scanning tool. ZAP: `https://plugins.jenkins.io/zap`
Arachni Scanner	Arachni Scanner is a dynamic web-scanning tool. Arachni Scanner: `https://plugins.jenkins.io/arachni-scanner`
Dependency Check plugin	The Dependency Check plugin detects vulnerable dependency components. Dependency Check plugin: `https://plugins.jenkins.io/dependency-check-jenkins-plugin`
FindBugs	FindBugs is a static code analysis tool for Java. FindBugs: `https://plugins.jenkins.io/findbugs`
SonarQube	SonarQube is a code quality analysis tool. SonarQube: `https://plugins.jenkins.io/sonar`
360 FireLine	360 FireLine is a static code scanning tool for Java. 360 FireLine: `https://plugins.jenkins.io/fireline`
HTML Publisher plugin	The HTML Publisher plugin generates the testing results in HTML. HTML Publisher plugin: `https://plugins.jenkins.io/htmlpublisher`
Log Parser plugin	The Log Parse plugin parses the testing results of security testing tools, such as the number of XSS detected or the number of errors. Log Parse plugin: `https://plugins.jenkins.io/log-parser`
Static Analysis Collector	The Static Analysis Collector plugin can consolidate the results from all other static code analysis plugins, such as Checkstyle, Dry, FindBugs, PMD, and Android Lin. Static Analysis Collector: `https://plugins.jenkins.io/analysis-collector`

Refer to `Chapter 13`, *Security Automation with the CI Pipeline*, for more details.

DevSecOps for the operations team

Q. What are the suggested open source security monitoring tools corresponding to the 20 CIS Critical Security Controls for Effective Cyber Defense?

Cyber security controls	Examples of security techniques
CSC1: Inventory of Authorized and Unauthorized Devices	Endpoint security, asset management
CSC2: Inventory of Authorized and Unauthorized Software	Endpoint security, asset management
CS3: Secure Configurations for Hardware and Software on Mobile Devices, Laptops, Workstations, and Servers.	CIS Security Benchmark, OpenSCAP
CSC4: Continuous Vulnerability Assessment and Remediation	OpenVAS: http://www.openvas.org/ Nmap: https://nmap.org/ OWASP Dependency Check: https://www.owasp.org/index.php/OWASP_Dependency_Check
CSC 5: Controlled Use of Administrative Privileges	Strong password complexity Auditing logs for root and administrator activities
CSC 6: Maintenance, Monitoring, and Analysis of Audit Logs	Syslog, event logs, SIEM ELK: https://bitnami.com/stack/elk GrayLog: https://www.graylog.org/security Security Onion: https://github.com/Security-Onion-Solutions Malicious Traffic Detection: https://github.com/stamparm/
CSC 7: Email and Web Browser Protections	Email protection, antispam, web application firewall ModSecurity: https://www.modsecurity.org/ Email Encryption Scramble: https://dcposh.github.io/scramble/ Linux Malware Detection: https://github.com/rfxn/linux-malware-detect
CSC 8: Malware Defenses	Endpoint protection, antivirus, HIDS/HIPS OSSEC: https://github.com/ossec/ ClamAV: https://www.clamav.net/

CSC 9: Limitation and Control of Network Ports, Protocols, and Services	NMAP, OpenSCAP
CSC 10: Data Recovery Capability	Bacula: `https://blog.bacula.org/`
CSC 11: Secure Configurations for Network Devices such as Firewalls, Routers, and Switches	CIS Security Benchmark: `https://www.cisecurity.org/cis-benchmarks/`
CSC 12: Boundary Defense	Firewall, IPS, HoneyPot Security Onion: `https://github.com/Security-Onion-Solutions`
CSC 13: Data Protection	OSQuery: `https://github.com/facebook/osquery/` Data Vault: `https://github.com/hashicorp/vault`
CSC 14: Controlled Access Based on the Need to Know	Data classification, firewalls, VLAN, logging
CSC 15: Wireless Access Control	VPN, SSL certificate, WAP2
CSC 16: Account Monitoring and Control	Log analysis tools Fail2ban: `https://github.com/fail2ban/fail2ban/`
CSC 17: Security Skills Assessment and Appropriate Training to Fill Gaps	Security training and labs resources Cybrary: `https://www.cybrary.it/` Git Awesome information security resource collections: `https://github.com/onlurking/awesome-infosec`
CSC 18: Application Software Security	OWASP: `https://www.owasp.org/index.php/` `Category:OWASP_Project`
CSC 19: Incident Response and Management	NIST SP800-61 Computer Security Incident Handling Guide **Fast Incident Response (FIR)**: `https://github.com/certsocietegenerale/FIR`
CSC 20: Penetration Tests and Red Team Exercises	Refer to some of the open source tools we suggested in the `Chapter 12`, *Security Testing Toolkits*.

Q: What are the recommended open source tools that can simulate the hacking attacks to test the effectiveness of the security monitoring?

Tools	Simulation of APT
DumpsterFire	DumpsterFire includes various kinds of simulated attack scenarios, such as account attacks, file downloads, drop files, command executions, and web access in Python. It provides a user-friendly menu to customize the security incidents, even for those who don't understand Python. DumpsterFire: `https://github.com/TryCatchHCF/DumpsterFire`
METTA	METTA allows the security team to customize the simulation of APT attacks based on MITRE ATT&CK. The simulated APT behaviors defined by YAML includes credential access, evasion, discovery, execution, exfiltration, lateral movement, persistence, and privilege escalation. METTA: `https://github.com/uber-common/metta` MITRE ATT&CK: `https://attack.mitre.org/wiki/Main_Page`
Red Team Automation (RTA)	RTA is a collection of Python and PowerShell scripts that can simulate over 50 malicious behaviors based on ATT&CK. RTA: `https://github.com/endgameinc/RAT`
Atomic Red Team (ART)	ART provides Windows, macOS, and Linux shell scripts to simulate a MITRE ATT&CK. ART: `https://github.com/redcanaryco/atomic-red-team`
APT Simulator	APT Simulator is a collection of Windows BAT scripts that simulate APT behaviors. APT Simulator: `https://github.com/NextronSystems/APTSimulator`
Network Flight Simulator	Network Flight Simulator can be used to generate malicious network traffic, such as DNS tunneling, C2 communication, DGA traffic, and port scans. Network Flight Simulator: `https://github.com/alphasoc/flightsim`

Q: What are the recommended industry references for the security incident responses?

- NIST SP 800-62 Computer Security Incident Handling Guide: `https://csrc.nist.gov/publications/detail/sp/800-61/rev-2/final`
- SANS Incident Handler Handbook: `https://www.sans.org/reading-room/whitepapers/incident/incident-handlers-handbook-33901`

- ENISA Cloud Computing—benefits, risks, and recommendations for information security: `https://resilience.enisa.europa.eu/cloud-security-and-resilience/publications/cloud-computing-benefits-risks-and-recommendations-for-information-security`
- MITRE Ten Strategies of a World-Class Cyber Security Operations Center: `https://www.mitre.org/sites/default/files/publications/pr-13-1028-mitre-10-strategies-cyber-ops-center.pdf`
- FIRST: `https://www.first.org/education/FIRST_PSIRT_Service_Framework_v1.0`

Q: What are the typical functions in a security operation team structure?

Key functions	Description
Security Incident Analysis and Forensic Analysis (Call Center)	The security incident analysis and forensic analysis team may include the Tier 1 case handling in the 24 x 7 security monitoring center. A Tier 1 case is typically handled by following the predefined checklist or SOP to perform an initial root-cause analysis or mitigation based on the incident.
Security Operations and Administration	The security operations and administration team involves the following routine security activities. These are regular security activities for checking the production environments: • Network scanning (Weekly) • Vulnerability scanning (Weekly) • Penetration testing (Monthly) • Security awareness training (Bi-monthly) • Security log trending analysis (Monthly) • Security administration and monitoring (Daily) • Patch or security signature update (Daily/weekly)
Security Tools Engineering	The security tools engineering team implements security tools for the security call center or security operations team. The security tools can be security automation, suspicious behavior detectors, forensic analysis tools, security configuration checkers, threat intelligence integration, threat signature creators, and so on.

Q: What are the recommended open source tools for the security forensics?

Category	Tools	Purpose and usage scenario
Log collection	OSX Collector	The macOS X Log Collector is an automated forensic evidence collector for macOS X. The Python script, `osxcollector.py`, is the code phrase that does all the collection jobs. The tool will generate a JSON file for the summary of the collected information. OSX Collector: `https://github.com/Yelp/osxcollector`
Log collection	IR Rescue	IR Rescue is a Windows and Linux script for collecting host forensic data. IR Rescue: `https://github.com/diogo-fernan/ir-rescue/`
Log collection	FastIR Collector	FastIR Collector for Linux only requires one Python script to collect all related logs in Linux. FastIR Collector: `https://github.com/SekoiaLab/Fastir_Collector_Linux` For Windows versions, it will require additional modules and tools. Refer to `https://github.com/SekoiaLab/Fastir_Collector` for more information.
Malware detector	Linux Malware Scanner	The Linux Malware Scanner is a free malware scanner for Linux. CalmAV: `https://www.calmav.net/downloads` **Linux Malware Detect (LMD)**: `https://github.com/rfxn/linux-maware-detect`
Suspicious files analysis	Cuckoo	Cuckoo is an automated malware analysis system. Cuckoo: `https://cuckoosandbox.org/`
Client/server log collector and analysis	GRR Rapid Response	Google Remote Live forensics for incident response will require the installation of a Python agent on the target hosts to collect the logs and the Python server to do the analysis. GRR Rapid Response: `https://github.com/google/grr`
Client/server log collector and analysis	OSQuery	The OSQuery works in a similar way to GRR. The key difference is that OSQuery provides an SQL query to do the endpoint analysis. OSQuery: `https://osquery.io/` Additional information: `https://osquery.readthedocs.io/en/stable/deployment/anomaly-detection/`

Q: What are the toolsets that can help to build a threat intelligence solution?

Category	Open source security tools
Log collector/sensor	Syslog-NG: `https://github.com/balabit/syslog-ng` Rsyslog: `https://github.com/rsyslog/rsyslog` FileBeat: `https://www.elastic.co/products/beats/filebeat` LogStash: `https://www.elastic.co/products/logstash`
SIEM/visualization	Kibana: `https://www.elastic.co/products/kibana` ElasticSearch: `https://www.elastic.co/` AlienValut OSSIM: `https://www.alienvault.com/products/ossim` Grafana: `https://grafana.com/` GrayLog: `https://www.graylog.org/`
Threat intelligence platform	MISP - Open source threat intelligence platform MISP: `http://www.misp-project.org` Additional information: `http://csirtgadgets.org/collective-intelligence-framework/`

Threat intelligence feeds	External threat feeds for blacklised IPs and firewall rule suggestions:
	`https://rules.emergingthreats.net/fwrules/`
	`https://www.spamhaus.org/drop/`
	`https://rules.emergingthreats.net/fwrules/emerging-Block-IPs.txt`
	`https://check.torproject.org/exit-addresses`
	`http://iplists.firehol.org/`

Q: What are the open source tools that can help us to perform security scanning?

Category	Open source security tools
All-in-one security scanning (host, network, visualization)	Security Onion includes several open source security tools, such as Elasticsearch, Logstash, Kibana, Snort, Suricata, Bro, OSSEC, Sguil, Squert, and NetworkMiner. Security Onion: `https://github.com/Security-Onion-Solutions`
All-in-one host-based IDS, secure configuration, and visualization	The Wazuh integrates the OSSEC (host-based IDS), OpenSCAP (secure configuration scanning), and Elastic Stack (threat visualization). Wazuh: `https://github.com/wazuh/wazuh` Rules: `https://github.com/wazuh/wazuh-ruleset/tree/master/rules`
Secure configuration	OpenSCAP: `https://www.open-scap.org/`

Vulnerability	OpenVAS: `http://www.openvas.org/`
Antivirus	CalmAV: `https://www.clamav.net/` LMD: `https://github.com/rfxn/linux-malware-detect`
Host IDS/IPS	OSSEC: `https://github.com/ossec/ossec-hids` OSSEC host IDS rules: `https://github.com/ossec/ossec-hids/tree/master/etc/rules` Samhain: `https://www.la-samhna.de/samhain/`
Web application firewall (WAF)	ModSecurity: `https://github.com/SpiderLabs/ModSecurity` Rules: `https://github.com/SpiderLabs/owasp-modsecurity-crs/tree/v3.0/master/rules`
Network IDS/IPS	Snort: `https://www.snort.org/` Snort rules: `https://snort.org/advisories/talos-rules-2018-06-05` Suricata: `https://suricata-ids.org/` Suricata rules: `https://github.com/OISF/suricata/tree/master/rules`
MySQL AUDITt	AUDIT Plugin for MySQL: `https://github.com/mcafee/mysql-audit` Security Plugins for MySQL: `https://dev.mysql.com/doc/mysql-security-excerpt/5.7/en/security-plugins.html`

Q: What are the security checklists and tools that are needed for every new release?

Security category	Security testing approaches	Suggested security testing tools
Hidden communication ports or channels	• Ensure there are no hidden communication ports or backdoors. • Ensure there are no hidden hard-coded secrets, passwords, or hard keys. • Ensure there are no unnecessary system maintenance tools. • Initiate a source code review for networking communication, such as Java-related API `connect()`, `getPort()`, `getLocalPort()`, `Socket()`, `bind()`, `accept()`, and `ServerSocket()`. • Listening to 0.0.0.0 is forbidden.	NMAP Graudit TruffleHog Snallygaster Hping masscan

Privacy information	• Search for the plaintext password and key in the source code. • Search for the personal information for GDPR compliance. • Check that the personal information can be modified and removed by the end user. • Check that the personal information can be removed within a defined period.	TruffleHog Blueflower YARA PrivacyScore Snallygaster
Secure communication	• SSH v2 instead of Telnet • SFTP instead of FTP • TLS 1.2 instead of SSL, TLS 1.1	NMAP WireShark SSLyze SSL/TLS tester
Third-party components.	• CVE check • Known vulnerabilities check • Hidden malicious code or secrets check	OWASP Dependency check LMD (Linux Malware Detection) OpenVAS NMAP CVEChecker
Cryptography	• Ensure there is no weak encryption algorithm • Ensure there are no secret files on the public web interfaces	Graudit SSLyze Snallygaster
Audit logging	Ensure the operation and security team can log the following scenarios: • Nonquery operations, including success and failure actions • Nonquery scheduled tasks • API access or tool connections to execute administration tasks	GREP
DoS attacks	The testing of the DOS is to ensure whether the application failure occurred as expected. The DOS scenario may cover the following: • TCP Sync flooding • HTTP Slow • HTTP Post flooding • NTP DOS • SSL DOS	Pwnloris Slowloris Synflood Thc-sll-dos Wreckuests ntpDOS

Web security	This can refer to the OWASP Testing Guide, and OWASP Top 10: • Injection • Broken authentication • Sensitive data exposure • XXE • Broken access control • Security misconfiguration • XSS • Insecure deserialization • Known vulnerabilities • Insufficient logging and monitoring	Refer to the OWASP Testing Guide v4. OWASP ZAP BurpSuite Arachni Scanner SQLMap
Secure configuration	Ensure the configurations of the applications, web services, databases, and OS are secure. The secure configurations are based on the CIS Security Benchmark and OpenSCAP.	OpenSCAP Docker Bench Security Clair
Fuzz testing	The purpose of fuzz testing is to generate dynamic testing data as input to check whether the application will fail unexpectedly.	API Fuzzer Radamsa American Fuzzy lop FuzzDB Wfuzz
Mobile app security	Refer to the OWASP Mobile App Security Testing Guide.	Mobile Security Framework
Top common issue	The list of the most common security issues based on the project's historical data.	CWE/SANS Top 25 Most Dangerous Software Errors
Security compliance	The security compliance based on business needs may also be included, such as the GDPR or PCI DSS.	Refer to the specific security compliance requirements.

Q. What are the open source tools that can be used to build a security analysis by a big data framework?

Project	Key features
TheHive Project	TheHive provides threat incident response case management, which allows security analysts to flag IOCs. The Cortex can analyze the issues using threat intelligence services such as VirtusTotal, MaxMind, and DomainTools. It supports over 80 threat intelligence services. The Hippocampe provides a query interface through a REST API or a Web UI. TheHive: `https://thehive-project.org/`
MISP	MISP is mainly a threat intelligence platform to share the IoC and indicators of malware. The correlation engine helps to identify the relationships between the attributes and indicators of malware. MISP: `https://www.misp-project.org/` The MISP provides over 40 threat intelligence feeds. Refer to `https://www.misp-project.org/feeds/` for more information.
Apache Metron	The Apache Metron is an SIEM (containing threat intel, security data parsers, alerts, dashboard) and also a security analysis (anomaly detection and machine learning) framework based on the Hadoop big data framework. Apache Metron: `https://metron.apache.org/` The typical technology components that are required to build a big data framework include the following: • Apache Flume • Apache Kafka • Apache Storm or Spark • Apache Hadoop • Apache Hive • Apache Hbase • Elastic Search • MySQL

Refer to `Chapter 18`, *Business Fraud and Services Abuses*, for further details.

Q. What are the common indicators of compromise and the detection techniques that are used to identify them?

Abnormal host behaviors	Potential threats
Multiple compromised hosts' data communication to external hosts.	The compromised hosts are sending data to external C and C servers.
The host connects to an external known APT IP address or URL. The host downloads a known malicious file.	The host shows an indication of compromise from an APT or malware attack.
Several unsuccessful login attempts.	One of the internal compromised hosts is trying to log in to access critical information.
An email message that includes a dangerous URL or malicious file.	The attackers may be using social engineering to send an email for targeted attacks. Enter the email senders into the watch list.
Rare and unusual filenames	The malware installs itself during the startup to continue to act even after reboot. Here are some of the common ways for malware to achieve persistence. • Program start • Services • Process injection • Login Script For Windows, it's suggested that you use AutoRuns to check whether the host is compromised with suspicious malware. AutoRuns: `https://docs.microsoft.com/en-us/sysinternals/downloads/autoruns`
Unusual event and audit logs alert	The following system event or audit logs may need further analysis: • Account lockouts • User added to the privileged group • Failed user account login • Application error • Windows error reporting • BSOD log • Event log was cleared • Audit log was cleared • Firewall rule change

The following table lists the detection abnormalities in the web access logs:

Web access analysis	Detection techniques
External source client IP	The source of the IP address can help to identify the following: • A known bad IP or Tor exit node. • Abnormal geolocation changes. • The concurrent connection from different geolocations. The MaxMind GeoIP2 database can be used to translate the IP address to a geolocation. MaxMind GeoIP2: `https://dev.maxmind.com/geoip/geoip2/geolite2/#Downloads`
Client fingerprint (OS, browser, user agent, devices, and so on)	The client fingerprint can be used to identify whether there are any unusual client or non-browser connections. The open source `clientJS` is a pure JavaScript that can be used to collect client fingerprint information. The JA3 tool provided by Salesforce uses SSL/TLS connection profiling to identify the malicious client. ClientJS: `https://clientjs.org/` JA3: `https://github.com/salesforce/ja3`
Website reputation	When there is an outbound connection to an external website, we can check the threat reputation of that particular website. This can be done by a web application firewall or web gateway security solutions. VirusTotal: `https://www.virustotal.com/`
Random domain name by DGA (domain generation algorithm)	The domain name of the C and C server can be generated by DGA. The key characteristics of the DGA domain can be high entropy, high consonant count, and long domain length. Based on these indicators, we can analyze whether the domain name is generated by DGA, and therefore be a potential C and C server. DGA detector: `https://github.com/exp0se/dga_detector/` In addition, to reduce false positives, we may also use the Alexa Top 1,000,000 sites as a website whitelist. Refer to `https://s3.amazonaws.com/alexa-static/top-1m.csv.zip` for more information.
Suspicious files download	Cuckoo Sandbox is useful for suspicious file analysis. Cuckoo Sandbox: `https://cuckoosandbox.org/`

DNS Query	For the analysis of a DNS query, the following are the key indicators of compromises: • DNS query to unauthorized DNS servers. • Unmatched DNS replies can be an indicator of DNS spoofing. • Clients connect to multiple DNS servers. • Long DNS query (for example, over 150 characters), which is an indicator of DNS tunneling. • Domain name with high entropy. This is an indicator of DNS tunneling or a C and C server.

Refer to `Chapter 18`, *Business Fraud and Services Abuses*, for further details.

Q: What are the common cybercriminal activities in business scenarios?

Business scenario	Cybercriminal activities
For the promotion of new user registration, the e-commerce site may give a $10 coupon or certain discounts.	**Account cheating:** Cybercriminals may register massive numbers of accounts to gain the coupon and discounts, and then, resell those coupons.
The shopping site may sell a limited number of special edition goods.	**Scalper:** The cybercriminals may register massive numbers of accounts to purchase the goods and resell them at higher prices.
The shopping search query results are sorted by the ratings and volume of sales of the online seller.	**Unreal orders:** The online sellers may make a deal with the cybercriminals to manipulate massive numbers of unreal orders and ratings in order to be listed in the top rankings of the query results.
A shopping site account is normally registered with an email address, phone number, and ID.	**Account takeover:** A computer criminal poses as a genuine user and gains control of an account to make unauthorized transactions. In addition, the cybercriminals may do brute-force attacks on the accounts and re-register with other email or phone details to gain financial benefits.

Refer to `Chapter 19`, *GDPR Compliance Case Study*, for further details.

Q. How can "profiling" help to detect business fraud and abuses?

Profiling	Description
IP profiling	IP profiling is used to identify the IP behaviors of the account and the device. IP profiling involves the following attributes: • Geolocation • VPN, Proxy, Gateway, or Tor (these IPs will require the user to do further verification) • Known blacklisted IP address
Device fingerprints	A device fingerprint is the information collected about a remote client device or browser for the purpose of identification. We use device fingerprints to know whether the remotely connected device is the usual one that is used by the user/account. For example, for the same account, a login to the e-commerce service with a different mobile phone every day is definitely a sign of abnormality. Here are some common device fingerprints: • Machine type, CPU, virtualization • OS version, software plugin, fonts • Concurrent connection for the same device fingerprints • Geolocation for the same devices on the same day • The same device fingerprints used by a number of different accounts • Multiple different device fingerprints used by the same user account
Machine versus human behaviors	The objective of the behavior analysis is to identify whether the source of the request is manipulated by a malicious program or a real human. There are several clues that are used to analyze the behavior of a user to determine whether they are a human or a machine: • Usage of keyboard • Mouse movement • User agent HTTPS fingerprints
Account profiling	The following attributes are related to the account. If one of the attributes is identified as suspicious, such as the email address, it's very likely that all the other accounts related to the email address may be suspicious as well. Therefore, we will build a watch list of the following privacy information: • Email address • Shipping address • Bank account number • Telephone number • Social networking friends • Payment

Usage profiling	Based on the historical usage, we can also identify whether it's a normal user or just a one-time user that is abusing the services or business promotion code: • Page-visit historical records • Historical communication with sellers • Purchase history and habits

Refer to `Chapter 19`, *GDPR Compliance Case Study*, for further details.

Summary

In this final chapter, we have summarized the key FAQs of the DevSecOps practices from different roles, such as security management, development, testing, IT, and the operations team.

Security management identifies the security requirements, and the need for security compliance to support the business's success. To achieve this goal, the security manager may define security awareness programs, security assurance programs, security guidelines, and processes or tools for the development, testing, and security monitoring team.

The objective of a development team is to build secure software and services with rapid delivery. The principles of security and privacy by design will apply to the whole development cycle, from the security requirements, secure architecture frameworks, hardening compiler options, secure coding, and the secure third-party dependencies. We have listed lots of industry best practices, suggested frameworks, and secure code scanning tools for the development team. The development team may apply security practices.

The security testing team ensures the security quality using several approaches, such as a white box code review, penetration testing, secure configuration, secure communication, sensitive information review, and so on. We have introduced several open source tools and testing methodologies to do the security testing. The security testing tools can also be used by other teams. For example, the development team may also use the code scanning tool to ensure secure coding in the construction stage and the operation team may also apply the secure configuration scanning tools during the deployment stage. The security is not just the testing team's responsibility but also requires the collaboration between the development and operation teams.

The security operation team needs to ensure the security of the cloud services 24/7. The security activities in the security operation team include security monitoring, security incident response, secure environment, vulnerabilities management, and service abuse monitoring. In addition to this, we also introduced the threat intelligence that provides the threat feeds to detect the known bad IP, file hash, or DNS. The security operation team is the frontier defense against threats and can give the development and testing team the most valuable feedback to improve security. Again, an effective loop also requires high collaboration between each functional team.

Moving toward DevSecOps requires high collaboration between the development, testing, IT, operation, and security monitoring teams. For example, the infrastructure operation team may apply the technology of Docker containers for their deployment. The security testing team will help to provide the secure configuration assessment tools, and the development team may define the security configurations of the Dockerfile. The security management will define the security requirements for the whole life cycle of the Docker adoption. Shifting security to the left—that is, the earlier stages of the process—requires a culture of collaboration and security awareness of every role. A well-defined role, responsibility matrix, and SOP (Standard Operating Procedure) may help to execute tasks with efficiency. However, the functional team barriers and the KPIs of each role may have a negative impact on everyone in taking an extra mile to move forward toward DevSecOps. The understanding of the importance of security and privacy for each functional team and the collaboration between each teams are key to the success of DevSecOps.

Further reading

Visit the following URLs for more information:

- **SANS DevSecOps PlayBook**: https://www.sans.org/reading-room/whitepapers/analyst/devsecops-playbook-36792
- **CSA Security Guidance for Critical Areas of Focus in Cloud Computing v4.0**: https://cloudsecurityalliance.org/guidance/#_overview
- **Awesome Information Security courses and training resources**: https://github.com/onlurking/awesome-infosec
- **Cybrary Security training courses**: https://www.cybrary.it/
- **Open Security Training**: http://opensecuritytraining.info/

- **Security 101 for SaaS Startups**: https://github.com/forter/security-101-for-saas-startups/blob/english/security.md
- **Firmware Security Training**: https://github.com/advanced-threat-research/firmware-security-training
- **Awesome Incident Response**: https://github.com/meirwah/awesome-incident-response
- **Awesome AI Security**: https://github.com/RandomAdversary/Awesome-AI-Security
- **Awesome Penetration Testing**: https://github.com/wtsxDev/Penetration-Testing
- **Awesome Pentest**: https://github.com/enaqx/awesome-pentest

Assessments

Chapter 1

1. Yes
2. GDPR
3. All of the above
4. Defining secure configuration of the OS, platform, databases, and so on
5. All of the above
6. Secure configuration
7. Spoofing

Chapter 2

1. Yes
2. All of the above
3. All of the above
4. GDPR
5. PIA Privacy Impact Analysis

Chapter 3

1. Yes
2. All of the above
3. Secure architecture
4. Security requirements
5. Large security team size—over 100 members

Chapter 4

1. All of the above
2. Service logs were ready for security analysis
3. Yes
4. Apache Ranger
5. False
6. Yes

Chapter 5

1. No
2. All of the above
3. Newsletter
4. Yes
5. Yes
6. Testing
7. Secure code scanning
8. Passport

Chapter 6

1. All of the above
2. CSA CAIQ
3. All of the above
4. Shiro doesn't require a Java Spring framework
5. Node.JS
6. Mbed TLS
7. Remove illegal characters

Chapter 7

1. False
2. All of the above
3. Authentication logging
4. SeaSponge
5. Java Commons Validator

Chapter 8

1. PHP
2. Java
3. All of above
4. Detection rate and false positive rates
5. CSRF Token
6. VisualCodeGrepper
7. MobSF
8. Flawfinder

Chapter 9

1. All of the above
2. Antivirus
3. All of the above
4. False
5. It's to perform the data masking of sensitive information
6. Open source licenses check

Chapter 10

1. All of the above
2. Moible Security Testing Guide (MSTG)
3. It defines the testing approaches for the high-risk functions
4. Installation
5. Nmap
6. SSH v1
7. Security testing tools
8. It's a purpose-built vulnerable web application for security testing practices

Chapter 11

1. Antivirus scanning results
2. Generating documents directly from source code
3. All of the above
4. fwrite
5. All of the above

Chapter 12

1. OSSEC
2. Web security
3. OpenVAS
4. GUI interface
5. All of the above
6. Appie
7. PentestBox

Chapter 13

1. All of the above
2. It is an IDE plugin for static code scanning
3. All of the above
4. Scans for known vulnerabilities
5. API fuzz testing

Chapter 14

1. Preparation -> Detection -> Containment -> Post-Incident Analysis
2. It's an incentive program for security researchers to submit security issues
3. All of the above
4. It defines the 20 security controls for the whole enterprise security
5. Monitoring and Analysis of Audit Logs
6. The malware detection capability
7. The primary objective of the Tier 1 call center is to perform malware analysis
8. Unauthorized use of a compromised host to mine cryptocurrency

Chapter 15

1. Encryption
2. All of the above
3. Unusual mail receivers or senders
4. Kibana
5. It's an all-in-one security scanning and monitoring tool (host, network, visualization)
6. YARA is a pattern-matching Swiss army knife for malware detection

Chapter 16

1. Full assessment
2. Security awareness training program
3. Searching for personal information
4. Telnet
5. CVE checking

Chapter 17

1. It's an indicator of a C&C connection
2. Indicator of Compromise
3. All of the above
4. All of the above
5. Domain Generation Algorithms
6. It's an indicator of a C&C server

Chapter 18

1. A computer criminal poses as a genuine user, and gains control of an account to make unauthorized transactions
2. All of the above
3. Crawler
4. All of the above
5. CPU type
6. All of the above
7. All of the above

Chapter 19

1. All of the above
2. The product must ensure not to collect data that is irrelevant to the product functions
3. The product must provide the Agree or Disagree options to the data subject after the data collection
4. Provide the data export mechanism to CSV or XML formats
5. All of the above

Other Books You May Enjoy

If you enjoyed this book, you may be interested in these other books by Packt:

Mastering Linux Security and Hardening
Donald A. Tevault

ISBN: 978-1-78862-030-7

- Use various techniques to prevent intruders from accessing sensitive data
- Prevent intruders from planting malware, and detect whether malware has been planted
- Prevent insiders from accessing data that they aren't authorized to access
- Do quick checks to see whether a computer is running network services that it doesn't need to run
- Learn security techniques that are common to all Linux distros, and some that are distro-specific

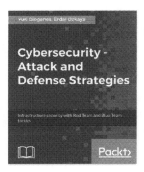

Cybersecurity – Attack and Defense Strategies

Yuri Diogenes, Erdal Ozkaya

ISBN: 978-1-78847-529-7

- Learn the importance of having a solid foundation for your security posture
- Understand the attack strategy using cyber security kill chain
- Learn how to enhance your defense strategy by improving your security policies, hardening your network, implementing active sensors, and leveraging threat intelligence
- Learn how to perform an incident investigation
- Get an in-depth understanding of the recovery process
- Understand continuous security monitoring and how to implement a vulnerability management strategy
- Learn how to perform log analysis to identify suspicious activities

Leave a review - let other readers know what you think

Please share your thoughts on this book with others by leaving a review on the site that you bought it from. If you purchased the book from Amazon, please leave us an honest review on this book's Amazon page. This is vital so that other potential readers can see and use your unbiased opinion to make purchasing decisions, we can understand what our customers think about our products, and our authors can see your feedback on the title that they have worked with Packt to create. It will only take a few minutes of your time, but is valuable to other potential customers, our authors, and Packt. Thank you!

Index